Begin with Christ

By

Prophetess
Adríenna Dionna Turner

Day Begins with Christ by Adrienna Turner.
First published September 2008, Author House.
Reprint March 11, 2009, Author House.
Revision Print, October 2009.
4th edition, retitled, **Begin with Christ** – A DYRP Devotional, 2017.

This book is a work of non-fiction.

All Scripture quotations and explanations are derived from King James Version, New Living Translation, New International Version, Life Application Study Bible, NKJV, New King James Version Holy Bible: Woman Thou Art Loosed edition, and Nelson Study Bible, NKJV unless otherwise noted.

Begin with Christ © 2017 by Adrienna Turner
eBook ISBN: 978-1-945822-04-9
Book ISBN: 978-1-945822-05-6

Begin with Christ Journal © 2017 by Adrienna Turner
eJournal ISBN: 978-1-945822-07-0
Paperback Journal: 978-1-945822-06-3

All Rights Reserved.

No part of this book may be reproduced, stored in a retrieval system, or transmitted by any means without the written permission of the author.

Dream 4 More Firm Websites: www.dream4more.org dream4more.us drean4more.net

Email: dream4morefirm@gmail.com

Author Site: http://www.adriennaturner.net

DYRP (Dream Your Reality Prophecies): http://www.dreamyourreality.webs.com

DYRP (Dream Your Reality Prophecies)

Printed in the United States of America. Sacramento, CA.

Foreword

It has been a pleasure and honor to work with Adrienna on this book about a lifestyle in Jesus. So much of our lives is learning, and this book covers a host of conundrums, from how we feel about ourselves to how we relate to others, and why.

You might see some unfamiliar terms as you read. You'll also witness an unbridled joy that comes from a relationship with the One who created us, through His spoken word.

As you read and begin to know more of Christ's rule in your life, you will see that life's experiences become stepping stones, and you'll look back on them to realize that, even before you knew Him, He was training you to trust Him. As life goes on, you'll see news and hear stories, and be able to understand what His words meant.

Parents, you will find ways to raise your children, and answers from a myriad of sources, including personal experiences. You can teach them well. You'll also see things that you might not have considered, and find new ways to communicate with your partner.

Young people, as you grow, you'll find yourself coming into your own, and confused about the demands of society and relationships. You'll find sage advice here, as well as the reasons behind it, backed up by biblical principles.

Mature believers will find themselves edified, and able to use these pages and graphs as a devotional. You'll be encouraged to turn to your Bible and explore stories and ideas that you've not considered for awhile.

Adrienna has done the hard work of gathering the words of the ancients, Bible Scholars, and advisors, and you'll feel as though you are listening to a group expounding on a walk with God.

Ministers of the Word, you will find this book to be a resource for sermons and Bible Study as well as a guide for youth groups.

Begin with Christ.

Karen Overturf

Introduction

Jesus is the good shepherd. His sheep (followers of Christ) are able to hear His voice. We can obtain the *mind of Christ* through the Holy Spirit. We can begin to know God's thoughts by talking to Him and expect His answers through our prayers.

To have an intimate relationship with Christ comes only from spending time consistently in His presence and in His Word (see *Philippians 2:5*).[5] Therefore, this book was specially written for this purpose: that people will be able to spend more time with Christ and to know His ways—through His Holy Word.

> Revelation 14:6, NKJV: *"...having the **everlasting gospel** to preach to those who dwell on the earth—to every nation, tribe, tongue, and people—."*

Some believe a final worldwide appeal is to spread the gospel of God's Word to all. Have you received Jesus Christ's Good News in your life and applied it? It is my hope that, after reading this book, you will recognize a change in your life and experience an eagerness to follow the footsteps of Jesus Christ!

Yahweh just wants us to get a closer and personal relationship with Him to hear from Him. Sometimes, He communicates with us in other forms such as *dreams and visions* like Daniel and Joseph; *hear His voice* like Elijah and Noah; *feel His Holy Spirit* like Saul later known as Paul. Furthermore, He loves you and wants a relationship with you. Remember Yahweh already knew you before the foundation of the world.

Congratulations! Today you will start a 273-day (9 month) journey. This is a birthing process in which your hopes of being a more mature believer in Christ will blossom.

Each Daily inspiration will give you the ability to meditate and gain divine wisdom from God's Holy Word. Some may call this book a "devotional," but I prefer that you view this book as a resource tool as you dedicate and devote your spiritual walk to Christ.

The previous book, entitled *The Day Begins with Christ,* was a 50-day journey. Now revised with a new title, *Begin with Christ* encourages the reader to personally take each day and dedicate it to Christ. The tables, charts, and other tools for further studies are in the appendixes. You can also purchase a *Begin with Christ* companion journal separately.

Prophetess *Adrienna Dionna Turner*

---

[5] Life Application Study Bible, NKJV, 1996.

Special Thanks

A prayer of thanks for all He is comes first, as He is the center of the first and greatest commandment.

"Dear Lord, it is a blessing and privilege to write an uplifting book to touch souls including those who do not really know You. Thank you, Lord, for allowing me to be a faithful servant, and to hear Your voice to do Your will. Thank you for allowing me the courage, and touching me with Your Holy Spirit to write *Begin with Christ.* You've designed this beautiful journey to help followers of Jesus Christ mature as believers through Your guidance and direction. May all who seek the gospel, looking for Your truth, also find edification in these pages. Amen."

I also would like to give a grateful thanks to those for the encouragement and the heartfelt emails to keep me going and trusting in the Lord that I can do it. I appreciate the reviews that I have received for the previous edition(s). I received a couple suggestions about extending the devotional book with shorter chapters (days) to gather the information. Some of the stats had to be updated too. Therefore, I have welcomed these suggestions and proceeded in this edition.

Additionally, I would like to thank all the previous editor(s) on the previous version(s). I am grateful for my latest editor, Karen Overturf for polishing this updated edition to His divine perfection.

I cannot forget my family members for all their love and support, especially my mother Diane Leslie (Battle) Turner. Maxine Battle spoke prayerful and loving words for my life. She is also trusting and believing that one day I will be on Oprah Winfrey Network. There are many more to name since we've found family members all over—and you all know who you are.

I especially want to thank God for the man of my dreams and the love of my life. He continues to encourage me to keep on pressing and pushing through the labor pains of writing/marketing my books. His devotion to God, his humility, and his love inspires me. At his request, his name is not published.

Begin Day 1:
God's Laws:
The Purpose of Following the Ten Commandments

At the foot of Mount Sinai, God showed His people the true lifestyle and beauty of His laws. Initially, the *Ten Commandments* were created to lead Israel to a life of holiness. The Israelites eventually understood the nature of God and that these commandments were intended to lovingly guide the community to meet the needs of every individual.

Some will argue not to abide by the Old Testament laws, but to only obey the New Testament laws because Jesus has fulfilled the prophecies of the Old Testament. Some refer to what Jesus was asked in the Bible: "What laws are we commanded to follow?"

Jesus responded:

Matthew 22:37-40, NKJV: *"...'You shall love the Lord with all your heart, with all your soul, and with all your mind. This is the first and great commandment. And the second is like it: 'You shall love your neighbor as yourself.' On these two commandments hang all the Law and the Prophets."*

Moses was a prophet who freed the Israelites from four hundred years of Egyptian rule through the inspiration and miracles of God. Through Abraham's bloodline, we are privileged with the laws of God and are the continuation from godly bloodlines. We can equally apply the Old Testament's *Ten Commandments* with the New Testament today.

Begin Day 2:
God's Laws:
Desire to Follow

It is up to you to have a great desire to follow God and what He commands you to do. Some of us do not have an eagerness to follow God's laws or commands. We continue to make excuses and are not willing to change our lifestyle. We are conditioned to believe what our society presents to us instead of turning to the Creator. We need to seek and read the Word that He has laid out for us. We need to ask Him for guidance in all that we do.

Abraham came from a family who relied on guidance and direction from many gods or idols. He yearned for more and desired to hear from the one and only God. From the first time Abraham heard God's voice in the midst, he knew that he had to obey God's command regardless of what others would think or say. God spoke to Abraham's heart, touched his spirit, and longed for Abraham to worship Him—the one and true living God. He also allowed God to direct his path and guide him during his travels. To proceed with God's request, Abraham had to remove familiarity and negativity to follow God wholeheartedly.

Are you willing to do the same? Will you go out on the limb to do God's will? Are you willing to leave the familiarity? Are you ready to leave the negativity and people of bad influences? Can you seek the true and living God who has a plan for your life? Do not look or turn back once God speaks to your heart. Get up and leave!

> Deuteronomy 4:8, NIV: *"And what other nation is so great as to have such righteous decrees and laws as this body of laws I am setting before you today?"*

Begin Day 3:
God's Laws: Guide Us

Deuteronomy 4:9, NIV: *"Only be careful, and watch yourselves closely so that you do not forget the things your eyes have seen or let them slip from your heart as long as you live. Teach them to your children and to their children after them."*

In *Deuteronomy 4:9*, Moses wanted to make sure that the people did not forget all they had seen God do. Therefore, Moses urged parents to teach their children about God's miracles. Parents are to remember God's faithfulness and share stories recounting God's greatness. It is easy to forget the miraculous acts God has worked in the lives of His people. You can remember God's great acts of faithfulness by telling your children, friends, or associates what you have seen Him do in your life.

Some argue that God's laws only applied to the Israelites. God's laws were devised to guide all people towards lifestyles that are healthy, upright, and devoted to God. The purpose was to point out sin, actual or potential sins, and to show the proper way to deal with sin. Therefore, the *Ten Commandments*, also known as the heart of God's laws, are just as applicable today as they were over three thousand years ago because they proclaim a lifestyle endorsed by God. They are the perfect expression of who God is and how He wants people to abide by them.

God gave other laws besides the *Ten Commandments*. You may be wondering if these laws are just as important and the answer is simple. God never issued a law that did not have a purpose. However, many of the laws we read in the Pentateuch (Jewish doctrine) were directed specifically to people of that time and culture. For example, no one practices sacrificing animals to cover our sins since Jesus Christ sacrificed himself as the 'Lamb' that removes our sins. Jesus also tells us, "Go on your way. From now on, don't sin."[6]

The New Testament refers to the death and resurrection of Jesus Christ. All the prophecies in the Old Testament have been fulfilled once Jesus Christ came and died for our sins. In other words, the Old Testament laws help us recognize our sins and correct our wrongdoings. Jesus Christ takes our sins away. Jesus is our primary example to follow because He alone perfectly obeyed the law and modeled its true intent.

---

[6] John 8:11, Message Bible

Begin Day 4:
God's Laws:
The First Commandment

The first four Commandments involve our relationship with God. The remaining six Commandments involve our relationship with others.

The *First Commandment* focuses on loving God first.[7] God exists in three spirits and/or persons: YHWH God, the Father; Jesus Christ, who came as a man on Earth and ascended back to Heaven; and the Holy Spirit. These three spirits and/or persons are also called the *Trinity* (Father, Son, and Holy Spirit). They are a set of three entities that form a unity.

God created everyone with the ability to worship. Everyone worships someone or something. However, God commanded us to worship only Him, and to serve no other gods before Him, who is worthy of all praise and worship. There are ways to guard ourselves against having other gods before the True God: seek first the Kingdom of God by making God your first priority; set your affections on things above; stay away from idols viewed as substitutes to God; and study and read your Holy Bible to know the true God.[8]

In the Old Testament, the Israelites were enslaved in a land of many idols and gods under Egyptian rulership. Egyptians worshipped the Sun God, and each god represented a different aspect of life. It was accepted as normal to worship and serve many gods to receive blessings. When God told His people to worship, trust, and believe in Him, Israelites had to remove all the Egyptians' rules and forms of worship from their way of living.

Ultimately, the Israelites assumed that God was just another god to serve and worship. Even though God commanded the Israelites to have no other gods before Him, it was difficult for them to accept. God led the Israelites out of bondage, escaping Egypt's stronghold and its rulership under Pharaoh to delete all confusion from the Israelite's religious assimilation.

God codified this devotion to Him, and Jesus clarified 'no other gods before me' as His *First and greatest Commandment*.

---

[7] Exodus 20:3
[8] Malone, Julius. *Introduction to the Ten Commandments*, Sermon at New Testament Church (Milwaukee, WI) notes taken by author, 2004.

Begin Day 5:
God's Laws: The First Commandment - No Other Gods Before Me

Who will you serve? Who do you love? Will you put God first in your daily functions and set aside all the other things that you once thought was greater than life itself?

Clearly, God is the one that blessed us with our husband or wife, with our children or those dear to us. We also forget and overlook Who gave us our spiritual gifts. Today, many of us rank other things as more important than spending time with God. Our roles, careers, or jobs may take up all our time and energy, and we forget about God. For example, someone might view his or her elder, pastor, reverend or bishop as a 'man of God,' and never seek God. In other words, you can view a 'prophet of God' or 'servant of God' as a god. If we concentrate too much on them, whether it is for personal identity or self-gratification to fit in a social organization (church), they become our *gods* or *idols*.

Some believe they are worshipping God by going to every church function held. However, whenever we devote more time to people or things for our gratification instead of lifting them up, the choice ultimately controls our thoughts and energies, not allowing God to hold the central place in our lives.

Begin Day 6:
God's Laws: The First Commandment - Religion can be a "god"

Deuteronomy 4:2, NIV: *"Do not add to what I command you and do not subtract from it, but keep the commands of the Lord, your God, that I give to you."*

In *Deuteronomy 4:2*, to presume you can make changes to God's law is to assume a position of authority over God, who gave the laws. As believers of Jesus Christ, we are consciously aware that text cannot be added or omitted from God's Word. However, many religions and many denominations of religions create their own perception of the Bible, by rewriting God's Word into their own translation. They may include their own writings to coincide with the Bible. Consequently, as followers of Jesus Christ, not only are we to read and study the Bible, but we are also to pray to the Lord for understanding and wisdom of His Word.

God loves us and wants to protect us. God created these laws for us. Moreover, we are to be careful of false religions and false prophets that appear in sheep's clothing. Their intentions are not of God. The Bible refers to these false prophets as wolves, ready to devour lost souls and weak believers. Their mission and goal are to seek you and have you follow their doctrine, belief system, or religious practices, effectively drawing your attention from God to place your faith in them. They do not have any light in them and no truth in their writings. Jesus said, "I am the light, I am the truth, and I am the way."

Ask God for discernment to show you the difference between falsehood and truth. Seek God to speak to your heart and mind to have clarity of these false teachings and confirmation.

There are three main categories of religion: monotheism, polytheism, and pantheism. All three of these types of religion were practiced before God engraved the Ten Commandments on stone tablets. *Monotheism* is the doctrine or belief that there is only one God. *Polytheism* is the belief in or worship of more than one god. *Pantheism* is the belief in and worship of all gods. This is also the belief that God is in everything and everything is God.

Begin Day 7:
God's Laws:
The Second Commandment

The *Second Commandment* refers to idolatry. There was a constant problem among the Hebrews, which led to the enslavement of Babylonian captivity.[9] God informed Abraham ahead of time that his nation would be held captive under Egypt jurisdictions and laws for four-hundred years.[10] Moreover, the *Second Commandment* is a prohibition against worshipping idols in deference to God.

Some examples are: Aaron building a golden calf to represent God,[11] and Jeroboam made two calves of gold, placing one in Bethel and the other in Dan.[12]
Aids to worship can also become objects of worship;[13] many pictures in the Tabernacle;[14] pictures inside the temple built by Solomon;[15] and even now there are pictures symbolizing the Triune God, which can be found in some artwork as a Rock, Fortress, Shield, Shelter, Shade, Shepherd, a mother hen, Eagle, Lion, Lamb, Consuming Fire, Wind, etc. Additionally, the Roman Catholics have statues, images, and pictures in their church.[16]

The *Second Commandment* relates to the Bible's description of God as a jealous God.[17] Those being disobedient against God and rebellious can be shown as hating God. In contrast, God blesses those who are obedient,[18] as well as those desiring to take advantage of God's mercy. The definition of *mercy* means we do not receive justice or get what we deserve. *Grace* means we receive what we do not deserve. *Justice* means we receive what we deserve. *Justice* also refers to God's compassion.[19]

Images limit God. No artificial image can represent the true God. God cannot be captured into an image.[20] The reason we cannot depict God and why images limit God are these: God is *omnipotent*,[21] God is *omniscient*,[22] and God is *omnipresent*.[23] In the *Roget's 21st Century*, *omnipotent* means all-powerful, almighty, divine, godlike, mighty, supreme, unlimited, and unrestricted. It also states that *omniscient* means all-knowing, all-seeing, almighty, infinite,

---

[9] Jeremiah 25:1-11
[10] Genesis 11
[11] Exodus 32:1-6
[12] 1 Kings 12:25-33
[13] Numbers 21:4-9; John 3:14-15; 2 Kings 18:1-5
[14] Exodus 25:1-31
[15] 1 Kings 6:21-35
[16] Malone, Julius. *Introduction to the Ten Commandments.* Sermon at New Testament Church. Milwaukee, 2004.
[17] Deuteronomy 4:24; Zechariah 1:14
[18] Deuteronomy 28:1-14; John 13:17
[19] Psalm 103:10; 130:3; Ezra 9:13
[20] Isaiah 40:18-25; Exodus 15:11; John 4:24; 1 Kings 8:27; Jeremiah 23:24; Acts 17:29; Romans 1:22-23; 1 Timothy 1:17
[21] Jeremiah 32:17; Psalm 93:4
[22] Psalm 139: 2-4
[23] Psalm 139:7-12

knowledgeable, panosophical, preeminent, and wise. In the *Webster's College Dictionary*, *omnipresent* means God is present in all places at the same time.

Rejoice that God is everywhere. God is too high and holy to be captured in an image, idea, or object. God is too wide and wise to be comprehended.[24]

---

[24] Malone, Julius. *Introduction to the Ten Commandments*. Sermon at New Testament Church. Milwaukee, 2004; Job 11:7; Romans 11:33.

Begin Day 8:
God's Laws:
The Second Commandment -Idol Worship

There were tribes throughout the Bible that worshipped idol gods:[25]

- Philistines (also known as Dagon)
- Amorites (also known as Molech)
- Moabites (also known as Chemosh)
- Babylonians (also known as Marduk)
- Canaanites (also known as Baal).
- Egyptians served many gods (e.g., Sun God). The Egyptian community also worshipped the Pharaoh.
- Greeks had nearly thirty thousand gods to avoid missing one 'Unknown God.'[26]
- Romans worshipped and followed many gods, and they persecuted those who worshipped the one and only true God. Some view the Romans as atheists. Today, most Romans are under the Roman Catholic Church. They do not only worship Jesus Christ but believe they have to speak to the Virgin Mary (idol statue form) to get their prayers to Jesus.

The New King James version (Exodus 20:4) states that God was not excusing other nations for their idol worshipping. God explains in His Word. While judgment was delayed for those other nations, it would be swift and complete for Israel since they knew God's laws. We must remember that idol worshipping is not just keeping statues around the house.

> Ideally, *idol worship* is a commitment to the other qualities, beliefs, and practices, or to strengths and attributes of humanity. We are *worshipping idols* when our focus is on the creation of or the evolution of the animal kingdom. We worship *idols* when the orderliness of stars is revered without reference to God, who created them.[27]

What does it mean to me? What are the "other" gods referenced in the second commandment?

Any person, place, or thing that one loves more than our Heavenly Father.

Other examples of these idols are: our family members, friends, celebrities, careers, homes, cars, boats, trucks, jewelry, and anything else that can cause us to lose sight of God.

What is higher than any worldly possession? What is higher than anything on earth? It is our Heavenly Father, Yahweh.

---

[25] Exodus 20:4
[26] Acts 17:23

[27] Life Application Study Bible, New King James Version, 1996.

Begin Day 9:
God's Laws:
The Third Commandment

The central behavior of *Third Commandment* is to avoid taking God's name in vain. First, the word *vain* is a translation of the Hebrew word *shav*. In Hebrew, according to the English *Lexicon of Brown, Driver, and Briggs*, *shav* means emptiness, nothingness, worthlessness, and vanity. Second, in this case, *vain* means to take, carry, or bear the Lord's name, using His name
- thoughtlessly,
- irreverently, or
- carelessly

and, according to *Lexicon of Brown, Driver, and Briggs*, to use 'to no good purpose.' Lastly, *to take the Lord's name in vain* means to bring the Lord dishonor by:
- one's lips,
- one's lifestyle,
- one's words, or
- one's walk.

In other words, anything that is said or done that brings dishonor or disrespect to the name of God.[28] The examples of taking the Lord's name in vain are when a person uses it with or as profanity, swearing by His name, or using other filthy or corrupt speech with His name. William Ward said, "Profanity is the use of strong words by weak people."[29] In addition, one can take the Lord's name in vain when it is emptied of its majesty, glory, honor, respect, and reverence to His name.

God's name can also be taken in vain when used in such expressions as shock, surprise, anger, amazement, disappointment, pain, etc. Examples are: 'Oh my God (OMG)!' 'Good Lord!' 'Jesus Christ!'
Thinking before speaking out thoughtlessly when using these names of *God* or *Jesus* helps to avoid such disrespect. Additionally, the Lord's name is expressed flippantly in worship or Christian expressions without considering the respect due to God. Another saying is 'God bless you' when someone sneezes.

Jesus spoke of people honoring Him with their lips, but their hearts were far away from Him.[30] There is a difference between speaking about God carelessly versus speaking about God prayerfully and reverently. Please start to take the time to be aware of using His name in vain, or bad habits that cause you to use His name in vain. Try to replace them with other words that do not refer to the Lord's name. If you find it difficult to do at first, pray to the Lord and ask for forgiveness, and God will show you the way to break this habit.

---

[28] Romans 2:21-24
[29] Ephesians 4:29 and Colossians 3:8
[30] Matthew 15:8

Another way to take the Lord's name in vain is by using euphemisms used in place of God such as 'gosh' or 'golly.' In addition, to take the Lord's name in vain is when it is used for personal gain by preachers, politicians, and other businessmen (or women), and through ill-gotten gains. God commands us to pray for our pastors, politicians, and officials or leaders in command, and those who have a wide influence over others that are not taking the Lord's name in vain for gain. Lastly, one can speak vainly by a failure to keep a promise, pledge, or vow made in God's name.[31]

---

[31] Matthew 5:33-37; James 5:12

Begin Day 10:
God's Laws: The Third Commandment
Dangers of taking the
Lord's Name in Vain

Exodus 20:7, NKJV: *"You shall not take the Lord, your God, in vain, for the Lord will not hold him guiltless who takes His name in vain."*

The *Third Commandment* refers to the sanctity of God's name.[32] Taking the Lord's (Yahweh) name in vain involves trivializing His name by regarding it as insignificant. For instance, some horror movies make jests, using words like 'Holy crap,' or 'Oh, my God.' They are simply using God's name in vain for evil purposes by coaxing God in violation to His character and purposes. Yet, punishment is usually not immediate.[33]

However, no one can hide from God.[34] Conversely, those who take God's name in vain are not fulfilling the purpose for which they were created.[35] While we may not say these exact words in prayer or an urgent moment in entreaty to Him, consider what might happen if we, who know better, had such a prayer of condemnation answered. Could we find ourselves cursing the things or people He has given us in blessing?

Using his name in anger can have effects that we don't see. It can hurt those who hear, as well as cause us to be more depressed and angry in a vicious circle.

God's name demonstrates His character, His mercy, and His greatness. Throughout the Bible, prophets and prophetesses names were associated with their character. Today, we try to get all fancy and unique with our children's names. When we do that, the names have no true meaning or relationship to their character when they mature. We may not know where our children's names derived from, or the definition of their names. For instance, the name *Abram* means 'exalted father,' which later was changed to *Abraham*, 'father of a multitude.'[36] The name *Esau* means red or hairy. *Jacob* stands for 'heel-catcher, trickster, deceiver,' and later was changed to *Israel*, which means prince with God, one who struggles with God.[37]

---

[32] Nelson Study Bible, NKJV.
[33] Ecclesiastes 8:11
[34] Psalm 139:7-12; Proverbs 15:3; Jeremiah 23:24; Daniel 5:23; Acts 17:28; Hebrews 10:31
[35] Isaiah 43:7, 21; Matthew 5:16; 1 Corinthians 10:31; Revelation 4:11
[36] Genesis 17:1-6
[37] Genesis 25:21-26; 32:24-30

Begin Day 11:
God's Laws: The Third Commandment: Guarding your Heart

Some of the defenses against taking the Lord's name in vain are:
- Choosing carefully the things you look at, or listen to or engage in
- As a person anointed with the Holy Spirit of God, trying to develop clean words to express emotions without God's name being a part of the expression.

We can practice using God's name reverently or respectfully because God is holy. We are to live a life that glorifies God's name. Look at these verses about the Name of God. They describe His name as:
- Safety – Proverbs 18:10
- Salvation – 2 Timothy 2:19 & Romans 10:13
- National Blessing – Psalm 72:17
- Healer – Exodus 15:26
- Peace – Judges 6:24
- Victory – Deuteronomy 20:4
- Protector – Psalm 91

Every time God describes himself in the Bible, He precedes it with the words "I AM."

Adríenna Dionna Turner

Begin Day 12:
God's Laws:
The Fourth Commandment

The *Fourth Commandment* is the most controversial of the *Ten Commandments*.

In the beginning of time, when Adam and Eve explored their paradise home, the scenery was breathtaking and beyond description. As beautiful as the world God created and completed, the greatest gift God gave to the newly created couple was the privilege of a personal relationship with Him.

Therefore, God gave them the *Sabbath*, a day of special blessing, fellowship, and communion with their Creator. The Sabbath is central to our worship of God. It reveals the reason God is to be worshipped: for He is the Creator, and we are His creatures. The true grounds of divine worship are found in the distinction between the Creator and His creation. This great fact can never be obsolete and must never be forgotten.[38]

In examining these texts, we find that, according to the *Fourth Commandment*, God set aside and made the seventh day of the week holy. It is the day we call "Saturday."

1. God rested on the Sabbath.
2. God blessed the Sabbath.
3. God sanctified the Sabbath.

The reasons God gave the Sabbath to the Jews:
- need for rest and to be refreshed;[39]
- remember the Sabbath day
- God rested on the seventh day.

God rested on the seventh day, not because he was weary, but because the work of creation was completed.[40] Additionally, God rested because He expected humans to rest in Him. He set an example for human beings to follow.[41] God not only made the Sabbath, He blessed it. The blessings on the seventh day implied that it was thereby declared to be a special object of divine favor.

---

[38] Seventh-Day Adventists Believe: A Biblical Exposition of 27 Fundamental Doctrines.
[39] Exodus 20:8-10; 31:17
[40] John 4:24; Psalm 121:4; Isaiah 40:28
[41] Exodus 20:11

Begin Day 13:
God's Laws: The Fourth Commandment –
God Sanctified the Sabbath

Last, but not least, God sanctified the Sabbath. To *sanctify* something means to make it sacred or holy, or to set it apart as holy and for holy use, to consecrate it. People, places, and time can be sanctified. The fact that God sanctified the seventh day means that this day is holy, that He set it apart for the lofty purpose of enriching the divine-human relationship.[42] God blessed and sanctified the seventh day Sabbath because He rested on this day from all His works. He blessed and sanctified it for humanity, not for Himself. His personal presence brings to the Sabbath God's blessing and sanctification.[43] Just as God has set the Sabbath aside for a holy purpose, so He has set His people apart for a holy purpose to be His special witnesses. Their communion with Him on the Sabbath day leads to holiness, where they learn to depend, not on their own resources, but on the God who sanctifies them.

True sanctification is harmony with God, oneness with Him in character. It is received through obedience to those principles that are the transcript of His character.

Without the Sabbath, all would be labor and sweat without end. Similar to the admonition to honor God's name, honoring the Sabbath has healthful benefits as well. People who work seven days a week quickly find themselves worn, mentally and physically. You will note that God, and Jewish tradition, started the new day in the evening. Consider the thought process of resting when we sleep. Would you rather rest from the day behind, or rest for the day ahead? Honor the Sabbath and keep it holy is to have a day to remember God forever.

The arrival of the Sabbath brings hope, joy, meaning, and courage. It provides time to commune with God through worship, prayer, song, the study of and meditation on the Word, and through sharing the gospel with others. The Sabbath is our opportunity to experience God's presence.

---

[42] Seventh-Day Adventists Believe: A Biblical Exposition of 27 Fundamental Doctrines, p. 250.
[43] Seventh-Day Adventists Believe: A Biblical Exposition of 27 Fundamental Doctrines, p.250.

Begin Day 14:
God's Laws: The Fourth Commandment - Sabbatical Law

Sabbath observance is an antidote for idolatry, illness, and evil of all kinds. Keeping the Sabbath then becomes the sign of our allegiance to the true God—a sign that we acknowledge His Sovereignty as Creator.[44]

Also, the Sabbath is the sign of obedience. He who, from the heart, obeys the *Fourth Commandment* will obey the whole law. He is sanctified through obedience. Following God's laws more than human principles and practices is far more important. The Bible, God's Word, is above the church and its fundamentals. The *Sabbath Commandment* is a seal of God's law because the person respecting God by observing the Sabbath gains enough rest, enough focus, and enough compassion to be a vessel through which God can spread His love to the world.

---

[44] Seventh-Day Adventists Believe: A Biblical Exposition of 27 Fundamental Doctrines, p.251.

Begin Day 15:
God's Laws:
Fourth Commandment – A Changed Day

The change in corporate worship from Saturday to Sunday was not made by the Pope, the Catholic Church, Christians in Rome, nor Constantine. The early Christians were worshipping on Sunday before the Pope and the Catholic Church, and the Romans did not have a Sabbath day. Constantine made Sunday a legal holiday in 321 A.D. since Christians were already worshipping on Sunday.

There were several reasons for the change. The first reason is that Jesus rose from the dead on Sunday, which is the first day of the week.[45] In other words, for early Christians, Saturday Sabbath commemorated God's rest, and Sunday commemorated Jesus' resurrection. *Luke 24:1* says that the day Jesus rose from the grave was the first day of the week. However, the Bible speaks about a three-day sequence: the day before the Sabbath (the day Jesus died); the Sabbath; and the first day of the week (the day Jesus rose from the dead). Everyone in the world is able to recognize Good Friday as the day Jesus died. The entire world recognizes Easter Sunday as the day He rose to life. The second reason is the first appearance of Jesus after His resurrection was on Sunday, the first day of the week.[46] The third reason is the appearance of Jesus to John on the Island of Patmos was on Sunday.[47] The early Christians called Sunday, *The Lord's Day*.[48] The fourth reason is the Holy Spirit descended, and the early church was born, and believers were added to the Church on the Day of Pentecost, which was on Sunday.[49] The fifth reason was that the early Church met for corporate worship on Sunday.[50] According to the Jews, Sabbath is sundown Friday until sundown Saturday. For the Romans, Sabbath is at midnight on Sunday until midnight on Monday. The sixth reason is freedom regarding the day of worship.[51] [52]

Since the Sabbath plays a vital role in the worship of God as Creator and Redeemer, it is not surprising that Satan has waged an all-out war to overthrow a sacred institution. Surprisingly, there is no verse in the Bible which authorizes a change from the day of worship God made in Eden and restated on Mount Sinai.

---

[45] Matthew 28:1-10; Mark 16:1-8; Luke 24:1-12; John 20:1-9
[46] Matthew 28:1-10; Mark 16:9-14; Luke 24:13-43; John 20:19-29
[47] Revelation 1:10

[49] Acts 2:1-47
[50] Acts 20:7; 1 Corinthians 16:2
[51] Romans 14:5-8; Galatians 4:9-10; Colossians 2:16-17
[52] Malone, Julius. *Introduction to the Ten Commandments*. Sermon at New Testament Church. Milwaukee, 2004.

Begin Day 16:
God's Laws:
The Fourth Commandment -Sun-Day

If there is no biblical evidence that Christ or His disciples changed the day of worship from the seventh day, then how did Christians come to accept Sunday in its place? The change from Sabbath to Sunday worship came gradually.

There is evidence that by the middle of the second century, some Christians were voluntarily observing The Lord's Day (Sunday) as a day of worship, not a day of rest. The Church of Rome, mainly Gentile believers,[53] led in the trend toward Sunday worship. In Rome, strong anti-Jewish sentiments arose, becoming stronger as time passed. Christians tried to distinguish themselves from the Jews, which trended away from the veneration of the Sabbath and moving towards the exclusive observance of Sunday. From the second to the fifth centuries, while Sunday was rising in influence, Christians continued to observe the Seventh-Day Sabbath nearly everywhere throughout the Roman Empire.

Ask yourself: Why did those who turned from worship on the seventh day choose Sunday and not another day of the week? Some believe since Christ was resurrected on Sunday, it was alleged that He had authorized worship on that day. Because of the popularity and influence of the Sun God, pagan worship practiced by Babylonians (and later the Romans), Sunday was a day of worship throughout their empires. Sun worship played an important role throughout the ancient world. It was one of the oldest components of the Roman religions. The popular religion had an effect on the early church through the new converts. Christian converts from paganism were easily attracted by the veneration of the Sun.

During the fourth century, Constantine saw the opportunity in Sunday laws. The first Sunday laws of a civil nature were issued, later known as *religious character*. Emperor Constantine decreed the first civil Sunday law on March 7, A.D. 321. Because of Sunday's popularity among the pagan sun worshipers and its esteem among many Christians, Constantine hoped that by making Sunday a holiday, he could ensure the support of these two constituencies for his government. Several decades later, the church followed this example as the Council of Laodicea (A.D. 364) issued the first ecclesiastical Sunday law. Many Christians honor Sunday. A.D. 538 was the year marked as the beginning of the 1260-year prophecy, where the Roman Catholic Third Council of Orleans issued a law even more severe than that of Constantine.[54]

---

[53] Romans 11:13
[54] Seventh-Day Adventists Believe: A Biblical Exposition of 27 Fundamental Doctrines, 258-260.

Begin Day 17:
God's Laws:
The Fourth Commandment - Preparation

We can set a day aside throughout the week for Sabbath and make the preparations necessary to observe it in a manner pleasing to God. Be careful not to exhaust our energies. Since this day is a special communion with God, we are to avoid anything that tends to diminish its sacred atmosphere. We are to cease our secular work and avoid all work we do to earn a living, and all business transactions.[55] In other words, we are to devote this day to God, instead of pleasing ourselves. We tend to be more involved in secular interests such as conversations and thoughts with our significant other or to be engaging in sports that would distract from communion with our Creator, and violate the sacredness of the Sabbath. We are to enjoy the blessings of the Sabbath.

Generally, the Sabbath begins at sunset on Friday evening and ends at sunset Saturday evening.[56] Scriptures refer to the day before the Sabbath which is preparation day. *Preparation day* is a day to prepare for the Sabbath so that nothing will interrupt its sacredness.[57] Therefore, we prepare food for the Sabbath, so that during its sacred hours, we can rest from our labors.[58] When the hours of the Sabbath approach, family members (or groups of believers) can get together on Friday evening to worship and invite the Spirit of Christ as a guest. We are to unite in worship requesting God's presence and guidance through the week.

The *Sabbath* is a day of delight, joy, and remembrance of our Holy Father. We are following the example of Christ, who regularly worshipped on the Sabbath, took part in the services, and gave religious instruction.[59] Jesus Christ did more than just worship, He also fellowshipped with others,[60] spent time outdoors,[61] and went about doing holy deeds of mercy. Wherever He could, He healed the sick and afflicted.[62] [63]

There are some things to put into practice on the Lord's Day. We are to rest the body, soul, and spirit. The *Sabbath principle* is to rest one day out of the seven days. This day of rest refreshes and restores us. Spiritual rest is found in God and results in physical rest. This is a time to rejoice – a balance between work and worship. Worship is to be a priority when serving God. We are to reflect on Jesus, who created man on the sixth day and required us to rest on the seventh day. On the day of rest, we can spend time with our family, friends, and/or

---

[55] Nehemiah 13:15-22
[56] Genesis 1:5; Mark 1:32
[57] Mark 15:42
[58] Exodus 16:23; Numbers 11:8
[59] Mark 1:21; 3:1-4; Luke 4:16-27; 13:10
[60] Mark 1:29-31; Luke 14:1
[61] Mark 2:23
[62] Mark 1:21-31; Luke 13:10-17; John 5:1-15
[63] Seventh-Day Adventists Believe: A Biblical Exposition of 27 Fundamental Doctrines, 261-262.

believers of Jesus Christ. Moreover, remember that God is the source of creation, salvation, and sanctification.[64]

---

[64] Malone, Julius. *Introduction to the Ten Commandments*. Sermon at New Testament Church (Milwaukee, WI) notes taken by author, 2004.

Begin Day 18:
God's Laws:
Fourth Commandment - The Sabbath Principle

"You shall delight yourself in the Lord." [65]

We are to look forward to what we delight in. These men found delight in God: David;[66] Asaph;[67] and Job.[68] God will honor your reverence once you delight in Him.[69] Next, God will provide you a full share of the blessings He promises. For example, He promises that you will feast on the inheritance of Jacob.[70] Plus, you will experience divine health.[71]

---

[65] Isaiah 58:14; Psalm 37:4
[66] Psalm 27:4
[67] Psalm 73:25
[68] Job 23:12
[69] Isaiah 58:14; Psalm 75: 6-7; 27:5; Proverbs 21:1; Habakkuk 3:17-19
[70] Isaiah 58:14, The Living Bible
[71] Exodus 15:26, Psalm 103:3

Adríenna Dionna Turner

Begin Day 19:
God's Laws:
The Fourth Commandment –
Breaking the Commandment

The *Fourth Commandment* stresses the word, "Remember." While most believers agree the other nine Commandments are still binding today and will be binding throughout all eternity, they feel the *Fourth Commandment* was done away with. The word, "*Remember*," tells us that God knew people were going to have enough trouble with the commandment that they would be tempted to forget it.[72]

In *Luke 6:3-5*, the priests tried to accuse Jesus of breaking the Sabbath Day. Contrary to their accusation, the story of David elaborates on how David and his men ate consecrated bread, was a need greater than any ceremonial regulations.[73] Jesus demonstrated a parallel principle with this story of David:

Human need is more important than regulations and rules.

Another Scripture tells us about Jesus (supposedly) breaking the Sabbath day, it was after Sabbath sunset:

> *"At evening, when the sun had set, they brought Him all who were sick and those who were demon-possessed. Moreover, the whole city gathered at the door. Then, He healed many who were sick with various diseases and cast out many demons, and He did not allow the demons to speak because they knew Him."*[74]

In the Sabbath healing of the blind man, recorded in *John 9*, Jesus extends to His followers the invitation to become links of the same redemptive chain.[75]
Although Jesus was criticized for His work of alleviating suffering, Jesus replied, "It is lawful to do well on the Sabbath."[76] Jesus' healing activities neither broke the Sabbath nor abolished it. God intended the Sabbath for humanity's spiritual refreshment and enrichment.

This reflects the relationship between the Sabbath and Christ's work of salvation alluded in two Sabbath miracles: the healing of the paralytic [77] and healing of the blind man.[78] Christ's justification is expressed through a memorable statement: "My Father is working until now, and I am working."[79]

---

[72] Shelton, Danny. *The Forgotten Commandment: A Battle For Our Loyalty To Christ Or Man*, p. 7.
[73] 1 Samuel 21:1-6
[74] Mark 1:32-34
[75] John 9:2*
[76] Matthew 12:12
[77] John 5:1-18
[78] John 9:1-41
[79] John 5:17; 9:4

Jesus answered, "The work of God is this: to believe in the one He has sent."[80] Therefore, we have to believe that God sent Jesus to do the works of the Father, which, according to Jesus, who said, "the Father is in me and I am in the Father."[81] Christ appeals to the 'working' of His Father not to nullify, but to clarify the function of the Sabbath. To understand Christ's defense, one must remember that the Sabbath is linked to both the creation [82] and redemption.[83]

While interrupting all secular activities, the Israelites were remembering the Creator God, by acting mercifully toward fellow-beings. They were imitating the Redeemer-God. For Jesus Christ, the Sabbath is the day to work for the redemption of the whole man. This comes from the fact that in both healings, where Jesus looked for the healed men on the same day and having found them, He ministered to their spiritual need.[84] Jesus' opponents cannot perceive the redemptive nature of His Sabbath ministry because they judge by appearances.[85]

To bring about the final Sabbath, the Godhead 'is working' for our salvation, but we must extend it to others. If your activities distract you from your purpose and let you turn the Sabbath into a holiday, make sure your intentions are proper according to God. The Lord of the Sabbath invites all to follow His example. Those who accept His call experience the Sabbath as a delight and spiritual feast. Week by week, the seventh day comforts our conscience, assuring us that despite our unfinished characters, we stand complete in Christ. His accomplishment at Calvary counts as our atonement. We enter His rest.[86]

---

[80] John 6:29
[81] John 10:37, 38; 4:34; 14:11; 15:24
[82] Genesis 2:2-3; Exodus 20:11
[83] Deuteronomy 5:15
[84] John 5:14; 9:35-38
[85] John 7:24
[86] Seventh-Day Adventists Believe: A Biblical Exposition of 27 Fundamental Doctrines, p. 264.

Begin Day 20:
God's Laws:
The Fifth Commandment

The *Fifth Commandment* is the first of the six commandments involving our horizontal relationship with others. This is how we learn to relate to others. Strong families equal strong churches, which equal strong communities, which equal strong countries. Originally, the command is to *honor your father and honor your mother*. *Honor* is derived from the translation of a Hebrews verb meaning, 'to be heavy or weighty.'[87] In other words, *honor* is to weigh someone down with respect, reverence, esteem, and significance. To *honor* means to 'place value on, to consider important.'

There are two promises granted by following this Commandment.[88] One promise is to live longer on the earth if we obey our parents, and show honor to them.[89] For instance, as I reflect on my great-grandmother, Gran, who lived until the age of 102, I strongly believe that Gran honored her parents to live slightly over a century. She was born April 27, 1902, died on July 27, 2004. The second promise is *that it may be well with you*.[90] [91]

---

[87] Exodus 20:12
[88] Exodus 20:23; Ephesians 6:2-3
[89] Exodus 20:12; Ezekiel 22:7; Ephesians 6:3
[90] Deuteronomy 5:16; Ephesians 6:3
[91] Malone, Julius. *Introduction to the Ten Commandments*. Sermon at New Testament Church. Milwaukee, 2004 and emphasis added by author.

Begin Day 21:
God's Laws:
The Sixth Commandment

The *Sixth Commandment* is the most misunderstood and misused since the Hebrew word *ratsach* or *rasah* in Exodus 20:13 are translated 'kill' rather than 'murder.' In the Bible, all murder is killing, but not all killing is murder.

According to the *Nelson's Illustrated Bible Dictionary*, *murder* is the unlawful killing of one person by another, especially with premeditated malice.

Some examples of murder:
- *Homicide* is the unlawful killing of one human being by another.[92]
- *Suicide* is self-murder.[93] Can a person who commits suicide go to heaven?[94]
- *Abortion* is the killing of the unborn in the womb. When does life begin?[95]
- *Euthanasia* is a Greek word *Eu*, which means 'good,' and *Thanatos* means 'death.' *Euthanasia* literally means 'good death.' Other names used are 'mercy killing' and 'doctor-assisted suicide.'

God will require each person to account for his or her actions.[96] We cannot harm or kill another human being without answering to the Creator. A penalty must be paid. Justice will be served. God's description of the humans he created explains why murder is wrong: to kill a person is to kill one made *in God's image*. Human beings are made in God's image, which all people possess the qualities that distinguish them from animals: morality, reason, creativity, and self-worth. When we interact with others, they are beings made by and to whom God offers eternal life. God wants us to recognize His image in all people.

---

[92] Numbers 35:15-18
[93] 1 Corinthians 6:19-20
[94] John 10:28-29; Romans 8:35-39; Judges 16:28-30
[95] Genesis 25:21-26; Exodus 4:11; Job 10:8-12; Jeremiah 1:5; Psalm 127: 3; 139:13-16; Matthew 18:10; Luke 1:41-44
[96] Life Application Bible, NKJV, 1996.

Begin Day 22:
God's Laws:
The Sixth Commandment - Suicide

Pastor Julius Malone states that suicide is a violation of the *Sixth Commandment.* Over twenty-five thousand Americans commit suicide each year. More Americans die from suicide than homicide. Suicide is listed among the top ten causes of death in the U.S. The model age for attempting suicide is thirty-two for men and twenty-seven for women, and the succeeding age is fifty through fifty-four for men and women. Sadly, current statistics are showing the ages for the sexes are much younger. Men generally kill themselves twice as often as women, but women attempt suicide twice as often as men do. There are over five thousand suicides among teenagers each year. Suicide is the second highest cause of death among young adults aged fifteen through twenty-four, surpassing accidents.

Some reasons or motives for suicide can be classified as d*epression*—usually, severely depressed individuals are potential suicides. Those described in the Bible who wanted to die are Jonah[97] and Elijah.[98] Other reasons or motives for committing suicide can be *retaliation,* where many young people take their lives trying to get back at a family member, friend, or loved one. *Reunion* is another reason for suicide. Some people take their lives to be reunited with someone who has deceased or died. *Reincarnation* is also a reason where some people believe that after death they will return in a different and better condition or circumstance. Some Native American and African rituals and beliefs refer to reincarnation as a cycle of nature and life. *Retroflex* is the killing of oneself in place of someone who is unreachable. One example in the Bible is Ahithophel.[99] *Retribution* is where some commit suicide in an effort to punish themselves. For example, Judas had strong feelings of guilt for what happened to Jesus Christ, and his carcass hung from the tree.[100] *Rejection* can be such as divorce, separation, or rejection by peers, parents and other family members, work, etc. *Pain* can be physical, emotional, or mental, thinking it will never end.

Warning signs: One will usually talk about suicide, death, or dying. In addition, someone in a suicidal state of mind will talk about being helpless, hopeless, and show signs of self-worthlessness, including withdrawal and isolation from family, friends, co-workers, peers, and other social contacts. Other signs can be *loss of interest* such as hobbies, personal appearance, mood swings, behaving recklessly, giving away valued possessions and writing out wills. *Recent losses* are layoffs and involuntary terminations of employment, deceased loved ones, disturbances in sleeping patterns, long periods of sadness, and drowning in drunkenness or getting high.

Please do not think suicide is your way of escaping your failure and half-forgotten dreams disappear by taking your own life. Moreover, taking your life is a selfish, independent act that

---

[97] Jonah 4:1-3
[98] 1 Kings 19:1-4
[99] 2 Samuel 17:23
[100] Matthew 27:3-5

takes God out of the equation. Do not think suicide is the final answer. God can unleash your destiny if you just ask, seek, and knock.

Prevention of suicide: If you see the signs of a loved one or person thinking suicidal thoughts or actions, please do not leave them alone. They need to seek professional help. Through prayers, whether it is praying in private or interceding with others is another way to prevent someone committing suicide. We can show love, appreciation, and concern, including a willingness to listen by allowing the person to talk and express his or herself freely without judging or ridiculing. Criticism or making them feel guilty can make matters worse. It does not minimize the problem. We have to take it seriously and cautiously with love. They may say they are fine, but even if they say they are, we can find encouraging words to edify and lift them up. Find creative things that would help this person overlook their problems or troubles. Through love, we are displaying God's love for His creation, and He wants the best for us all and loves us. There is a time for healing in which we are to believe and trust in God.

Begin Day 23:
God's Laws: The Sixth Commandment - Biblical reasons to reject suicide

In an effort to escape a temporary problem, one may run themselves into a permanent problem.[101] There is no problem greater than eternal torment in hell.

Instead of accepting suicide or his death, the Philippians' jailor turned to Jesus.[102] There is rest in Jesus.[103] Suicide causes pain and shame for friends and family. For the saved, *suicide* is a violation of the *Sixth Commandment*. Our life belongs to God, who is our Creator and Redeemer.[104] Suicide is not a part of God's plan for a life.[105] Suicide dishonors God.[106] Loss rewards will be suffered at the Judgment Seat of Christ.[107]

If you are having suicidal thoughts, do not isolate yourself from others.[108] We are to rest in the sovereignty of God and to seek God's grace.[109] Some argue that Christian music can be both uplifting and depressing.[110] However, we can sing songs from the heart,[111] speak the Word into our lives, and give thanks to the Lord.[112]

When dealing with a suicide, one is concerned about the deceased. Some believe that suicide is the only unpardonable sin because it cannot be repented after one has taken one's life. The *unpardonable sin* is to die without Jesus Christ.[113] All other sins can be forgiven. Murderers who were forgiven: Moses[114] and David.[115] *Salvation* is by grace through faith.[116] A relationship with Christ determines one's destiny, not the last thing that one did before death. God's grace saved us. The meaning of justification, sanctification, and glorification is found in *Romans 3:21-28*. *Justification* is deliverance from the penalty of sin—past, present, and future.[117] *Justification* is also a declaration of righteousness because of what Jesus did on the cross.[118] There are no degrees of justification. *Justification* is the result of

---

[101] Luke 16:19-24
[102] Acts 16:27
[103] Matthew 11:28-30
[104] Psalm 24:1; Romans 14:7-8; 1 Corinthians 6:19-20; Ephesians 2:10; 1 Peter 1:18-19
[105] Jeremiah 29:11; John 10:10; Revelation 4:11
[106] 1 Corinthians 10:31; Revelation 4:11
[107] Romans 14:10-12; 1 Corinthians 3:11-15
[108] 1 Kings 19:3; Hebrews 10:24-25
[109] 2 Corinthians 12:9-10
[110] 1 Samuel 16:14-23
[111] Psalm 34:1; 42:5; 103:1-5
[112] 1 Thessalonians 5:18
[113] John 14:6; Acts 4:12; Romans 1:20-23
[114] Exodus 2:11-15
[115] 2 Samuel 12:9-14
[116] Ephesians 2:8-9
[117] Romans 6:23
[118] Isaiah 53:5-6; Romans 3:21-28; 2 Corinthians 5:21; Romans 10:1-4; Philippians 3:7-14

predestination.[119] *Sanctification* is proof of justification. *Sanctification* is deliverance from the power of sin.[120] *Glorification* is deliverance from the presence of sin.[121] [122]

---

[119] Romans 8:28-30
[120] Philippians 2:12-13; 1 Thessalonians 4:3
[121] Romans 13:11
[122] Malone, Julius. *Introduction to the Ten Commandments*. Sermon at New Testament Church (Milwaukee, WI) notes taken by author, 2004.

Begin Day 24:
God's Laws:
The Sixth Commandment – Eternal Life

John 5:24, NKJV: *Jesus says, "Most assuredly, I say to you, he who hears My word and believes in Him who sent Me has everlasting life, and shall not come into judgment, but has passed from death into life."*

The verb in the above verse, *passed*, is translated from the Greek word, *Metabebeken*, and means "changing my place."

Everlasting life is living forever with God, which begins when you accept Jesus Christ as your Savior. At that moment, new life begins in you.[123] It is a completed transaction. You will face physical death, but when Christ returns, your body will be resurrected to live forever.[124]

The verb in the following verse, *perish*, is translated from the Greek word, *apolontai*, meaning "shall never be lost."

John 10:28, NKJV: *Jesus says, "And I give them eternal life, and they shall never perish; neither shall anyone snatch them out of My hand."*

A shepherd protects his sheep.[125] Jesus protects His people from eternal harm. While believers can expect to suffer on earth, Satan cannot harm their souls or take away their eternal life with God. There are many reasons to be afraid here on earth because this is the devil's domain.[126] However, if you choose to follow Jesus, He will give you everlasting safety.

In *Jeremiah 31:3*, nothing can separate a true believer from the love of God. God reaches toward His people with kindness motivated by deep and everlasting love. He is eager to do the best for them if they will only let Him. After many words of warning about sin, this reminder of God's magnificent love is a breath of fresh air. Rather than thinking of God with dread, look carefully and see Him lovingly drawing toward Himself.

The verses in Romans 8:35-39 contain one of the most comforting promises. Believers have always had to face hardships in many forms: persecution, illness, imprisonment, even death. These could cause them to fear that Christ has abandoned them. However, Paul exclaims that it is impossible to be separated from Christ. His death for us is proof of His unconquerable love. Nothing can stop Christ's constant presence with us. God tells us how great His love is so that we will feel secure in Him. If we believe these overwhelming assurances, we will not be afraid.[127]

---

[123] 2 Corinthians 5:17
[124] Life Application Study Bible, New King James Version, 1 Corinthians 15.
[125] Life Application Study Bible, New King James Version; John 10:28-29.
[126] 1 Peter 5:8

Begin Day 25:
God's Laws:
The Sixth Commandment – Samson's Suicide

Samson committed the act of suicide.[128] The question many of us ask is: Will Samson go to heaven after committing such an act?

We experience victory through faith in Christ. Our victory over oppressors may be like those of the Old Testament saints, but more likely, our victories will be directly related to the role God wants us to play. Even though our bodies die and deteriorate, we will live forever because of Christ. In the promised resurrection, even death will be defeated, and Christ's victory will be made complete.

Samson lost his legendary strength and subsequently, his eyesight because he was deceived by a harlot (Delilah). Blind, he prayed to God for the return of his strength, and, once his hair grew back, he was strong again. The Philistines made fun of his strength, requiring him to perform acts of strength to entertain them as they praised their god, Dagon. Asking his guide to place his hands between pillars, Samson prayed for strength enough to kill the Philistines in attendance. The Bible records him as having died with them as the roof fell, and that many more died in his death than while he lived.[129]

After analyzing the scenario, is it suicide and killing when you are granted the strength to destroy the evildoers instead of allowing the Lord to take care of it in a supernatural way? We tend to want to help God out when the Lord tells us that, "Vengeance is the Lord's," and sometimes we want to take matters into our own hands. Samson received insight on how to destroy these people, including him, which for him, was exactly what he felt was necessary.

God will allow things to happen in our lives for many reasons. Usually, things of the world blind us, and until we seek *Him* for guidance, we are unable to see His purpose. Open your eyes and mind, and seek the Lord Jesus.

---

[128] Hebrews 11:32
[129] Judges 16

Begin Day 26:
God's Laws: The Sixth Commandment – Great Men of Faith Sought Death

Hebrews 11:32-40 summarizes the lives of other great men and women of faith. Some experienced outstanding victories, even over the threat of death. Nevertheless, others were severely mistreated, tortured, and even killed. Having a steadfast faith in God does not guarantee a happy, carefree life.

On the contrary, our faith almost guarantees us some form of abuse from the world. While we are on earth, we may never see the purpose of our suffering. However, we know that God will keep His promises to us. Do you believe that God will keep His promises to you? God understands our fears, our weaknesses, and our disappointments. God promised never to leave us,[130] and He intercedes on our behalf. In the times of pain, persecution, or suffering, we should trust confidently in Christ.

Many think that pain is the exception in the Christian life. When suffering occurs, they say, "Why me?" They feel as though God deserted them, or perhaps they accuse Him of not being as dependable as they thought. God will allow some followers of Christ to become martyrs for the faith, and He allows others to survive persecution. Our faith, the values of the world, is on a collision course. If we expect pain and suffering to come, we will not be shocked when it hits. However, we can also take comfort in knowing that Jesus also suffered. In reality, however, we live in an evil world filled with suffering, even for believers. Think of Elijah, with his suicidal thoughts, when he wanted death to come on him. Jezebel and her worshippers were after him with a death sentence. However, God was still in control.

---

[130] Matthew 28:18-20

Begin Day 27:
God's Laws:
The Sixth Commandment: Killing Examples

Under the old covenant, twenty-six crimes punishable by death were written in the Bible. Eleven of those are mentioned below:[131]

1. Murder of another [132]
2. Striking father or mother [133]
3. Rebelling against one's parents [134]
4. Kidnapping [135]
5. An aborted child because of a fight [136]
6. Negligence resulting in the death of a person [137]
7. Adultery [138]
8. Cursing one's parents [139]
9. Incest [140]
10. Rape [141]
11. Homosexuality [142]

Capital punishment in the New Testament:[143] [144]
1. Accidental killing is not murder [145]
2. Killing in self-defense is not murder [146]
3. Killing plants and animals for food and shelter is not prohibited by the Sixth Commandment [147]
4. Killing of insects
5. Killing someone in war is not murder. What is a just war? [148]

---

[131] Malone, Julius. *Introduction to the Ten Commandments*. Sermon at New Testament Church (Milwaukee, WI) notes taken by author, 2004.
[132] Genesis 9:6; Exodus 21:12-14; Leviticus 24:17, 21; Numbers 35:16-21, 30-33
[133] Exodus 21:15
[134] Deuteronomy 21:18-21
[135] Exodus 21:16
[136] Exodus 21:22-23
[137] Exodus 21:28-29
[138] Leviticus 20:10; Deuteronomy 22:22
[139] Exodus 21:17
[140] Leviticus 20:11
[141] Deuteronomy 22:23-24
[142] Leviticus 18:22; 20:13; Romans 1:24-28; 1 Corinthians 6:9-11
[143] Romans 13:1-5; 1 Peter 2:13-14
[144] Malone, Julius. *Introduction to the Ten Commandments*. Sermon at New Testament Church. Milwaukee, 2004.
[145] Numbers 35:9-15; Deuteronomy 19:4-15; Joshua 20:1-6
[146] Exodus 22:2
[147] Genesis 3:21; 9:3: 1 Timothy 4:3-5
[148] Exodus 17:8-16; 1 Samuel 15:1-3

Begin Day 28:
God's Laws: Sixth Commandment - War

Killing in a just war is not murder. In the fourth century, St. Augustine developed the *Just War theory* and the eight principles are:[149]

1. *Proper authority* is a war that must be declared by a legitimate government, and not by private individuals and groups.[150]
2. *Proper cause* is a war for defense, protection, etc., and would be a just cause.
3. *Right intention* is goals for peace, safety, freedom, not revenge, plunder, and conquest.
4. *Comparative justice* is the evil that is fought and must be sufficient to justify killing.
5. *Murder* is the deliberate taking of an innocent human life that is forbidden, even in wartime.
6. *Proportionality* is where the government waging war must be sure that the destruction caused by their responses to aggression does not exceed the destruction caused by the aggression itself. Annihilation of a country that is retaliated against because of an attack on a city would be *disproportion*.
7. *The probability of success* must be a confident expectation that the action will achieve its objectives.
8. *Last resort* is when war should not be waged unless all negotiation possibilities have been exhausted.

There are wars which defend against evil aggression.[151] There are Scriptures elaborating further on deliverance from evil aggression,[152] and to deter the spread of evil when in battle.[153] President George W. Bush had our soldiers in Iraq under digress by seeking counsel from government officials and leaders that can either start and/or end a war.[154] Is there a reasonable sense of hope of the success in war? Is there a confident expectation that going to war will end more evil than it will cause? Should we serve in the military?

The New Testament does not condemn soldiers for serving in the military. Some examples are listed below.

1. John the Baptist responds to the soldiers that came to him[155]
2. Jesus to the centurion who came to Him[156]
3. Peter to Cornelius[157]
4. Picture of the soldier is used in the letters of Paul to describe the Christian life[158]

---

[149] Malone, Julius. *Introduction to the Ten Commandments*. Sermon at New Testament Church. Milwaukee, 2004.
[150] Romans 13:1
[151] 2 Chronicles 20:1-30; Romans 13:1-7
[152] Genesis 14:1-24; 1 Samuel 30:1-19; and Judges 6:11-16; 13:5
[153] Numbers 33:55-56; Deuteronomy 20:16-18; Deuteronomy 20:10-12; Ecclesiastes 3:8; Romans 12:18
[154] Proverbs 20:18; 24:6
[155] Luke 3:14
[156] Luke 7:1-10
[157] Acts 10:1-48
[158] Ephesians 6:13-17; 2 Timothy 2:3-4

Begin Day 29:
God's Laws: The Sixth Commandment - Pray for Leaders on War

Believers are to pray for our leaders in office and for our soldiers in war.

1 Timothy 2:1-8, NIV: *"I urge, then, first of all, that requests, prayers, intercession and thanksgiving be made for everyone—for kings (president, officials, government) and all those in authority, that we may live peaceful and quiet lives in all godliness and holiness. This is good, and pleases God our Savior, who wants all men to be saved and to come to knowledge of the truth. For there is one God and one mediator, the man Christ Jesus, who gave Himself as a ransom for all men and His testimony was given in its proper time. And for this purpose I was appointed a herald and an apostle—I am telling the truth, I am not lying—and a teacher of the true faith to the Gentiles (everyone that is not a Jew). I want men everywhere to lift up holy hands in prayer, without anger or disputing."*

Believers of Christ choosing to participate in the governmental process do so by voting. One must be respectful when voicing an opinion.[159] We rest in His sovereignty.[160] Security of a nation is not in its wealth, wisdom, weapons, warriors, but in God.[161] We are to witness to the lost and to those who are anxious.

---

[159] Romans 13:1-7; 1 Peter 2:13-14
[160] Psalm 37:7; Isaiah 26:3-4; Daniel 4:35
[161] Psalm 20:7; 33:12, 16-17; 90:1-16; 121:1-8; 127:1

Begin Day 30:
God's Laws:
The Sixth Commandment - Rumors of Wars

The wars will not cease until Jesus returns in Matthew 24:6-8, NKJV: *"And you will hear of wars and rumors of wars. See that you are not troubled; for all these things must happen, but the end is not yet. For nation will rise against nation, and kingdom against kingdom. Moreover, there will be famines, pestilences, and earthquakes in various places. And these are the beginning of sorrows."*

When the Prince of Peace returns, there will be peace in the valley, and nations will study war no more.[162] Internal peace can be experienced now.[163]

---

[162] Isaiah 2:1-4; 11:6-9; Micah 4:1-3
[163] John 16:33; Romans 5:1; Philippians 4:6-7; Ephesians 2:14; Isaiah 26:3

Begin Day 31:
God's Laws: The Sixth Commandment – Reasons for Valuing Human Life

Human life is sacred because we are made in the image of God.[164] God is the source of all life. He also has the right to end life when He chooses, and no one has the right to take a life unless God grants it to him or her.[165] We are created to bring glory to God.[166] A life that is taken cannot be restored. However, some murderers were forgiven by God. Some murderers who were forgiven are Moses;[167] David;[168] and Paul.[169]

The *Sixth Commandment* is a prohibition against murder. The New Testament prohibits the emotions of anger and hatred of which are attributes that leads to murder.[170] The Bible teaches that the source of evil is from the heart. Therefore, God looks at the heart. We are commanded to guard the heart. The act of murder with the hands starts with the attitude of murder in the heart. The form of murder in the heart is unrighteous or unjustified anger.[171] The anger that is prohibited by Jesus is the anger that is nurtured, that is not allowed to die, that holds grudges, that refuses to forgive, that does not desire reconciliation, that holds on to resentment, and that results in a 'root of bitterness.'[172]
Some examples of unrighteousness anger:
1. The anger of Cain because of jealousy [173]
2. The anger of King Saul because of jealousy [174]
3. The anger of Jonah against God because of God's grace, mercy, and kindness to save Nineveh [175]
4. The anger of the Prodigal Son's brother because of how his father treated the lost son on his return home [176]

Not all anger is a sin.[177] Three things that caused Jesus to become angry is the hardness of hearts of the Pharisees;[178] the hindering of children from coming to Jesus;[179] and the hindering of worship in the house of God.[180] However, unrighteous anger is dangerous to us and to others. Studies show that men who have an anger problem are four times more likely

---

[164] Genesis 1:26-27; 9:6
[165] Romans 13:1-5
[166] Isaiah 43:7, 21; 1 Corinthians 10:31
[167] Exodus 2:11-12
[168] 2 Samuel 12:9-12
[169] Acts 8:1-3; 1 Timothy 1:12-17; Proverbs 28:13; 1 John 1:9
[170] Matthew 5:21-22; 1 John 3:15
[171] Matthew 22
[172] Hebrews 12:15
[173] Genesis 4:1-8; 1 John 3:11-15
[174] 1 Samuel 18:6-9
[175] Jonah 4:1-11
[176] Luke 15:25-32
[177] Psalm 4:4; 7:11; Ephesians 4:26
[178] Mark 3:1-6
[179] Mark 10:13-16
[180] Matthew 21:12-13; John 2:13-17

to die young than the average person. Unresolved and uncontrolled anger can cause ulcers, heart attacks, high blood pressure, and many other diseases. To deal with unrighteous anger, one has to confess it,[181] to control it,[182] and channel their anger. *Channeling* to stop the destructive effect of anger is achieved by walking away, refusing to argue, or be involved in anything that would make you upset, and to, instead, find something constructive to do.

---

[181] 1 John 1:9
[182] Galatians 5:23

Begin Day 32:
God's Laws:
The Sixth Commandment - Slander

Slander is a form of murder.[183] *Raca* is translated as 'empty-headed,' 'you good for nothing,' 'brainless idiot,' 'worthless,' and other crucial words that can kill a person's spirit, reputation, and relationships with others, including self-esteem.

Another form of *slander* is gossip. How many people have been murdered with words said by someone else?[184] Also, words spoken in unrighteous anger can be destructive.[185]

Additionally, condemning the character of a person is a form of murder.[186] One way to condemn someone's character is by calling him or her a 'fool.' *Fool* meaning stupid. It is from the Greek word *Moros*, where we get the English word *moron*. According to Webster, *moron* is a mentally retarded person, who has a potential mental age of between eight through twelve years old. Jesus prohibits calling a person a fool out of anger and hatred. *Hatred* is another form of murder.[187] Unrighteous hatred is a sin because we are commanded to love, and hatred usually results from unrighteous anger.[188]

Solutions to the sin of murder are:
- the new birth;[189]
- to forgive;[190]
- seek reconciliation quickly;[191]
- experiencing the presence of the Holy Spirit;[192]
- and the fruits of the Holy Spirit.[193]

We must love because love is the antidote to hate.[194] [195]

---

[183] Matthew 5:22
[184] Matthew 12:36-37
[185] Proverbs 12:18; 18:8, 21
[186] Matthew 5:22
[187] 1 John 3:15
[188] Matthew 5:43-44; John 13:34-35; 15:12
[189] 2 Corinthians 5:17; John 1:12-13; 1 John 3:9
[190] Matthew 6:14-15; Mark 11:25-26; Ephesians 4:31-32
[191] Matthew 5:24-26
[192] Ephesians 5:18; Galatians 5:16
[193] Galatians 5:22-23
[194] Galatians 5:22; 1 John 3:14-15
[195] Malone, Julius. *Introduction to the Ten Commandments*. Sermon at New Testament Church (Milwaukee, WI) notes taken by author, 2004.

Begin Day 33:
God's Laws: The Seventh Commandment: Physical Adultery

The *Sixth Commandment* protects the sacredness of life, and the *Seventh Commandment* protects the sacredness of marriage.

Adultery was punishable by death in the Old Testament.[196] Definition of *adultery* is a voluntary sinful sexual act, where a person engages in sex with someone other than his or her spouse.

There are different forms of adultery:
1. Physical
2. Mental
3. Divorce

Physical adultery involves two physical bodies that engage in sexual activities such as oral, anal and vaginal. [197] Some people do not want to consider oral sex as sexual contact with their partner, but it is a form of sex to satisfy or fulfill lustful thoughts and feelings. The Bible speaks against anal sexual activities too.

Genesis 19:4-5, NKJV: *"Now before they lay down, the men of the city, the men of Sodom, both old and young, all the people from every quarter, surrounded the house. They called to Lot and said to him, "Where are the men who came to you tonight? Bring them out to us so that we can have sex with them carnally."*

The phrase *'that we may know them carnally'* means the men wanted sexual relations with Lot's male guests.

---

[196] Leviticus 20:10; Deuteronomy 22:23-24
[197] Genesis 19:4-5; Judges 19:22

Begin Day 34:
God's Laws:
The Seventh Commandment - Fornication

Fornication is another form of adultery. *Fornication* involves voluntary sex between unmarried people. *Fornication* is a sin that is to be avoided.[198] The Greek word *neia* means two people who are not married. Incest and homosexuality are also sinful sexual acts for people who are not married.

---

[198] Acts 15:20; 1 Corinthians 6:13, 15-18; 10:8; Galatians 5:19; Ephesians 5:3; Colossians 3:5; 1 Thessalonians 4:3-7; Hebrews 13:4

Begin Day 35:
God's Laws: The Seventh Commandment: Homosexuality (and Transgenders)

God had a purpose in making us uniquely male and female. God's plan for natural sexual relationships is His idea for His creation. Unfortunately, sin distorts the natural use of God's gifts. Sin often means, not only denying God, but also denying the way we are. When people say that any sex act is acceptable if nobody gets hurt, they are fooling themselves. In the end, sin hurts people such as individuals, families, and whole societies.[199]

Or dressed up as a transsexual, according to Deuteronomy 22:5: *"A woman shall not wear anything that pertains to a man, nor shall a man put on a woman's garment, for all who do so are an abomination to the Lord your God."*

Scripture commands men and women not to reverse their sexual roles.[200] Today, role rejections are common. Ideally, there are men who want to become women and women who want to become men. It is not the clothing style that offends God but the acting out of a different sex role. For example, a man dressing in women's clothing, wearing makeup, and/or transforming their body parts to emerge as a woman.

Moreover, these desires are sins of sexual immorality and sorcery, including less obvious sins such as hatred, selfish ambition, and envy. Those who ignore or refuse such sins will have to deal with them, and they have not received the gift of the Spirit that leads to a transformed life.[201]

God views lesbians and homosexuals to have a depraved mind, according to Romans 1:26-28, NIV: *"Because of this, God gave them over to shameful lusts. Even their women exchanged natural relations for unnatural ones. In the same way, the men also abandoned natural relations with women and were inflamed with lust for one another. Men committed indecent acts with other men, and received in themselves the due penalty for their perversion. Furthermore, since they did not think it worthwhile to retain the knowledge of God, he gave them over to a depraved mind; to do what ought not to be done."*

Homosexuality was as widespread in Paul's day as it is in ours. Many heathen practices encouraged it. Yet, homosexuality is strictly forbidden in the Scripture.[202] Many consider homosexuality as an acceptable practice today, even in some churches. However, society does not set the standard for God's law. Many homosexuals believe that their desires are normal and that they have a right to express them. Nevertheless, God does not obligate nor encourage us to fulfill all our desires. Our lustful desires violate His laws. We must seek the Holy Spirit for it to be controlled. If you have these desires, flee from fornication and resist. Consciously avoid places or activities you know will kindle these temptations. Do not

---

[199] Life Application Study Bible, NKJV.
[200] Life Application Study Bible, NKJV, 1996.
[201] Malone, Julius. *Introduction to the Ten Commandments.* Sermon at New Testament Church (Milwaukee, WI) notes taken by author, 2004.
[202] Leviticus 18:22

underestimate the power of Satan to tempt you, nor the potential for serious harm if you yield to temptation.

One must consider the reason for sex. The future of the world is in the hands of each, and one only need to refer to Jesus' second greatest commandment to remind oneself.

Children are gifts; young people for you to protect and nurture for a successful future. God specifically made men and women to nurture the future of their children, guiding them throughout life, and then for them to be an example for their grandchildren. In so doing, one not only assures their future, but the health of the nation, and ultimately the world.[203] Consider the mental anguish you will inflict on children or grandchildren (even those not your own) when you or the person who is or will be your sexual partner leaves their lives.

God is willing to receive anyone who comes to Him in faith, and believers are to love and accept others regardless of their background. God can and will forgive our sexual sins, just as He forgives other sins. Surrender yourself to the grace and mercy of God, asking Him to show you the way out of sin, and into the light of His freedom and His love. You can count on God to hear your prayer. Strong support in a Christian church can help you to gain strength to resist these powerful temptations. If you are already deeply involved in homosexual behavior, seek help from a trustworthy professional pastoral counselor.

---

[203] Matthew 18:6

Begin Day 36:
God's Laws:
The Seventh Commandment - Mental Adultery

Mental adultery can be found in Matthew 5:27-28, NJKV: *"You have heard that it was said to those of old. You shall not commit adultery. But I say to you that whoever looks at a woman to lust for her has already committed adultery with her in his heart."*

The Old Testament law said that it was wrong for a person to have sex with someone other than his or her spouse. Jesus explained that the desire to have sex with someone other than your spouse is *mental adultery*. Jesus emphasized that if the act is wrong, then so is the intention. To be faithful to your spouse with your body, but not your mind, is to break the trust is so vital to a strong marriage. Jesus is not condemning natural interest in the opposite sex, or even a healthy sexual desire, but the deliberate and repeated filling of one's mind with fantasies that would be evil if acted out. Some think that if lustful thoughts are a sin, a person can go ahead and fulfill the lustful actions too.[204]

Allowing sinful desires is harmful in several ways:
1. It causes people to excuse sin
2. Destroys marriages, since the mental image is often a lofty "grass is greener" daydream
3. It is deliberate rebellion against God's Word
4. It will hurt someone else besides the sinner, because of higher expectations

Nevertheless, sinful desire is just as damaging to righteousness. Left unchecked, wrong desires result in wrong actions and turn people away from God.

'Look' is a translation of the Greek verb *blepo*, which is referring to the continuous action of looking (discerning with the bodily eye). *New Strong Concise Concordance* and *Vine's Concise Dictionary of the Bible* states that *blepo* means primarily 'to have sight, to see,' then 'observe, discern, and perceive.' Overall, Jesus is prohibiting, not a momentary glance, but a continuous gaze resulting in a bodily reaction. Adultery starts in the mind or the heart.[205]

Matthew 15:18-20, NJKV: *"But those things which proceed out of the mouth come from the heart, and they defile a man. For out of the heart proceed evil thoughts, murders, adulteries, fornications, thefts, false witness, (and) blasphemies. These are the things which defile a man, but to eat with unwashed hands does not defile a man."*

Mark 7:20-23, NKJV: *"And He said, 'What comes out of a man, that defiles a man. For from within, out of the heart of men, proceed evil thoughts, adulteries, fornication, murders, thefts, covetousness, wickedness, deceit, lewdness, and evil eye, blasphemy, pride, foolishness. All these evil things come from within and defile a man.'"*

---

[204] Life Application Study Bible, NKJV, 1996.
[205] Matthew 15:18-20 and Mark 7:20-23

These two Scriptures are saying every evil action begins with a single thought. If we permit our minds to dwell on lust, envy, hatred, or revenge, the result is sinful action. Do not defile yourself by focusing on evil. Instead follow Paul's advice in *Philippians 4:8*. *Lust*, the Greek term *epithumia*, denotes 'strong desire' of any kind.[206] The word *lust* is used in reference to a *good desire* in *Luke 22:15*; *Philippians 1:23*; and *1 Thessalonians 2:17* only. Everywhere else, the word *lust* is used in a bad sense. In *Romans 6:12*, there is the injunction against letting sin reign in our mortal body to obey the 'lust' thereof, refers to those evil desires, which are ready to express themselves in bodily activity. They are equally the *lusts* of the flesh. Moreover, the term *lust* describes the emotions of the soul, the natural tendency towards things evil.[207] Such *lusts* are not necessarily base and immortal, they may be refined in character, but are evil if inconsistent with the will of God.

---

[206] New Strong Concise Concordance and Vine's Concise Dictionary of the Bible.
[207] Romans 13:4; Galatians 5:16, 24; Ephesians 2:3; 2 Peter 2:18; 1 John 2:16

Begin Day 37:
God's Laws:
The Seventh Commandment - Divorce Adultery

The scriptures clearly state that the marriage bed is binding and sacred. However, many people are divorcing for irrevocable differences or filing for separation to see if they will reconcile the relationship or finalize the separation by dissolving the marriage. Once the ink dries on the divorce certificate, some people already have established new relationships even intimacy that leads to fornication. Even in celebrity news, during separations, these spouses have already established another relationship and possibly conceived an illegitimate child in the process. Moreover, they have engaged in spousal affairs before, during, or after the divorce.

Matthew 5:31-32, NKJV, tells us, *31 "Furthermore it has been said, 'Whoever divorces his wife, let him give her a certificate of divorce.' 32 But I say to you that whoever divorces his wife for any reason except sexual immorality causes her to commit adultery and whoever marries a woman who is divorced commits adultery."*

Matthew 19:8-9 NKJV states, *"He said to them, "Moses, because of the hardness of your hearts, permitted you to divorce your wives, but from the beginning it was not so. 9 And I say to you, whoever divorces his wife, except for sexual immorality, and marries another, commits adultery; and whoever marries her who is divorced commits adultery.""*

This law Jesus refers to is found in Deuteronomy 24:1-4. This same principle applies today. Some people marry for all the wrong intentions and motives; usually to satisfy their fleshly needs and not godly ones. Therefore, divorce was a civil law designed to protect the women.

Once we realize God designed and created marriage to be indissoluble, we know married couples are to find ways to stay together. Seek God's will before plunging into a lifelong commitment to marriage. Know God's reason for marriage is not to satisfy your desire for a companion.

To keep the romance alive in your marriage read Proverbs 5:15-19; 1 Corinthians 7:3-5.

Begin Day 38:
God's Laws: The Seventh Commandment - Defenses against Adultery

Deal drastically with the things that tempt you to sin.[208] Second, guard your heart and mind.[209] Be careful about the things that you look at.[210] Avoid books, movies, videos, websites, television programs, or anything that arouse or stimulate lust in you. Be careful what you listen to.[211] Consider places that you linger.[212] We can fill our minds with good thoughts.[213] Avoid idleness.[214] Someone has said, 'an idle mind is the devil's workshop.' Keep the armor of God in mind.[215] Watch and pray.[216] Pray without ceasing. We are to walk in the Spirit.[217] Remember that your body is the temple of the Holy Spirit.[218] Stay away from the edge.[219] Avoid being alone with someone of the opposite sex who is not a relative.[220] Avoid flirting with those attractive to you.[221] Do not play with fire, you might be burned. Run if necessary.[222] Be aware that God knows all that we think, and He sees all that we do. All sins are committed in the sight of God.[223]

Remember that God can expose your sin whenever He is ready. You will eventually be caught.[224] For instance, those who were caught in the Bible (and some in our society today) is David, Adam and Eve, Joseph's brothers, Achan, Jonah, Ananias and Sapphira, Bill Clinton, and Anthony Weiner, to name a few. Be aware of the consequences of adultery. Remember that forgiveness does not erase all the consequences of adultery.[225] [226]

David's consequences for committing adultery with Bathsheba were demonstrated through his family troubles. God said that murder would be a constant threat to his family, his family would rebel, and someone else would sleep with his wives. All this happened as prophet Nathan had predicted. The consequences of sin affect not only us, but also those we know and love. Remember that the next time you are tempted to sin.

---

[208] Matthew 5:29-30; 1 Corinthians 6:12; 9:27
[209] Proverbs 4:23; Matthew 15:18-20; Mark 7:21-23; Luke 6:45
[210] Job 31:1; Psalm 119: 37; Daniel 1:8
[211] Psalm 1:1
[212] Psalm 1:1-2; 1 Corinthians 15:33
[213] 2 Corinthians 10:5; Philippians 4:8; Psalm 119:9, 11
[214] 2 Samuel 11:1-5
[215] Ephesians 6:10-17
[216] Ephesians 6:18; Colossians 4:2; 1 Thessalonians 5:17
[217] Galatians 5:16-23
[218] 1 Corinthians 6:18-20
[219] 1 Corinthians 10:12
[220] Genesis 39:10
[221] Proverbs 6:27-29
[222] Genesis 39:12; 1 Corinthians 6:18; 2 Timothy 2:22
[223] Psalm 51:4; 139:1-4, 7-12; Proverbs 15:3; Jeremiah 23:24; Hebrews 4:13
[224] Numbers 32:23, Luke 8:17
[225] 2 Samuel 12:1-20
[226] Malone, Julius. *Introduction to the Ten Commandments*. Sermon at New Testament Church (Milwaukee, WI) notes taken by author, 2004.

We can look to the story of David for a clear example:
David's wife, Michal, Saul's daughter, was childless. David gave her five nephews to the Gibeonites to be killed because of Saul's sins.

David's second wife, Ahinoam, from Jezreel, gave David his firstborn son, Amnion. David's other wife, Maacah, who was the daughter of King Talmai of Gusher, gave birth to Absalom, who was David's third son and she also gave birth to a daughter, Tamar. Amnion raped Tamar (his half-sister). Amnion was later murdered by Absalom in revenge. Later Absalom returned, only to rebel against David. Absalom set up a tent on his roof and slept with ten of his father's concubines. Shortly later, Absalom's pride led to his death.

Next, his wife, Haggith, had David's fourth son, Adonijah. He was very handsome but was never properly disciplined. He set himself up as king before David's death. Adonijah's plot was exposed. David spared his son's life, but his half-brother, Solomon, later had him executed. Bathsheba's unnamed son died in fulfillment of God's punishment for David and Bathsheba adultery. Later, Bathsheba had a son called Solomon, who became the next king of Israel. However, Solomon had many wives who caused his downfall. This defined sin can be labeled 'short-term gain with long-term pain.'

Begin Day 39:
God's Laws:
The Seventh Commandment - Results of Adultery

Adultery is the cause of 65% of divorces.

It can cause:
- ✓ Anguish: A heartfelt, deep pain that some say is greater than the loss of a spouse in death.
- ✓ A loss of spousal trust.
- ✓ A loss of respect from children and other relatives.

God will judge adulterers (Hebrews 13:4.) As in all sins, save one, there is deliverance from the sin of adultery.[227]

---

[227] John 8:1-11 and 1 Corinthians 6:9-11. Other Scriptures: 2 Thessalonians 3:5, 16-22; 1:2, 5

Begin Day 40:
God's Laws: The Eighth Commandment

The *Eighth Commandment* is a prohibition against stealing. How many of you have been victims of identity theft? We all have had something stolen from us. We all have pilfered something from others. Many stores have security systems, detectors at the exit doors, and security guards because of the problem of stealing. *Stealing* means "taking what belongs to others." *Robbery* is taking from others openly and by force.[228]

The *manifestations of stealing* are:
- failure to render to others what is due;[229]
- failure pay employees their agreed wages;[230]
- failure to give employers the proper amount of work.[231]
- failure to pay the proper amount of taxes;[232]
- failure to give honor and respect to those to whom it is due (which includes the taking of things like paperclips, paper & pens from your employer;[233]
- failure to give glory to God;[234]
- failure to give tithes and offering to God through a local church.[235] [236] God determines tithe. We determine what our offering will be. Grace goes beyond the law, more than 10%.
- failure to return what is borrowed;[237]
- failure to return the correct amount of change; taking of someone's good name through slander or gossip;
- taking the virginity of someone who is not one's spouse;
- knowingly receiving stolen goods,
- plagiarism and violation of copyright laws. The copying of tapes, CD's, DVD's, and software for profit, or to sell illegal merchandise is stealing.

Some motives for stealing are:
- lack of patience or failure to delay gratification;
- lack of understanding of the difference between need and greed (covetousness – an intense desire to own what belongs to someone else);[238] [239]
- the belief that what is stolen is desired;

---

[228] Luke 10:30
[229] Romans 13:7
[230] Leviticus 19:13; Deuteronomy 24:14-15; Jeremiah 22:13; Colossians 4:1; James 5:4
[231] Colossians 3:22-24
[232] Romans 13:6-7; Matthew 22:21
[233] Romans 13:7; 1 Peter 2:17
[234] Isaiah 42:8; 43:7; 1 Corinthians 10:31
[235] Malachi 3:7-12; Matthew 23:23; 5:20; Mark 12:41-44; Luke 19:8
[236] Malone, Julius. *Introduction to the Ten Commandments*. Sermon at New Testament Church (Milwaukee, WI) notes taken by author, 2004.
[237] Psalm 37:21
[238] Philippians 4:19
[239] Joshua 7:19-21

- the belief that stealing is okay because everyone else is doing it.

Some methods of breaking the habit of stealing:
- Practice the principle of replacement. Bad habits are to be replaced with good habits.[240] Note that when we are commanded to 'put off,' we are also commanded to 'put on' something else.[241] Learn to be content.[242]
- Obtain possessions God's way by working (labor) to pay for possessions.[243]
- Save your money for possessions.[244]
- Learn to make some of the things you need.[245]
- Receive possessions such as gifts or an inheritance.[246]
- Receive possessions from investments.[247]

---

[240] Ephesians 4:28
[241] Ephesians 4:17-32; Colossians 3:5-17
[242] Philippians 4:11; 1 Timothy 6:6-8; Hebrews 13:5
[243] Ephesians 4:28
[244] Proverbs 6:6-8
[245] Proverbs 31:13, 18-24
[246] 1 Kings 10:10; Proverbs 13:22
[247] Matthew 25:20-21

Begin Day 41:
God's Laws: The Ninth Commandment – Bearing False Witness (Lying)

The *Ninth Commandment* is a prohibition against perjury. *Perjury* is lying under oath in a court of law. In the ancient times, the courts depended on witnesses to arrive at the truth so that justice could be rendered. There were no lawyers. There was no evidence such as fingerprints and DNA. False witnesses could cause the innocent to be punished and the guilty to go free. At least two witnesses were required to establish a verdict.[248] In capital punishment cases, the witnesses were to cast the first stone.[249] Note that the witness who lies to cause the death of an innocent person is also the witness who would be guilty of the sin of murder.

Lying is stating what one knows is not true. A nationwide telephone survey revealed that 91% of Americans survey confessed to regularly lying about their income, weight, age, and true hair color. Some of the reasons people lie are d*epravity;*[250] d*emonic influence;*[251] and *deception*. Satan deceived Eve with lies;[252] Jacob lied to deceive his father, Isaac, to steal his brother's birthright;[253] Gibeonites lied to deceive Joshua,[254] and the enemies of Daniel lied to deceive the King of Babylon.[255]

One can destroy someone by lying. Two examples are; Jezebel destroyed Naboth with false witnesses,[256] and Mrs. Potiphar sought to destroy Joseph with lies.[257] Consequently, some will lie or tell a 'white lie' to protect one's self. Abraham and Isaac lied about their wives to protect themselves.[258] Peter denied Jesus to protect himself.[259] Lies were told during World War II to protect the Jews from being killed by German soldiers. The Hebrew midwives, Shiphrah and Puah, lied to Pharaoh to protect Hebrew boy babies.[260] Rahab lied to protect the spies from being put to death by the King of Jericho.[261]

The Bible says those who lie:
- imitate the devil, the father of lies;[262]
- lose the manifest presence of God;[263]

---

[248] Numbers 35:30; Deuteronomy 17:6; Matthew 18:16; 2 Corinthians 13:1; 1 Timothy 5:19; Hebrews 10:28
[249] Deuteronomy 17:6-7
[250] Psalm 58:3; 51:5; Matthew 15:19
[251] Acts 5:1-11
[252] Genesis 3:1-7; 1 Timothy 2:14
[253] Genesis 27:1-46
[254] Joshua 9:3-27
[255] Daniel 6:1-28
[256] 1 Kings 21:1-29
[257] Genesis 39:1-23
[258] Genesis 12:9-20; 26:6-11
[259] Matthew 26:69-75
[260] Exodus 1:15-21
[261] Joshua 2:1-24; Hebrews 11:31; James 2:25
[262] John 8:44; John 1:12
[263] Psalm 15:1-3; 101:7; Revelation 21:8; 22:15

- lose the trust of others
- are condemned to hurt (iniquity and being hated). See the references to lying in Proverbs.[264]

One of the remedies for lying is to have a personal relationship with Jesus Christ.[265] As disciples of Jesus Christ, we imitate God, who cannot lie.[266] We will not lie if we are filled with the Holy Spirit.[267] Practice the principle of replacement.[268] We can meditate on what is true,[269] pray for God's help,[270] and love your neighbor.[271]

---

[264] Proverbs 6:16-19 12:17; 14:5; 19:28; 25:18; 24:28
[265] John 1:14; 14:6; 2 Corinthians 5:17; 1 Corinthians 6:9-11
[266] Ephesians 5:1; Titus 1:2; Numbers 23:19
[267] John 16:13; Ephesians 5:18; Galatians 5:16
[268] Ephesians 4:22-29; Colossians 3:5-16
[269] Philippians 4:8; Proverbs 4:23
[270] Psalm 19:14; 141:3
[271] 1 Corinthians 13:5-6

Begin Day 42:
God's Laws:
The Ninth Commandment – Toxic Talk

The *Ninth Commandment* is a prohibition against gossip and slander. *Gossip* involves rumor or idle talk about the affairs of others. We shall not engage in gossip, nor listen to gossip.[272] *Slander* is speaking evil of others.[273] *Slander* is making statements that damage the character or good name of another person. We do the work of the devil when we slander. *Diabolos* means to 'accuse falsely and slanderously' in secular Greek usage.[274] *Diabolos* is translated 'devil' thirty-five times, 'false accuser' twice,[275] and 'slanderers' ('backbiters') once.[276]

The most dangerous lie ever told is that there are many ways to God.[277] Jesus states, "I am the way, the truth, and the life; no man can come to the Father except by Me." People take many paths to the recognition of Christ as their Savior, but He is the only Way.

---

[272] Matthew 12:34-37
[273] Ephesians 4:31; 1 Peter 2:1-2; James 4:11
[274] New Strong's Concise Concordance and Vine's Concise Dictionary of the Bible.
[275] 2 Timothy 3:3; Titus 2:3
[276] 1 Timothy 3:11
[277] John 14:6; Acts 4:12

Begin Day 43:
God's Laws: The Tenth Commandment

The *Tenth Commandment* differs from the other nine since it involves our inner attitude rather than the outer actions. *Covetousness* is an unrighteous desire to possess something or someone when the authority of possession is not given.

Some causes of *covetousness* are:
- a corrupted heart;[278]
- comparison of your possessions with the possessions of others;
- advertisements that cause people to covet.

Billions of dollars are spent each year to get people to act on their desires for knowledge, wealth, societal status, health, products, and ease, among other things. Companies gather your demographics. They compile what you've clicked on, what you've searched for, and whether you are related to someone. This information is sold, along with your phone number and address to those interested, or to Internet advertisers who want to tailor their ad to you.

The consequence of *covetousness* is discontent, of which a covetous person is never satisfied.[279] *Covetousness* is a sin that leads to many other sins. David coveted Bathsheba, who was married to one of his soldiers. His sin led to adultery, lying, deception, stealing, and murder.[280] Achan's covetousness resulted in the stealing of forbidden materials, the death of thirty-six soldiers, and the death of Achan and his family.[281] Ahab's covetousness led to false witnesses and murder.[282] Micah points out that covetousness led to the taking of the property of others by violence.[283] Paul also points out that *covetousness* is a form of idolatry.[284] Moreover, covetousness causes the Word of God to become unfruitful after it is heard.[285] Covetousness leads to conflicts.[286] Covetousness cause financial difficulties. Someone has said, "Some people buy what they do not need, with money they do not have, to impress people they do not like."

Some cures the Bible lists for covetousness are: A clean heart,[287] Delight in the Lord,[288] Replace evil desires with good desires, or redirect your desires,[289] Set your mind on things above,[290] Lay up treasures in heaven, not earthly treasures,[291] Seek first the Kingdom of

---

[278] Jeremiah 17:9; Mark 7:20-23
[279] Ecclesiastes 5:10
[280] 2 Samuel 11 & 12
[281] Joshua 7:1-26
[282] 1 Kings 21:1-29
[283] Micah 2:2
[284] Ephesians 5:5; Colossians 3:5
[285] Mark 4:18-19
[286] James 4:1-2
[287] 1 Corinthians 6:9-11; Psalm 51:10; 1 Samuel 16:7
[288] Psalm 37:4
[289] Psalm 27:4; 73:25-26
[290] Colossians 3:1-2; Ephesians 2:6; Philippians 3:20
[291] Matthew 6:19-21; 1 John 2:15-17

God,[292] Learn to be content with what you have,[293] You can practice being thankful for what you have,[294] Stay on guard against covetousness,[295] Pray for deliverance from covetousness,[296] and Love your neighbor.[297] [298]

---

[292] Matthew 6:33
[293] Philippians 4:11-13; 1Timothy 6:6-10; Hebrews 13:5
[294] Philippians 4:6-7; Colossians 3:15-17; 4:2; 1 Thessalonians. 5:18; Daniel 6:10; Psalm 100:4
[295] Luke 12:15-21; Mark 8:36-37; Proverbs 4:23
[296] Psalm 119:36
[297] Matthew 22:36-40; Romans 13:8-10; 1 Corinthians 13:1-13
[298] Malone, Julius. *Introduction to the Ten Commandments*. Sermon at New Testament Church (Milwaukee, WI) notes taken by author, 2004.

Begin Day 44:
God's Laws: Keeping God's Commandments

1 John 3:22, NKJV: *"And whatever we ask we receive from Him, because we keep His commandments and do those things that are pleasing in His sight."*

This Scripture simply says that we come to God without fear and because of that, we are confident that our requests will be heard. Our desires will be fulfilled once we seek God first.[299] It does not mean that you will get everything that you want, but if you are seeking God's will, there are some requests that you will not even make (doing things that are pleasing in His sight).

God placed his finger on the tablets of stone when creating the *Ten Commandments*.[300] We cannot worry then, that they appear earlier in the story of the Exodus than the knowledge that they were hewn in tablets of stone. The *Ten Commandments* were His good intentions for His people, and now, as then, translated for us in the 'Holy Word,' 'God's Word,' or the 'Bible,' which was written by men and prophets of God that were inspired by the Holy Spirit. The reasons that we obey God's law are found in *Galatians 2:16-21*. Moreover, Paul recognized that 'the law is holy.'[301] In other words, Paul is saying that the law can never make us acceptable to God. The law still has an important role to play in the life of a Christian. The law guards us against sin by giving us standards for our behavior. The law convicts us of sin, leaving us the opportunity to ask for God's forgiveness. In addition, it drives us to trust in the sufficiency of Christ because we can never keep the *Ten Commandments* perfectly. Through personal experience and reason, we can see the necessity of avoiding the hurt we cause by not following the simple commands, to Love God first, and then to love our neighbor as we would want to be loved.

---

[299] Matthew 7:7; 21:22; John 9:31; 15:7 and Psalm 37:4
[300] Exodus 31:18
[301] Romans 7:12

Begin Day 45:
God's Laws: Reasons for the Law

Some of the reasons for the law are given for protection. Obedience to the law protects others and us. The law reveals the will of God.[302] The law reveals sin.[303] The law reveals our need for Christ.[304] However, the law cannot possibly save us. The law was given to people who were chosen.[305] The law was not given for salvation.[306] [307]

Nevertheless, once we become new creatures in Christ, God's laws can guide us on how to live according to what God requires. What is a Christian? *Christian is* a person professing belief in Jesus as the Christ or the teachings of Jesus.[308] *Christian is* a decent, respectable person of Jesus Christ or His teaching; or professing the religion with these teachings; having the qualities demonstrated and taught by Jesus Christ, which are love, kindness, and humility.[309] According to Jesus, though, His people are those who experience the second birth, and the Father's laws are written on their hearts.[310]

On a further note, Paul realized that he could not be saved by obeying God's laws.[311] The prophets knew that God's plan of salvation did not rest on keeping the law. Because we are born sinners, we cannot keep God's law flawlessly. Fortunately, God has provided a way of salvation that depends on Jesus Christ, not on our own efforts. Although we know the truth, we must guard our heart and minds against the temptation of using service, good deeds, charitable giving, or any other effort as a substitute for faith.[312]

---

[302] Psalm 119:97-100
[303] Romans 7:7
[304] Galatians 3:24-25
[305] Exodus 19:4; 20:2
[306] Romans 3:20; 10:1-4; Galatians 2:16; Ephesians 2:8-9; Philippians 3:7-9; Titus 3:5
[307] Life Application Study Bible, NKJV, 1996.
[308] Webster's New World College Dictionary.
[309] Webster's New World College Dictionary.
[310] Jeremiah 31:33
[311] Galatians 2:17-21
[312] Life Application Study Bible, NKJV, 1996.

Begin Day 46:
Crucify the Flesh & Abide in Christ under the Law

How have we, as Christians, been crucified with Christ? Ideally, God looks at us as if we had died with Christ. Because our sins died with Him, we are no longer condemned.[313] Relationally, we have become one with Christ, and His experiences are ours. Our Christian life began when, in unity with Him, we died to our old life.[314] In our daily life, we must regularly crucify sinful desires that keep us from following Christ.[315]

Another law mentioned in the Bible that seems to be carried out today in various countries [316] refers to the poor and debtors. They could pay their debts by selling themselves or their children as slaves. God ordered rich people and creditors not to take advantage of these people during their time of extreme need.[317] Evidently, the woman's creditor in 2 Kings 4 was not acting in the spirit of God's law. Elisha's kind deed demonstrates that God wants us to go beyond simply keeping the law.[318] We must also show compassion, just like Jesus showed His compassion for us.

Lastly, religion can compel people to include synthetic laws, believing that God has favor over those who obey these additional laws created.[319] However, these laws usually are religious doctrine and not supported by scripture. It is obvious that those who create additional hardships through religious laws are not trusting Jesus Christ completely. It takes God to change man or woman through sanctification, resting in God's power to save man or woman through justification. If those synthetic laws treat members as saved if they are good people, then Jesus Christ did not have to die for us. Jesus' death on the cross was, and is, the only way to our salvation.

---

[313] Colossians 2:13-15
[314] Romans 6:5-11
[315] Life Application Study Bible, NKJV, 1996.
[316] 2 Kings 4:1
[317] Deuteronomy 15:1-8
[318] Life Application Study Bible, NKJV, 1996.
[319] Galatians 2:21

Begin Day 47:
Three Laws Given By God To The Prophets

The three types of laws given by God are *civil laws*, *ceremonial laws,* and *moral laws*.[320] Read Matthew 5:17-20.

In Matthew 5:17, we are able to see that Jesus did not come to destroy the law but to fulfill it. In the Old Testament, there were three categories of law. *Civil laws* are dealing with the legal and social life of the Israeli nation. These laws contained a temporal punishment because there were no prisons among the Israelites. These laws have disappeared, yet, they were used as an example. *Ceremonial laws* are dealing with the priesthood, sacrifices, and rituals. All foreshadowed by Jesus Christ, who fulfilled the laws. These laws are no longer necessary since the promised death and resurrection of Jesus Christ has been fulfilled and set us free from following these laws. Although we are not bound to ceremonial laws, we are still bound to worship and love God.[321] *Moral laws* are a direct command of God and require strict obedience. Yet, it reveals the nature and will of God, which still applies today. Jesus obeyed this law entirely. *Moral laws* also deal with God's rules for holy living.[322]

What are these laws used for? These laws do focus on telling people to take orders and to follow them, but they also emphasize that obeying God's laws are more important. Today, it is easy to quote the *Ten Commandments* or even the *Two Greatest Commandments*, but we find ourselves unable to put them into practice on a regular basis. We sometimes focus on the fellow man or fellow woman for the answers. Or sometimes, we will focus on other members in the church and even our pastor for the answer. That behavior does not put God first.

You are accountable for your own actions and words. God is counting on you to follow His commandments and laws, which will show how much you truly love your Heavenly Father. Jesus made the sacrifice for our sins so that we may have an eternal lifetime with Him. He wants to see your face, and wants to see you happy and to remember God loves you. Nevertheless, He deserves our love for Him, for others, and our duty to be obedient servants.

---

[320] Matthew 5:17-20
[321] Colossians 2: 16-17; Hebrews 5-10
[322] Exodus 20:1-17

Begin Day 48:
Love for Others

Think of how your parents feel about you. They want you to be able to listen and obey their rules. Our parents or guardians want to protect you from harm or past mistakes because they love you. You are a part of them, just like we are a part of God's creation. We are all His children, and God wants the best for us. He created these laws to protect us, and to show how much He truly loves us. Remember that He did it out of love.

Why is love for others so important to God? We are children of God and are reminded how Jesus Christ lavished His love on the Cross for us, poured out His spirit and flesh for us. How can we repay Him? In return, we are to show love to our neighbor and our enemies. First, let us ask ourselves, what is a neighbor and an enemy, or are these words interchangeable? The word *neighbor* is a person who lives near another; a fellow human being; any person; to have friendly relations.[323] *Enemy*, on the other hand, means a person who hates and wishes, or tries to injure us; a military or wartime adversary; and/or a hostile nation.[324] Of course, the two words have differences. However, the similarity in the descriptions of the words *neighbor* and *enemy* is 'any person.' In other words, we are to learn to accept and to love everyone, whether they are your neighbor or enemy.[325]

Jesus, in Matthew 5:43-48, exhorts us to love our enemies. In doing so, He keeps us from taking the law into our own hands. By loving and praying for our enemies, we can overcome evil with good. Once you are able to love your enemies, it shows that Jesus Christ is the Lord in your life. It shows us that we are unselfish and able to trust the Lord to show us how to love those we dislike, even if we do not think we can show love towards them. We will grow in character, in holiness, and be able to spiritually mature in love. In character, we are showing characteristics more like Christ by loving all, including our enemies or people we strongly dislike. Those who persecuted Jesus Christ, He remained humble and loving throughout his sufferings. Our enemies can cause us to suffer emotionally, mentally, spiritually, and even physically. With Jesus Christ in our lives, we will be able to overcome what they dish out. If you show love in replace of hate, how would that make them feel? I would hope that it will break that person's hardness, and recognize the cruel and evil deeds enough to be able to repent for those sins. Then, to be able to ask you for forgiveness and show love or gratitude in return. A smile in place of a frown or hateful words, despite what your enemy is throwing at you. In time, God will make a way, especially if you show love towards them. Let go, and let God. Over time, your character will be Christ-like.

This is not to say that you should accept the begging of a mentally unstable abuser for forgiveness. The love of Christ demands that you keep others safe. If the abuser injures or kills you, he or she may kill others as well as themselves. You must consider that love sometimes means "no," and distance is the wisest choice. Seek God, and seek help. If you truly love and truly forgive, you will be delighted to see him or her in heaven. Don't mistake forgiveness for the power of God.

---

[323] Webster's New World College Dictionary.
[324] Webster's New World College Dictionary.
[325] Matthew 5:43-48 and Luke 6:27-36

Begin Day 49:
Following the Lead to Holiness

Next, it will lead to holiness, once we are able to separate ourselves from worldly sins and values. As followers of Christ, we are to be devoted to God's will and desires for our lives, rather than what we want for ourselves. Then, we are able to carry out God's will, and then we are able to show love and mercy in this cruel world. By becoming more like Christ and living holy and righteous, we are able to mature spiritually. However, we may have a hard time being holy and achieve a godly character right away. However, in time, we will grow maturely and in complete wholeness. God will mold us. It will build our character by going through trials, temptations, and tribulations to strengthen us, and to be able to love one another unconditionally as Jesus loves us.

> *[5] For this very reason, make every effort to add to your faith goodness; and to goodness, knowledge; [6] and to knowledge, self-control; and to self-control, perseverance; and to perseverance, godliness; [7] and to godliness, mutual affection; and to mutual affection, love. [8] For if you possess these qualities in increasing measure, they will keep you from being ineffective and unproductive in your knowledge of our Lord Jesus Christ. 2 Peter 1:5-8 (NIV)*

That is why we seek to love others as much as Jesus loves us. We can act perfectly on the outside or around others, but from time to time, we tend to sin again.

Even though Christ calls us to excel, to rise above all temptations, trials, and tribulations, mature in every area, and to become more like Him. Jesus was tempted. Jesus turned to the Word, for it is written, and He loved His Heavenly Father so much that He would not fall into sin. Let us meditate on how much we truly love our Father when we are tempted.

After watching the movie, *The Passion of Christ*, does it make you want to change your lifestyle and represent Jesus Christ to the fullest? Every time that you go through a trial or tribulation think of Job, how he overcame his trials through faith and truly loved his Heavenly Father. Daniel still praised the Lord three times a day, even though King Nebuchadnezzar wanted everyone to worship and praise him. King Nebuchadnezzar thought of himself as a god, to worship an image made of gold that all were required to worship. There are other examples throughout the Bible that demonstrate perseverance over temptations, trials, and/or tribulations with the grace of God.

Begin Day 50:
Love in the Commandments

Nine of the *Ten Commandments* are repeated in the New Testament under grace:[326] Read Romans 13:8-10. Therefore love is the fulfillment of the law.

Loving others means *actively seeing that their needs are met*. However, people who worry about others may suffer from low self-esteem but must have some degree of self-care to appropriately determine the proper care for others.[327] Furthermore, believers of Christ are to obey the law of love that supersedes both religion and civil laws.[328] We are to go beyond human law regulations and focus on the laws of God. In the Old Testament, civil laws are filled with deep spiritual meanings that are written for our benefit today.[329] When we step out of God's law, we step into Satan's territory. We are not only to obey God's laws, but also to love one another. However, 95% of us do not practice neighborly love towards one another. We are known for the battles and wars between one another, sibling rivalries and gang-related wars.

In 2 Peter 3:1-2, we know the commandments, but do not remember it because we allow something or someone else to take first place in our minds. If we are mindful of our Lord and Savior, we will follow His commandments, and in everything we do, will abide in love.

---

[326] Romans 13:8-10, NIV, with commentary below.
[327] Commentary: Life Application Study Bible, NKJV, 1996.
[328] Commentary: Life Application Study Bible, NKJV, 1996.
[329] 1 Corinthians 9:8-9

Begin Day 51:
Our Faith yields Health

Our health is a vital part of our lives. The Bible speaks about our health further in 3 John 1:2: *"Beloved, I pray you may prosper in all things and be in health, just as your soul prospers."* Health principles are important to God since man's body, mind, and spiritual well-being are all interrelated and interdependent. If our bodies are misused, our minds and spiritual natures cannot become what God ordained they should be.

John was concerned for Gaius' physical and spiritual well-being. Today, many people still fall into that way of thinking that there is a separation of spirit and matter, despite the physical side of life. A non-Christian attitude logically leads to one of the two responses: neglect the body and physical health, or indulgence of the body's sinful desires. God is concerned for both your body and soul. As a responsible Christian, you should neither neglect nor indulge yourself, but care for your physical needs, and discipline your body so that you are at your best for God's service.

God knows what is best for the human body. Following God's rules results in saving health,[330] and a more abundant life.[331] The diet God created, in the beginning, was fruit, grain, and nuts (Eden's diet). Vegetables were added a little later.[332] Plus, the Bible offers ample evidence that there were clean and unclean animals from the very dawn of Creation. During Noah's day, he took into the ark the clean animals by 'sevens' and unclean by 'twos.' Revelation 18:2 refers to some birds as unclean before the second coming of Christ. The death of Christ had not an altering effect on all who break, but they will be destroyed when Jesus returns.[333] Alternatively, these health laws are for all people for all time.

---

[330] Psalm 67:2
[331] John 10:10
[332] Genesis 3:18
[333] Isaiah 66:15-17

Begin Day 52:
Discipline

Discipline has derived from the Greek word, *sophronismos. The root word of sophronismos* is *sophron*, meaning 'saving the mind,' primarily an admonishing or calling to soundness of mind, or to self-control, which is also used in 2 Timothy 1:7, 'a sound mind.'

"For God has not given us a spirit of fear, but of power and of love and of a sound mind."

When we allow people to intimidate us, we neutralize our effectiveness for God. The power of the Holy Spirit can help us overcome our fear so that we can continue to do God's work. Furthermore, in 2 Timothy 1:7, Paul mentions three characteristics of the effective Christian leader: power, love, and a sound mind (wisdom). These three characteristics are available to us because of the Holy Spirit that dwells in us. Do we acknowledge that our bodies are the temple of the Lord?

1 Corinthians 6:19-20, NKJV: *"Or do you know that your body is the temple of the Holy Spirit who is in you, whom you have from God, and you are not your own? For you were bought at a price; therefore glorify God in your body and in your spirit, which are God's."*

What did Paul mean when he said that our bodies belong to God? Many people say that they have the right to do whatever they want with their own bodies. Although they think of that as freedom, they are really enslaved to their own desires. When we become followers of Christ, the Holy Spirit fills and lives in us. Therefore, we no longer own our bodies. For instance, 'bought at a price,' refers to slaves purchased at auction. With His death, Jesus Christ paid the cost to redeem us from our slavery of sin. Christ's death freed us from sin, but also obligated us to His service. Because your body belongs to God, you must not violate His standards of living.[334]

Exodus 15:26, NKJV: *"…If you diligently heed the voice of the Lord, your God, and do what is right in His sight, give ear to His commandments and keep all His statutes, I will put none of the diseases on your which I have brought on the Egyptians. For I am the Lord who heals you."*

---

[334] Life Application Study Bible, NKJV on 1 Corinthians 6:19, 20.

Begin Day 53:
Bodies Are The Temple Of The Lord

The temple also was referred as *palace temple*. A construction often very beautiful and ornate, it was the dwelling place of a king or a god. The Temple in the Old Testament was built for the true God. The word *palace* in English versions is defined as a residence for a king.[335] Paul told believers that each one of their bodies was a *naos*, a Greek word meaning 'a sanctuary for God.'[336] Paul also said that the church, as Christ's body, is a spiritual temple for God.[337] What a special privilege it is to be God's spiritual dwelling place, both individually and corporately. The glory of God filled the tabernacle and the temple. Now the glory of God is present when the Holy Spirit indwells every believer,[338] and thus inhabits the entire church. In the New Jerusalem, there will be no need for a physical temple because God and the Lamb will be the eternal temple.[339]

---

[335] 2 Kings 20:18; Nahum 2:6
[336] 1 Corinthians 6:19
[337] 1 Corinthians 3:16, 17; 2 Corinthians 6:16; Ephesians 2:21
[338] John 14:16, 17
[339] Revelation 21:22

Begin Day 54:
Free from Disease Through Obedience

God promised that if the people obeyed Him, they would be free from the disease that plagued the Egyptians. Little did they know that many of the moral laws, which He later gave them, were intended to keep them free from sickness? For example, following God's law against prostitution would keep them free of venereal diseases. God's laws for us are often designed to keep us from harm. Men and women are complex beings. Our physical, emotional, and spiritual lives are intertwined. Modern medicine now is acknowledging what these laws assumed. If we want God to care for us, we need to submit to his directions for living.[340] What do we do?

Romans 12:1, 2, NKJV: *"I beseech you therefore, brethren, by the mercies of God, that you present your bodies a living sacrifice, holy, acceptable to God, which is your reasonable service. And do not be conformed to this world, but be transformed by the renewing of your mind, that you may prove what is that good and acceptable and perfect will of God."*

When sacrificing an animal according to God's law, a priest would kill the animal, cut it in pieces, and place it on the altar. Sacrifice was important, but even in the Old Testament, God made it clear that obedience from the heart was much more important.[341] God wants us to offer ourselves, not animals, as living sacrifices by daily laying aside our own desires to follow Him, putting all our energy and resources at His disposal and trusting Him to guide us. We do this out of gratitude that our sins have been forgiven. God has good, acceptable, and perfect plans for His children. He wants us to be transformed people with renewed minds, living to honor and obey Him. God wants only what is best for us and because He gave His Son to make our new lives possible. We joyfully give ourselves as living sacrifices for His service.[342]

1 Corinthians 10:31: *"Therefore, whether you eat or drink, or whatever you do, do all to the glory of God."*

God's love must permeate our motives that all we do will be for His glory. Keep this as a guiding principle by asking, "Is this action glorifying God?" Alternatively, you might ask, "How can I honor God through this action?"[343]

---

[340] Life Application Study Bible, NKJV, 1996.
[341] 1 Samuel 15:22; Psalm 40:6; Amos 5:21-24
[342], [347] Life Application Study Bible, NKJV, 1996.

Begin Day 55:
Food High In Fiber And Low In Fat:
Original Diet

Dietary fiber is the part of the plant foods such as vegetables and grains that are not broken down by digestive juices in the intestine, as are other food elements. It is important for normal functioning of the digestive tract. Fiber in the digestive tract holds water in the intestine, adds bulk, softens stools, and regulates the time it takes for food wastes (toxic) to move through the body. There are two major types of dietary fiber: insoluble fiber and soluble fiber. Insoluble fiber helps prevent constipation and hemorrhoids. It also helps satisfy the appetite by creating a feeling of fullness. Soluble fiber plays a role in reducing blood cholesterol and blood glucose (sugar level).

Sugar, unbelievably, will not make you gain weight. In fact, studies show that overweight people eat less sugar than lean people do. Although obesity has increased, sugar consumption has remained constant. Yet, this does not mean you can stuff yourself with sugary candies, which are made of refined and/or processed sugar and have no nutritional value, plus it is also terrible for your teeth.

Sugar alone makes your blood glucose level go up very fast, and drop just as fast, leaving you as hungry as you were before. Instead, enjoy natural, simple sugars occurring in apples, grapes, pineapples, and other fruit, which provides vitamins and minerals with fiber to satisfy your hunger. Eat as much of them as you like. However, the odd sugary treat will not hurt your weight loss, if the sugars are not accompanied by fat. Cakes, cookies, brownies, and chocolate bars, all are high in fat that will make you gain weight. The occasional vanilla wafer or sugar in your tea will not slow down your weight loss.

Your needs are 20-35 grams of dietary fiber a day. Good sources of fiber include whole grain; cereals, breads and pasta, bran, fruits and vegetables, legumes, nuts, and seeds. Bran cereal is a concentrated source of fiber. You can get about 20 grams of dietary fiber if you choose at least three servings a day of vegetables, plus two servings a day of fruit, plus three servings a day of whole grain products. In addition, drink eight to twelve glasses of water or other fluids such as 100% juices, herbal or non-caffeine teas. Milk or soy protein products such as Rice Dream, Soy Dream, and other soy brand names are also recommended daily. Today, I prefer to drink Silk Milk which is almond milk or coconut milk. No soy in my diet. It is important to drink plenty of fluids when increasing fiber intake. If fluids are not taken, severe constipation will result.

See the companion book for the charts on dietary fiber recommended and 30 foods to help with weight loss.

Begin Day 56:
Eden Diet (Raw Diet)

The Eden diet started in the Garden of Eden when Adam and Eve roamed the earth in such a paradise created by God and ate a diet that He had fit for them. This diet consisted of plants, fruit, and some nuts and seeds. In Genesis 1:29, God was speaking to Adam in the Garden of Eden, the first human life: *"And God said, 'See I have given you every herb that yields seed which is on the face of all the earth, and every tree whose fruit yields seed; to you it shall be for food."*

Genesis 2:15: *"Then the Lord God took the man and put him in the Garden of Eden to tend and keep it."*

The Garden was perfectly prepared. It was man's home, and he had to tend to it and keep it. Even paradise required work.[344] Therefore, we are to tend to the bodies that God has blessed us with and to be healthy. Today, some people are following the plant-based diet.

In *Genesis 5:5*, it shows that Adam lived to be 930 years old. This appears that one will live longer if we follow God's standards concerning our diet, whether it is Eden diet (or plant-based), or meat-eaters diet, including fruits, grains, nuts, and vegetables. However, Adam only ate fruit and nuts (of seed-bearing plants) until he was removed from the Garden of Eden. Men did not, apparently, eat meat until after the flood, at which time God allowed the eating of animals,[345] and then ate whatever seeds grew such as fruits and vegetables. Animals were used as a sacrifice.[346]

---

[344] Genesis 1:28
[345] Genesis 9:2-3
[346] Leviticus 1:1-17

Begin Day 57:
The Daniel Diet

Isaiah 55:2, NKJV: *"Why do you spend money for what is not bread, and your wages for what does not satisfy? Listen carefully to Me, and eat what is good, and let your soul delight itself in abundance."*

Food only lasts for a short period and is meant to meet our physical needs. However, God offers us free nourishment that feeds our soul. We come,[347] listen,[348] seek, and call on God.[349] God's salvation is freely offered, but to nourish our souls, we must eagerly receive it. We will starve spiritually without Him as surely as we will starve physically without our daily bread.[350] Not only does God's salvation supply what is necessary for life, but it also provides what brings joy. Salvation cannot be bought but can be readily received when desired.[351] [352]

Daniel 1:12: *"Please test your servants for ten days and let them give us vegetables to eat and water to drink."*

The Babylonians were trying to change the thinking of the Jews by giving them a Babylonian education, their loyalty by changing their names, and their lifestyle by changing their diet. Without compromising, Daniel found a way to live to God's standards in a culture that did not honor God. Wisely choosing to negotiate rather than to rebel, Daniel suggested an experimental ten-day diet of vegetables and water, instead of the royal foods and wine the king offered. Without compromising, Daniel quickly thought of a practical, creative solution that saved his life, and the lives of his companions. As God's people, we may adjust to our culture, so we do not compromise God's laws.[353]

Choosing a diet like Daniel did requires recognition of our choice to focus on the richness of the food rather than the richness of God. Health is in Christ, and it is He who places the nutrient in the food.

If you doubt such truth, try fasting a day without focusing on God, but on some other goal, like losing weight. You will find yourself in a very hard day. However, if you focus on Him instead, you will find the time going much more smoothly.

---

[347] Isaiah 55:1
[348] Isaiah 55:2
[349] Isaiah 55:6
[350] Life Application Study Bible, commentary, NKJV, 1996.
[351] Isaiah 52:3; Deuteronomy 8:3; Romans 6:23
[352] Nelson Study Bible, commentary NKJV and emphasis added by the author.
[353] Life Application Study Bible, NKJV, 1996.

Begin Day 58:
Eating Meat

Genesis 9:3-5: Three new realities mark the post-Flood world: meat may be eaten with plants; blood is not to be eaten with meat, and taking of a person's life is not punishable by death.

- 9:3: argues that men and women ate only vegetables.
- 9:4: blood – is a prohibition against God. Blood represents animal's life was used for rituals or sacrifice, for all life belongs to the Lord (Old Testament).
- 9:5: lifeblood is more sacred than the life of an animal because it is the life of a person. Animals may be slain for food, but the wanton slaying of a human is not allowed.[354]

A good discussion of why God allowed meat after the flood is online. The basic premise is that the flood had destroyed the landscape as well as shortened the lifespan of man. Plants would be inferior as nutrition for many years, and man would need good proteins to subsist.[355]

---

[354] Nelson Study Bible, NKJV.
[355] http://www.aish.com/atr/Meat-After-the-Flood.html

Begin Day 59:
Forbidden & Allowed Foods

Leviticus 3:17: "This shall be a perpetual statute throughout your generations in all your dwellings: you shall eat neither fat nor blood."

Perpetual in all dwellings: some regulations in the Law of Moses were observed only in the land that God was giving the Israelites. However, the prohibition of eating fat or blood applied wherever an Israelite might live. There were no exceptions. These sacrificial regulations consistently emphasize the theme of *'only the best for God.'* As it was in ancient Israel, so it is today. Only our best is good enough to give to God.[356]

On the other hand, *Leviticus 11:2-43*, shows what foods are forbidden and what we are able to eat according to God.

- 11:2: On the earth: as distinct from the sea and the air. A similar grouping of animal life is found in Genesis 1:20-31.
- 11:3: Those chewing the cud (regurgitating it back and chew it a second time): that is the ruminants, like cows, sheep, goats, deer, and antelope. The ruminants eat only plants, mainly grasses, and grains. No meat-eating animal chews the cud. The animals allowed for food are not mentioned by name as they are in the book of Deuteronomy.
- 11:4, 5. Cattle, sheep, and goats provided most of the meat for the ancient Israelites. They ate meat much less often than we do, usually only on special occasions such as the sacrificial feasts or to honor guests in their home.
- 11:4: The camel was eaten by some of Israel's neighbors, who considered it a delicacy. However, the camel would not have been an important source of meat for Israel even if it had been permitted, for it never was a numerous in Israel or as important to Israel's economy as it was to their neighbors. The camel does have a split hoof, but its sole or pad is so thick its imprint is like a single pad.
- 11:5: The rock hyrax lives in colonies among the rocks.[357] Though it is sometimes called a rock badger, it is not a badger. The rock hyrax is about the same size as a rabbit. Hyraxes appear to chew constantly while sitting outside their dens sunning themselves.
- 11:6: The hare is not a ruminant, although it does appear to chew constantly. It lacks a hoof.
- 11:7: The swine is the best known of the unclean animals and continues to be avoided by both Jews and Muslims. Israel's neighbors in both the Old and the New Testament periods most commonly ate the swine. All the reasons for labeling an animal as unclean fit the swine:
    - Inadequately cooked pork could transmit disease to humans
    - Pigs were sacrificed to pagan deities
    - Because pork tasted so good, refusing it would be a suitable test of faithfulness and obedience

---

[356] Nelson Study Bible, NKJV.
[357] Proverbs 30:26

- - Pigs are omnivores. They will eat anything, including flesh. They eat what is unfit for human consumption.
- 11:8: In case of these unclean animals, eating their meat or touching their dead carcasses caused an Israelite to be unclean or ritually impure. However, touching a live animal did not make a person unclean, and an Israelite could raise and use a donkey or camel as a beast without becoming unclean.
- 11:9: A water creature had to possess both fins and scales to be eaten. Only true fish, and not all of them, fit this description. Oysters, clams, crabs, lobsters, and eels were unclean. Whether in the seas or in the rivers, this applied to God's command to both saltwater and freshwater species.
- 11:10-12: Abomination is a stronger word than unclean. It implies that not just avoidance, but active, fierce repulsion. Fins and scales are 'appropriate' water creatures. Fish that have them are clean. Water creatures that appear to mix categories—suggesting disorder, are not merely unclean. They are an abomination. There are good health reasons for being cautious in eating some of these creatures, but this was not the main reason for classifying them as unclean.
- 11:19: The hoopoe is a migratory bird. It spends its winters in tropical Africa and its summers in Israel and farther north. The bat is not a bird. However, in the pre-scientific age, it was grouped with birds because it has wings and flies.
- 11:20: Creep on all fours is an idiom for crawling on the ground, as insects do on their six legs. Many insects move about in filth and eat droppings. Their association with death, impurity, and disorder made them unclean.
- 11:21: Insects with jointed legs, those who leap, were permitted to be eaten. The joints are the enlarged third legs of locusts and grasshoppers that enable them to leap. Locusts and grasshoppers do not live in filth or eat dung. They eat only plants.
- 11:24: This refers to the flying insects of the previous paragraph or to all the unclean animals discussed so far. Merely to touch an unclean carcass caused a person to be unclean until evening when the new day began for the Israelites.
- 11:25: If a person carried or picked up a carcass or part of a carcass, that person's uncleanness was greater. Therefore, the remedy had to be more thorough.
- 11:26: The word, carcass, is not in the Hebrew text, but clearly, that is what is meant here. A live unclean animal, such as a donkey or camel, could not make a person unclean simply by touching it. Otherwise, many people would have been unclean all the time.
- 11:27-28: Whatever goes on its paws is unclean because it lacks a cloven hoof. As with the previous group, to touch a carcass was to be unclean and to carry a carcass was to be even more unclean, requiring thorough cleansing. The reason is the bacteria and disease carried by carrion birds and flies.
- 11:29-30: Another group of animals is introduced here. Many of these animals could be found in or around human dwellings. Since these animals were unclean, it was important to know how to deal with them and with objects and utensils they touched. These are small creatures crept the earth. This refers not only to their great numbers but also to their quickness of movement. The group includes small rodents such as mice, voles, shrews, and hamsters, also some kinds of lizards.
- 11:31: When they are dead: literally 'in their death' or 'in their dying.' The Israelite farmer was more likely to kill a small rodent during chores than any other creature

named in this chapter. It was important to remember as they killed these pests that they would be unclean until evening if they touched them.
- 11:32: Expensive vessels of wood, fabric, leather, or fiber were to be put in the water. Whether they were only to be washed or soaked until evening is unclean. However, at evening, the start of the new Jewish day, they would be clean.
- 11:33: Any earthen vessel…you shall break: Pottery was plentiful, cheap, and easily replaced. Vessels made of pottery were also used for food preparation and eating. Again, hygiene is an important result of avoiding the unclean. We are to wash dishes and food when preparing to avoid bacteria and salmonella or other diseases.
- 11:34: The contents of any vessel made unclean in this way became unclean as well.
- 11:35: These ovens were made of clay and so had to be broken also.
- 11:36: A spring or a cistern could hardly be emptied. Only the person removing the carcass became unclean -- until evening.
- 11:37-38: Dry planting seed did not become unclean.
- 11:39-40: If an animal dies: This refers to animals that died of natural causes, and not those killed for food. The carcass caused the person who touched it to be unclean because its blood had not been drained. Eating or carrying the carcass involved more than merely touching it and required a greater remedy --washing one's clothes by waiting until evening. Eating meat without draining its blood apparently was not as serious an offense as eating and drinking blood by itself.[358] Carrying the carcass would have been unavoidable in many situations such as removing the animal for burial. Uncleanness often was not a moral issue at least in the way a person became unclean.
- 11:41-43: Crawls on its belly and has many feet are new descriptions. They were not mentioned in the previous ban on eating creeping things.

—Scriptures were a breakdown from the Nelson Study Bible

Even though the Jews had to follow these practices of preparation and foods under God's standards that were allowed, we also find that Noah knew how to distinguish the clean from the unclean.[359] The pairs of every animal that joined Noah in the ark; seven pairs were taken of those animals to be used for sacrifice— the 'clean' animals. Scholars estimated that almost forty-five thousand animals could fit in the ark.[360] You may be asking or thinking to yourself, *"why do I have to follow the diet that God has required?"*

---

[358] Leviticus 7:26-27
[359] Genesis 7:2-3
[360] Life Application Study Bible, NKJV, 1996.

Begin Day 60:
Obey with Food

Exodus 15:26, states that if we obey God standards on what we eat, we will be free of diseases and sickness. Daniel 1:15, describing Daniel and his friends as "fairer and fatter," God had clearly allowed them to be healthier than the young men who ate of the king's delicacies. Some of us do not want to change our eating habits because we grew up as meat eaters or vegetarians. As adults, we are able to make better conclusions or remain stubborn to old habits. God is concerned about our eating and our bodies to become healthier.

Paul explains why in 1 Corinthians 6:19. Our bodies contain the Holy Spirit. God's breath exists within us.

Begin Day 61:
Criticism on Foods

Paul knew the danger of criticism on this issue in Romans 14.

1) Accept believers who are weak in faith, and do not argue with them about what they think is right and wrong.
2) For instance, one person believes it is all right to eat anything. However, another believer who has a sensitive conscience will eat only vegetables.
3) Those who think it is all right to eat anything must not look down on those who will not. Additionally, those who will not eat certain foods must not condemn those who do, for God has accepted them.
4) Who are you to condemn God's servants? They are responsible to the Lord, so let him tell them whether they are right and wrong. The Lord's power will help them do as they should.
5) Those who have a special day for worshipping the Lord are trying to honor him. Those who eat all kinds of food do so to honor the Lord since they give thanks to God before eating. Those who will not eat everything also want to please the Lord and give thanks to God (like Daniel).
6) For we are not our own masters when we live or when we die.
7) While we live, we live to please the Lord. In addition, when we die, we go to be with the Lord. Therefore, in life and death (our eternal life), we belong to the Lord.
8) Christ died and rose again, for this very purpose, so that he might be Lord of those who are alive and of those who have died.
9) So why do you condemn another Christian? Why do you look down on another Christian? Remember, each of us will stand before the Judgment Seat of God.
10) For the Scriptures read, "As surely as I live, says the Lord, every knee will bow to me and every tongue will confess allegiance to God."[361]
11) Yes, each of us will have to give a personal account to God.
12) So, do not condemn each other anymore. Decide to live in such a way that you will not put an obstacle in another Christian's path.
13) I know and am perfectly sure on the authority of the Lord Jesus that no food, in and of itself, is wrong to eat. But, if someone believes it is wrong, then for that person, it is wrong.
14) If another Christian is distressed by what you eat, you are not acting in love, if you eat it. Do not let your eating ruin someone, for whom Christ died.
15) Then you will not be condemned for doing something you know is right.
16) For the Kingdom of God is not a matter of what we eat or drink, but of living a life of goodness and peace and joy in the Holy Spirit.
17) If you serve Christ with an obedient attitude, you will please God. Additionally, other people will approve of you, too.
18) So then, let us aim for harmony in the church and try to build each other up.

---
[361] Isaiah 45:23

19) Do not tear apart the work of God over what you eat. Remember, there is nothing wrong with these things in themselves. However, it is wrong to eat anything if it makes another person stumble.
20) Do not eat meat, drink wine, or do anything else if it might cause another Christian to stumble.
21) You may have the faith to believe that there is nothing wrong with what you are doing, but keep it between yourself and God. Blessed are those who do not condemn themselves by doing something they know is right.
22) If people have doubts about whether they should eat something, they should not eat it. They would be condemned, for not acting in faith before God. If you do anything you believe is not right, you are sinning.[362]

Some would ask why God created the hog (others in the swine family are wild boar, warthog or domestic pig) if we are not meant to eat pork. He made it for the same purpose that He made the buzzard as a scavenger to clean up garbage, and the hog serves this purpose admirably. In Romans 14, Verse 3 and 6 are a discussion of those who eat certain things versus those who do not. The passage does not say it is right to eat pork but rather counsels us not to pass judgment on another who eats it. Instead, let God be the judge.[363]

---

[362] New Living Translation (NLT) found on BibleGateway.com.
[363] Romans 14: 4, 10, 12

Begin Day 62:
Abstain from Unclean Foods?

Upon a reading of Old Testament laws, we are aware that foods first offered to idols would be unclean.[364] The point made is that food is 'unclean' or 'impure' because it was first offered to the gods, which is 'part of worldly ways.'[365] If a Christian's conscience bothers him or her for eating such a food, he or she needs to leave it alone. Paul makes a point, that even if it merely offends a brother, it is a service to God for us to abstain from it in order to help the weaker brother.

1 Timothy 4:3-5, NKJV: *"…and commanding to abstain from foods which God created to be received with thanksgiving by those who believe and know the truth. For every creature of God is good, and nothing is to be refused if it is received with thanksgiving; for it is sanctified by the Word of God and prayer."*

In a review of 1 Timothy 4:3-5, it makes sense that we also abstain from processed foods and other foods that were not created by God, if we want to remain healthy, look and feel great. Regarding kosher foods which may be preserved, you should be able to look at the ingredients label and see only the original food as God created it, and it's preservation process. Additionally, a superb book to read is *The Seven Pillars of Health* by Dr. Don Colbert.

---

[364] 1 Corinthians 8:1, 4, 10, 13; Romans 14:14, 20
[365] 1 Corinthians 8:4

Begin Day 63:
Health Laws Overview

Eat your meals at regular intervals and do not use animal fat or blood.[366] "Eat in due season."[367] Do not overeat.[368] Jesus Christ warns against *surfeiting*, which means "an excessive amount of something" in the last days. Overeating or gluttony is responsible for many degenerative diseases. The original Greek translates to "dissipation," meaning squandering of resources, of which overeating is one.

Do not harbor envy or hold grudges.[369] Jesus Christ even commands us to clear up grudges that others may hold against us.[370]

Maintain a cheerful disposition, which imparts health and prolongs life.[371] Many diseases are a result of mental depression. In Proverbs 22:24–25, Solomon warns that the people we choose to associate with can affect our disposition and our health. This also means that we must be careful how we associate with people on Social Media. Many people feel that the anonymity of the net hides them, but you are not hidden from God. Spend more time in activities that help others around you.

Put full trust in the Lord. Trust in the Lord strengthens health and life.[372] Therefore, health comes from obedience to God's commands, and from putting full trust in Him.

Balance work and exercise with sleep and rest.[373] "The sleep of a laboring man is sweet."[374]
1. Keep your body clean.[375]
2. Be temperate in all things.[376] "Let your moderation be known to all men."[377] A believer of Christ will completely avoid all things that are harmful and eat or drink in moderation. Some foods or things such as alcohol, tobacco, and drugs that are bad for our bodies are like committing suicide on an installment plan.
3. Avoid all harmful stimulants. Medical science confirms that tea, coffee, and soft drinks contain the addictive drug caffeine and other harmful ingredients that are positively harmful to our bodies. Stimulants give a dangerous, artificial boost to the body. Many Americans are sickly because of their addiction to coffee, tea, and caffeinated soft drinks. However, the real tragedy is that men and women seek peace and strength through drinks such as caffeine tea and coffee, as cheap substitutes. This delights the devil and wrecks the human life.

---

[366] Leviticus 3:17
[367] Ecclesiastes 10:17
[368] Proverbs 23:2; Luke 21:34
[369] Proverbs 14:30
[370] Matthew 5:23-24
[371] Proverbs 17:22; 23:7
[372] Proverbs 19:23, Proverbs 4:20-22
[373] Exodus 20:9, 10
[374] Ecclesiastes 2:22-23; 5:12; Psalm 127:2
[375] Isaiah 52:11
[376] 1 Corinthians 9:25
[377] Philippians 4:5

4. Make mealtime a quiet and happy time.[378] Unhappy scenes at mealtime hinder digestive system, so try to avoid them.

The people of God's new kingdom will obey His health laws, and there will be no sickness or disease. They will be blessed with eternal vigor and youth and will live with God in supreme joy and happiness throughout all eternity. Moreover, God wants us to seek healthy thoughts and motives, not just healthy food and exercise.

---

[378] Ecclesiastes 3:13, Proverbs 17:1

Begin Day 64:
Help Those in Need

Help those who are in need. Read Isaiah 58:6-8. We help the poor and needy, but we need to improve our own health. It would be good to join a club, gym or a health partner, to get advice on healthy eating tips and exercise, and ways to lose weight or restore your health. One might choose to join volunteers at the local soup kitchen, both receiving and giving of time and health.

Begin Day 65:
Clean Foods

1 Timothy 4:4: *"Every creature of God is good, and nothing to be refused..."*

This Scripture refers to meats that God created to be received with thanksgiving. God accepted these animals, sanctified by God's Word, to say they are consecrated or 'made clean,' by a prayer of blessing when offered before the meal.[379] This will avoid poisoning or defiling the body in any way, once it has been blessed and prepared, with no blood or fat. God will destroy people who try to 'sanctify themselves' and then turn to eating unclean food.[380]

Matthew 15:11, NIV: *"What goes into a man's mouth does not make him 'unclean...'"*

---

[379] Leviticus 11; Deuteronomy 14
[380] Isaiah 66:17

Begin Day 66:
Washing Hands

Matthew 15:2-3, 10, 16-20, refers to those eating without washing their hands first. The focus here is not so much about eating, but washing. The Scribes taught that eating any food without a special ceremonial washing defiled the eater. Yet, as Jesus pointed out to the Scribes (religious leaders), it is not the refusing to wash your hands that defiles you, but what you harbor in your heart that defiles you. In Verse 2, it speaks about the tradition of the elders, not the Law of Moses.[381] It was an oral tradition with the interpretations of the law. Here you can refer back to yesterday's discussion of how people wash to be clean, then turn to unclean behavior. The Scribes and Pharisees washed their hands ceremonially to remove defilement, not for hygiene.[382]

Jesus answered the accusations of the Scribes and Pharisees with a question, "Why do you also transgress the commandment of God because of your tradition?"[383] Do we find ourselves caught up in tradition or following God's commandments? Pharisees challenged Jesus for His disciples' violation of the teachings of former rabbis. Jesus challenged them back with their traditions that focused on creating a hardship, instead of abiding by the commandments of the Lord. Moreover, the Scribes and Pharisees placed their own views above the revelation of God and yet claimed to be following Him. Jesus rebuked the Scribes and Pharisees for being so obsessed with traditions that they failed to observe basic commandments.[384] Jesus chided them for being so concerned with external ceremonial washings and dietary regulations that they failed to deal with character. It is what you say and think that makes you unclean. Does this statement, coming from the mouth of Jesus Christ, offend you as much as it did the Pharisees who heard it originally? Please heed God's Word.

In Matthew 15, Verse 20: *"These are the things, which defile a man, but to eat with unwashed hands does not defile a man."* We work hard to keep our outward appearance attractive, but what is in our hearts is even more important.[385] The way we are deep down, our souls, our spirits, where others cannot see, what truly matters to God. What are you like inside? When people become believers of Jesus Christ, God makes them different on the inside. He will continue the process of change inside them if they only ask.

By the way, Jesus is not, by any means, telling you that you cannot or should not wash your hands. Caring for your outside without caring for the temple within will leave your soul hungry and thirsty. Please, for your neighbor, wash your hands.

---

[381] Mark 7:3
[382] See Mark 7:2-4
[383] Matthew 15:3
[384] Mark 7:11-13
[385] Mark 7:16-20

Begin Day 67:
Personal Hygiene

Isaiah 52:11, MSG: *"Just leave, but leave clean. Purify yourselves in the process of worship, carrying the holy vessels of God."*

This passage is letting the worshippers know that they were to leave that which defiles, and to clean themselves from the filth, then to go through the purification process in the temple with the priests. You can see this process in the command Jesus gave to the lepers, to go and show themselves to the priests.

Similarly, in our modern times, we know that which is not healthy for our souls. We need to leave it behind, wash anything from our skin and clothes, and confess our sin, and to purify ourselves in worship. We also have to be pure within to be considered holy people of God. Ultimately, personal hygiene is important.

Begin Day 68:
Improving your Body Image

First, we will look at ways to improve your body image. Remember that we are to love our body. It is the temple of God:

1. *Exercise*: can do wonders. 87% of women say exercise improves the way they feel about their bodies. Try dancing, yoga, walking, biking, etc. The average woman should get 30-60 minutes of exercise a day and at least three times a week.
2. *Accentuate the positive*: even the toughest self-critics can take pride in their eyes, hair, hands, or some other body part. Zero in on what you like rather than what you hate. Try not to give yourself time to criticize the home God gave your soul.
3. *Pamper yourself*: enjoy your body by indulging in small, sensual pleasures such as soaking in a scented bath, lather on lotion, get a massage, and wear sexy attire.
4. *Use Visualization*: Imagine yourself stripping the negative labels you've internalized. Do not let those people who've been shallow with you come to mind, as God will work with them. Your job is to give Glory to Him, and thank Him for all the tools He's given your soul. Visualization is a key to becoming comfortable and at peace with your body and yourself.
5. *Give yourself time*: transforming the way you feel about your body is a slow process. Each day, determine that you will do one good thing to make each day a little better than the last. Remember 2 Peter 1:5-11, where we are admonished to make every effort to add. Goodness is one of those!

Begin Day 69:
Checklist on Weight

Second, answer these questions below. Are you hung up about your weight?

1. My life would be better if I would focus on exercise instead of how much I weigh. *True* or *False*?
2. I often eat when I am upset, depressed, anxious, or angry, to feel better. *True* or *False*?
3. I tend to eat too little in social situations because I am afraid people will talk. *True* or *False*?
4. I avoid mirrors. *True* or *False*?
5. I've learned to focus on keeping water close by. It staves off my hunger. *True* or *False*?
6. If I ate a handful of food whenever I wanted to, I would get very fat. *True* or *False*?
7. I choose clothes that make me feel beautiful. *True* or *False*?
8. I often feel guilty after I eat. *True* or *False*?
9. I am afraid to have a taste of dessert because I might lose control and eat too much. *True* or *False*?
10. I have tried many diets. *True* or *False*?
11. I prefer to dress (or undress) alone in intimate situations because I'm not comfortable with my body. *True* or *False*?
12. I eat when I can't sleep. *True* or *False*?
13. I compare my body unfavorably with those of others. *True* or *False*?
14. I look at the health numbers more than I do my weight. If my body is healthy, and I'm happy, the amount I weigh isn't as important. *True* or *False*?
15. I eat normally when I am with friends, but when I am by myself, I tend to pig out on things that aren't good for me. *True* or *False*?
16. I find that I am less likely to munch when I'm focused on a goal or mission. *True* or *False*?
17. I am embarrassed about the fact that I like to eat. *True* or *False*?
18. I've learned to enjoy flavors and the exercise that cooking from raw foods gives me. I don't gain any weight because I watch what goes in. *True* or *False*?
19. I garden for fresh fruits and vegetables. I love talking to my plants and watching them grow, and I love their flavor. *True* or *False*?

In the questions above, I've inserted some positive ways people deal with their calorie and eating issues. If you missed those, look at them again, and think of using one of those positives to practice each day. You are loved by the One who knew you before you were formed in the womb. He made your trip to earth a special one, and will indeed make your return to Him even more so!

Begin Day 70:
Get Plenty of Exercise

The Bible talks about avoiding overeating. Proverbs cautions about eating with an influential person (or attempting closeness in a social gathering) since it may cause you to eat more (or take actions to flatter that person).[386] No good will come from the meal. Why exercise? It takes more than physical components to look good. Exercising and eating healthy can prevent high blood pressure, heart disease, high cholesterol levels, strokes and some cancers. Many people wait until their physician to inform them of the at-risk conditions before engaging in any physical activities. Then, one wants to find the nearest gym, or sign up for some physical activity program, expecting physical trainers to provide them with results.

It could all be avoided by practicing self-discipline and self-control. Exercising on a consistent basis, at least 3-5 days a week, will lower blood pressure, increase energy level, build muscle mass, reduce risk factors for stroke and heart disease, and much more. Anyone who lives a sedentary lifestyle needs to incorporate some form of exercise into his or her daily life. Do it for your loved ones. You will be amazed at the way you will feel after a day of exercising. There are benefits of exercise: it's a prescription for prevention. If your doctor gave you a prescription or medication, would you take it? Obesity is the fastest growing health threat.

Below is a list of the benefits of taking your prescription of exercise. A person exercising:

- Improves working memory, reaction time and working IQ
- Feels sick 30% less often
- Relieves stress
- Eight (8) times less likely to die from cardiovascular disease
- Four (4) times less likely to die from cancer
- Decreases blood pressure
- Improves lipid profile
- Improves body composition, increases muscle mass and decreases fat
- Increases metabolic rate
- Improves tolerance of arthritis
- Helps prevent bone loss and osteoporosis
- Slows down muscle atrophy which occurs with age
- Decreases the need for insulin (if diabetic)
- Helps relaxation in response to stress
- Helps smokers in kicking the habit
- Moderates depression and increase a sense of optimism
- Improves sex life
- Fifty (50%) less likely to get breast cancer
- Less likely to develop varicose veins
- Improves skin
- Improves sleep and helps prevent insomnia

--SB (Spiritually Beautiful) Fitness Inc.

---

[386] Proverbs 23:1-3

Begin Day 71:
Body Fat And Its Relationship To Your Health

Get a scale that measures not only your weight but also your body fat percentage. What this can do is encourage you to drink more water which, in turn, will help your body rid itself of excess *everything*. Weigh yourself daily, and note, in particular, how much water your body is carrying. *Livestrong.com* recommends a water percentage of 45 to 60 percent water. The more water your body carries, the less fat you will carry.

Too much body fat can cause serious health problems, diabetes, cancer, heart disease, etc.
1) *Apple shaped*: stores fat around abs increases risk of developing heart disease and diabetes
2) *Pear-shaped*: stored fat around hips and thighs have lesser risk
3) *Overweight*: increased body weight relative to height
4) *Obesity*: high amount of fat relative to lean muscle

How to reduce body fat?
1) Cardiovascular exercises or strength training
2) Diet
3) Eat throughout the day (small portions)
4) Consistency of all above—very important
5) Drink Water
   —SB (Spiritually Beautiful) Fitness Inc.
   (See full chart on the four body types that refers to the required exercise routine(s) in the appendices)

Genetics play a key role in determining your physical potential. If you exercise according to your particular body type to reduce body fat, improve your cardiovascular fitness level, and increase lean muscle mass—you will look and feel great no matter what size you are.

Begin Day y 72:
Three Step Guide To Losing Weight And Feeling Great

Step 1: Eating Smart
- Eat a variety of foods.
- Balance the food you eat with physical activity to maintain or improve your weight.
- Choose a diet with plenty of vegetables, fruits, and grain products.
- Choose a diet moderate in sugar.
- Choose a diet moderate in salt and sodium.
- If you drink alcoholic beverages, do it in moderation.
- Choose a diet low in fat, saturated fat, and cholesterol.

Step 2: Energize with Exercise
The Activity Chart (see appendix)
- *Keep a daily tracker:* Exercise 3-5 times per week for 20 to 30 minutes is recommended for overall health and fitness. Weight loss will occur more quickly if exercise is increased to 5 times per week for 40 to 60 minutes. Keep track of your daily exercise: calories burned in various activities.
- Target your heart rate: during your exercise session, pause, and take your pulse to check your exercise intensity or training heart rate -- check your carotid artery (on either side of the center of your neck), or your radial artery (wrist). You can find your rate by subtracting your age from 220. (See appendix for target heart rate chart).

Step 3: Go for the Goals
- Short term goals:
  - Eating a piece of fruit instead of a doughnut
  - Walking during your lunch break instead of sitting in the cafeteria
  - Using jelly or jam on your bagel instead of peanut butter or cream cheese
- Long-term goals:
  - Maintaining a healthy weight
  - Establishing a regular exercise routine
  - Maintaining a healthy eating pattern

Setbacks: Do not put yourself down for setbacks; we all have them. If you ate six chocolate chip cookies yesterday, just forget about it and move on. A common mistake made after overeating is that people fast or skip meals, which causes hunger and frustration. Follow your healthy eating plan with your next meal.

Rewards: You can reward yourself each time you reach a goal; just make sure it is not food. Take a long, luxurious bubble bath or get a professional massage.

Begin Day 73:
Simple Solutions

Before turning to medical professionals for help to lose weight, try some of these simple solutions:
- Support from family, peers, and friends by encouraging one another to lose weight, or find someone with similar issues who is on the way to losing weight too. You are able to share secrets, methods that work, stories about how one feels about being overweight, struggles, and strategies to want to lose the weight.
- Simply limit food choices by not having any chocolate, candy, or ice cream in the house. Read food labels, check the sugar level, partially hydrogenated fats or MSG (also check for other terms relating to MSG). Read the ingredients or chemicals that are listed on the labels of the food your purchase. For instance, 'partially hydrogenated' in potato chips will cause you to remain overweight. Find other snacks that are healthy and good for your body, remember our bodies are God's temple we have to take care of.
- Ban nighttime eating; try not to snack after 8:30 p.m. At first, it may seem difficult to break bad habits, but take a step at a time, and have faith that you will reach your goal once you take that first step to stopping. You will be able to see the weight results once you decide to stop eating snacks late.
- Stop dieting and start eating. Restricting calories by more than 500 a day, (conversant mode), slowing down metabolism by 20%, equals starvation. Eating regularly and exercising moderately burns more calories than someone who skips a meal and exercises.
- Aerobic exercise: 30-45 minutes can burn 400-500 calories per session.
- Weight training increases lean body mass and boosts metabolic rate (best results after aerobic, bicycling, or pumping your heart rate).
- Metabolic rate=calories
  - Formula: $665+(4.36*weight (lbs))+(4.32*height (in.))-(4.7*age (yrs))$
- Plenty of sleep stimulates the body to burn more fat.

For every pound you carry, you need 100 calories to maintain it. So, if you're following one of the many calorie counting diets, and it tells you to limit your choices to 300 calories for breakfast, you're going to fail fast. You're only eating to maintain 3 pounds!

Try this instead: You read the menu at breakfast, and you're hungry. You see a healthy breakfast with whole grain and avocado and eggs is 640 calories. That maintains 6.4 of your pounds, so you add enough to make you full. You add a side and eat slowly. Enjoying your food and your companion is much better than worrying that you've overstepped your diet.

Begin Day 74:
Stay Slim Tips

Stay Slim Tips:
- Try making a change for three weeks.
- 3-5 oz. of meat (size of your palm), half cup of potatoes, rice or pasta, medium piece of fruit (size of a fist).
- Spicy foods will speed up your metabolism and satisfy you with small portions.
- Eat fruits and vegetables: receive your vitamins, minerals, fiber, fewer calories, and no fat. Five servings a day.
- Quench your hunger (hungry between meals, drink a glass of water, wait for 10 to 15 minutes before a meal, cuts appetite).
- Switch to light bread, sugar-free gelatin, read pasta sauce labels.
- Fry in cooking spray: sprit of canola or olive oil.
- Sauté stir-fry in bouillon, omit butter or margarine in rice, pasta, dried potatoes (baked).
- Low-fat or fat-free products.
- Snooze to lose (sleep more).

You may be wondering why water works, or why sleeping will work. People will substitute food for the water their body needs, thinking they won't urinate as often. Water washes out what one doesn't need. When you are awake, you're using calories. You're more likely to be hungry and raid the fridge late at night. Try chamomile tea instead, and get your rest!

Begin Day 75:
48 Steps on Releasing the Weight

48 Steps To Losing Weight
1. Double veggies (3-5 servings daily), which will appease hunger and shrink your waistline.
2. Skinless chicken can be marinade in BBQ sauce, basting sauce such as Teriyaki, and eat no more than 3 oz. of lean meat.
3. Drink less juice and eat more fruit. For example, orange juice has more calories than cola. Eat bananas, oranges, apples, watermelon, and other types of fruits.
4. Eat whole grains: whole wheat bread, pasta, or multigrain at least once a week.
5. Add veggies to lunch.
6. Dump the donut; replace it with English Muffins. You can add all-natural peanut butter or light cream cheese instead of butter or margarine.
7. Easy on the cheese: Low-fat, feta, parmesan.
8. More veggies in your sandwich (salad/tomatoes)
9. Lean ground turkey or chicken.
10. Skip the soda and try flavored water.
11. Match grains with veggies (cup of rice or pasta is about 200 calories).
12. Switch to low-fat milk, soy milk, almond milk, or Rice Dream.
13. Munch on pre-dinner veggies: carrots, celery, etc.
14. Veggie Pie: veggie pizza or more veggies than meat.
15. Scream for less ice cream: Cut back on the scoops (try 2).
16. Dress down salad (2-3 tablespoons of dressing).
17. Do not desert dessert.
18. Smaller bags of chips.
19. Snack smartly.

<u>Exercises to Try:</u>
20. Walk a lap around the mall.
21. Get off the bus a block early.
22. Music and dance around the house.
23. Buy exercise gear: athletic shoes can lose their cushion after 6 months of regular use, causing knee or ankle injury.
24. Unload one bag at a time when grocery shopping.
25. Quick walks (5 minutes a day, at least 35 minutes a week).
26. Outdoor activities: mow lawn, rake, or shovel.
    a. Raking burns 111 calories in a ½ hour.
    b. Mowing burns 225 calories in a ½ hour.
    c. Shoveling burns 557 calories in an hour.
27. Wash car weekly at least up to 30 minutes, which will burn 120 calories or 4 calories a minute.
28. Walk while you talk.
29. Deliver message by hand.
30. Take a long walk or long way.

31. Choose activities such as softball, volleyball, etc.
32. Exercise with family and friends.
33. Stop sitting at the TV or computer. Do Stretching, Tai Chi, or Yoga instead.

<u>Habits to Change:</u>
34. Eat breakfast.
35. Shop smartly.
36. Hide serving bowls (not to eat extra).
37. Walk off anxiety.
38. Put your fork down (enjoy your food).
39. Measure your portions once a week. For example, eat 3 oz. of meat for lunch and dinner (women's palm), and a cup of rice, pasta, veggies (women's fist).
40. Snacks: crackers, popcorn, pretzels, and corn chips (avoid vending machine snacks).
41. Sleep (at least 7-8 hours a day).
42. Stop munching, find things to do instead.
43. Eat before you drink alcohol.
44. Stop before getting stuffed.
45. Keep out of the kitchen.
46. Chart your success (food log).
47. Celebrate without food.
48. 3 meals, 2 snacks a day.

<u>Get the Exercise and help out, too</u>

Volunteering will give you opportunities to move and give at the same time. Non-profits like Habitat for Humanity allow you to learn and help people build a place to live. Non-profit stores that rely on volunteers need someone who will dust, clean or organize products. Walk a dog at the Humane Society. Organize a fundraiser. The opportunities to learn, exercise, and care at the same time are everywhere.

Begin Day 76:
Stop Postpartum Weight Gain

Many women find they have become obese after pregnancy. They think that they ate too much, or did not exercise hard enough. However, studies show that women who gain weight after delivery, typically moms who are 60-70 pounds overweight, may have inherited the tendency toward post-pregnancy heaviness. Women can outsmart her genetics. Here are some tips below.

During pregnancy:
- Watch your calories: Pregnant women need to add calories for the baby to grow on through tomorrow. Don't overdo, as a nine-pound baby would only need 900 extra calories, which comes from healthy meals. Listen to your body and your prenatal physician, and know that you are carrying water as well. Take 400 mcg of folic acid.

After pregnancy:
- Breastfeed your baby: Women who nurse return to their pre-pregnancy weight faster than those who do not. Breastfeeding burns 500 calories a day.
- Do not eat too much: Women who gained weight were eating more after their pregnancy than before – a more stressful lifestyle could be the reason.
- Keep active: Many first time mothers say they cannot find the time to exercise. However, doing everyday activities may require you to roll up your sleeves by mopping the floor, gardening, walking the dog, and cleaning the house, this will make a significant difference.

Where does the weight go? What expectant mothers can expect on the scale: The weight gain that occurs during pregnancy may be easier to accept if you understand where it is coming from. During the first trimester, most women gain 3-4 pounds. During the second and third, it is normal to put on a pound a week, resulting in a gain of 20-30 pounds.

- Blood volume: 3-4 lbs (usually in the breasts)
- Body fluid: 1-3 lbs (usually in the breasts)
- Uterus expansion: 1-3 lbs
- Amniotic fluid: 1-2 lbs (stomach)
- Baby: 7-8 lbs
- Placenta: 1-2 lbs (in womb)
- Fat and protein: 6-8 lbs (usually in the hips)

One should get plenty of exercise and fresh air.

Begin Day 77:
Harmful Substances for Your Body

The soothing comfort of alcohol is temporary. Real relief comes from dealing with the cause of the anguish and sorrow and turning to God for peace.[387] Do not lose yourself in alcohol. For instance, Israel was a wine-producing country. In the Old Testament, winepresses bursting with new wine were considered a sign of blessing. Wisdom is even said to have set her table with wine.[388] Nonetheless, the Old Testament writers were alert to the dangers of wine. It dulls the senses, it limits clear judgment,[389] it lowers the capacity for control,[390] it destroys a persons' efficiency.[391] To make wine, usually as a means of self-indulgence or an escape from life, is to misuse it and invite the consequences of the drunkard.[392]

Proverbs 20:1: *"Wine is a mocker, strong drink is a brawler, and whoever is led astray by it is not wise."*

This is a warning against the abuse of wine as well as excessive drinking. A wise person takes the danger seriously. There is no wisdom in drunkenness; only brawling and confusion.[393] Please take heed that God loves you, and does not want you to misuse your bodies with liquor, drugs, or other harmful substances. It leads to confusion and more depression, and temporary relief is not the answer, Jesus is the answer. Do you want eternal happiness or temporary enjoyment that will not last once the liquor or drugs wear off? Harmful substances are slowly destroying your body to death when you can be filled with the Holy Spirit forever. You can read more information about these substances that are harmful to your body in *Does Your Social Life Seem Empty?*

---

[387] Proverbs 23:29-35
[388] Proverbs 9:2, 5
[389] Proverbs 31:1-9
[390] Proverbs 4:17
[391] Proverbs 21:17
[392] Life Application Study Bible, NKJV, 1996.
[393] Nelson Study Bible, NKJV.

Begin Day 78:
Is God Involved In Your Home?

Job prayed that God would bless his home.[394] Through our daily prayers, we can ask God to bless our homes while we are away, raising our children, and taking care of our significant other, and to keep a peaceful environment within the boundaries of our home. Homes can be a place of worship. We can lift our praise and have a secret place for our prayers. Additionally, our homes can be a place for business, homeschooling, and church services, and/or conducting Bible studies.

According to John 14:22-23 the disciples were still expecting Jesus to establish an earthly kingdom and overthrow Rome. Yet, the disciples found it difficult to articulate why Jesus did not tell the world that He was the Messiah. Judas, one of the disciples, had high expectations that the Messiah would free them from the horrifying earthly realm and make the earthly home a paradise. However, Jesus was referring to our heavenly home, not here on earth. Not everyone could understand Jesus' message because He spoke in parables. From the time of the Pentecost, the gospel of the kingdom has been proclaimed in the whole world, but not everyone is receptive to it. Jesus saves the deepest Revelation of Himself for those who love and obey Him.[395] Make your home with Him.

---

[394] Job 29:4
[395] Life Application Study Bible, NKJV and emphasis added by the author.

Begin Day 79:
Fellowship

If a believer loves and obeys the Lord, he or she will experience the true fellowship with God.[396]

Fellowship in Revelation 3:20, NLT: *"Look! I stand at the door and knock. If you hear my voice and open the door, I will come in, and we will share a meal together as friends."*

Jesus is knocking on the door of our hearts. Every time that we sense His presence, we can rely on Him. Jesus wants fellowship with us, and He wants us to open up to Him. He is patient, not persistent, in trying to get through to us to come to Him. He is knocking at the door, small taps at our hearts, and is only waiting for us to open up to receive Him. He is not breaking and entering, but knocking. He allows us to decide to come to Him. Do you intentionally keep His life-changing presence and power on the other side of the door?[397] This fellowship with the Lord can start in your home. There is open fellowship. *Open fellowship* can also be viewed as hospitality.

In Philemon 1:2, the early churches often would meet in people's homes. Because of sporadic persecutions and great expense involved, church buildings were typically not constructed then.[398] Paul reflected on Philemon's love and faith. Philemon had opened his heart and his home to the church. We should do likewise, opening ourselves and our homes to others, offering Christian fellowship to refresh people's hearts.[399]

Hebrews 13:2, NLT: *"Don't forget to show hospitality to strangers, for some who have done this have entertained angels without realizing it!"*

There were three Old Testament people who "unwittingly entertained angels."[400] They appeared to Abraham,[401] Gideon,[402] and Manoah.[403]

---

[396] Nelson Study Bible, NKJV and emphasis added by the author.
[397] Life Application Study Bible, NKJV, 1996.
[398] Life Application Study Bible, NKJV, 1996.
[399] Philemon 4-7, Life Application Study Bible, NKJV, 1996.
[400] Life Application Study Bible, NKJV, 1996.
[401] Genesis 18:1, Genesis 19:1-4
[402] Judges 6:11
[403] Judges 13:2

Begin Day 80:
Hospitality

Some people say that they cannot be hospitable because their homes are not large or adequate enough. If you have a table and two chairs in a rented room, there are people who would be grateful to spend time in your home. Are there visitors to your church with whom you could share a meal? Do you know single people who would enjoy an evening of conversation? Is there any way your home could meet the needs of traveling missionaries?

Hospitality simply means making other people feel comfortable and at home.[404] We can also conduct small group sessions in our homes. We even welcome choir practices and other social outlets with believers.

Acts 5:42: *"And daily in the temple, and in every house, they did not cease teaching and preaching Jesus as the Christ."*

Jesus told his disciples to accept hospitality graciously because their work entitled them to it. Ministers spreading the gospel of Jesus Christ deserve to be supported, and it is our responsibility to make sure they have what they need. While serving in the ministry, they need several things to remain encouraged. First, they should make a decent salary. Second, they need a support system or an event planner. Third, lift their spirits with special surprises occasionally. Our ministers deserve to know that we are giving to them cheerfully and generously. Jesus gave two rules for the disciples to follow as they traveled. They were to eat what was set before them by accepting hospitality without being picky, and they were commanded to heal the sick. Because of their gentle nature, and God's healing, people were willing to listen to the gospel.[405]

---

[404] Genesis 12:14-16; 24:12-33; Ruth 2:14; Judges 19:1-10; 1 Kings 10:11-13; 2 Kings 6:18-23; Job 31:32; Psalm 101:7; 1 Corinthians 16:10-11; 1 Peter 4:9
[405] Life Application Study Bible, NKJV, and emphasis added by the author.

Begin Day 81:
Service/Serving

Home Bible studies are not new. As babes in Christ, we are to grow in our new faith. Therefore, a home Bible study will meet a new believer's needs.

Serving also introduces new believers to the Christian faith. During times of persecution, meeting in homes is the primary method of acquiring and sharing biblical knowledge. Persecuted followers of Jesus Christ throughout the world still use this approach to upsurge and support believers.[406]

Jesus said that those who minister are to be cared for. The disciples could expect food and shelter in return for spiritual service they provided. Who ministers to you? Make sure you take care of the pastors, missionaries, and teachers who serve God by serving you.[407]

Moreover, the disciples' mission was short-term. In essence, they were to do a national survey to determine the people's response to Jesus as the Messiah. Each of the twelve disciples covered an area of about 75-125 miles radius. They did not need extensive provisions since people would provide meals or food on their journey and open their homes to meet their needs.[408]

In Luke 10:7-10, Jesus direction to stay in one house avoided certain problems for the disciples.[409] Shifting from house to house could offend the families who first took them in. Some families might begin to compete for disciples' presence. Some might think they were not good enough to hear their message. If the disciples appeared not to appreciate the hospitality offered them, the town might not accept Jesus, when he followed them there. By staying in one place, the disciples did not have to worry continually about getting good accommodations. They could settle down and do their appointed task.

So, as a person who welcomes the disciple, you also should expect to lend support for the short time they are in your area.

---

[406] Life Application Study Bible, NKJV, emphasis added by author.
[407] See 1 Corinthians 9:9-10; 1 Timothy 5:17; also derived from Life Application Study Bible, NKJV, 1996: Matthew 10:10.
[408] Nelson Study Bible, NKJV and emphasis added by the author.
[409] See also Hospitality, Jesus is speaking to his disciples: Matthew 10: 9-10, 40-42; Luke 10:5-8

Begin Day 82:
Ministry Leadership: Hospitality

Church leadership (hospitality) in Titus 1:5: *"The things that are lacking,"* is the unfinished work of establishing correct teaching and appointing elders in every town. Paul had appointed elders in various churches during his journeys.[410] Furthermore, Paul was unable to stay at each church that was built, but he knew these new churches needed strong spiritual leadership. The men chosen were to lead the congregation by teaching sound doctrine, helping believers mature spiritually, and equipping them to live a life for Jesus Christ, despite opposition.[411]

Additionally, Paul briefly described some qualifications that the elders or church leaders should have. For example, Paul had given Timothy a similar set of instructions for the church in Ephesus.[412] Most of the qualifications involve character, not knowledge or talent.

A person's lifestyle and relationships provide a window into his or her character. Consider these qualifications as you evaluate a person for a position of leadership in your church. It is important to have leaders who can effectively preach God's Word, but even more important to have those who can live out God's Word and be examples for others to follow.[413] Other references to hospitality can be found in the book of *Judges 19:12-21*.

---

[410] Acts 14:23
[411] Life Application Study Bible, NKJV, and emphasis added by author.
[412] 1 Timothy 3:1-7; 5:22
[413] Life Application Study Bible, NKJV, 1996.

Begin Day 83:
Women in Church Leadership

1 Corinthians 14:34, 35: *"Let your women keep silent in churches, for they are not permitted to speak: but they are to be submissive, as the law also says. And if they want to learn something, let them ask their own husbands at home: for it is shameful for women to speak in the church."*

Corinthian women were not allowed to confront men in public. Apparently, some of the women who had become followers of Jesus Christ gave them the impression that they had the right to question the men during public worship service. However, this was causing division in the church. Women of that day did not receive a formal religious education as men did. Women may have been raising questions during worship service, which could have been answered at home without disrupting the church service. Plainly, Paul was asking women not to flaunt their Christian freedom during worship. The purpose of Paul's words was to promote unity within the body of Christ, not to teach women about their roles in the church.[414]

Does this mean that women are not to speak in church services today? Women prayed and prophesied in public worship.[415] It is also clear that women are given spiritual gifts and is encouraged to exercise them in the body of Christ.[416] Women have much to contribute and can participate in a worship service. When we consider the proper exercise of our faith, listening to the lesson learned before asking questions is paramount.

Today, there are women pastors, women evangelists, and other ministries are led by women. If God calls on women to do His business, men cannot scrutinize a woman's role in the church or a ministry. The Bible speaks against judging one's role in the church. In addition, we are to edify and encourage believers, not to exclude women pastors and women evangelists from participating in leadership roles in the church because we've misconstrued a verse in the bible. Many people lose sight of the true focus of God's Word by focusing on a single verse.

---

[414] Life Application Study Bible, NKJV, and emphasis added by author.
[415] 1 Corinthians 11:5
[416] 1 Corinthians 11:12-14

Begin Day 84:
Refusal of Hospitality

The Scriptures warn us not to envy the lifestyles of those who have become rich. We want to get stingy with our tithes and offerings. Furthermore, we will gain their favor by fawning over them. Here, their friendship is fake, by which they will just use you for their own gain.[417] They only want to know how God is in you and how you were so blessed beyond human measure.

On the other hand, when you extend hospitality to those who cannot repay, you are rewarded. Jesus advised people not to rush to the best places at a feast. People today attempt to raise their social status by appearances, whether by being with the right people, dressing for success, or driving a luxury car. Whom do you try to impress? Rather than aiming for prestige, look for a place where you can serve. If God wants you to serve on a wider scale, He will invite you to take a higher place.

Jesus taught two lessons: He spoke to the disciples, telling them not to seek places of honor. Service is more important in God's kingdom than status. Second, He told them that the host shouldn't be exclusive about whom he invites. God opens His kingdom to everyone that wants to receive God's gifts, blessings, and to live with Him one day in the heavenly realm of true paradise.[418]

---

[417] Life Application Study Bible, NKJV, and emphasis added by author.
[418] Mark 10:37, Luke 14:8, Luke 14:12

Begin Day 85:
Dedicating Your Home

We are to dedicate our homes to the Lord.[419] A man or father is the *head of the household*, which he can guide his family into the leadership under the Heavenly Father's covering. His family can follow his path or direction, and pray for spiritual wisdom, knowledge, and insight to continue to raise his family in the Lord, by following the duties set aside for him. However, if you are a single female parent, this makes you the head of your household, and the one to make decisions in your home.[420]

Joshua told his family that we would always glorify the Lord in his home. Will you follow Jesus' footsteps for you and your family? In taking a definite stand for the Lord, Joshua again displayed spiritual leadership. Regardless of what others thought, Joshua decided to stand on a commitment to God, and he was willing to set the example with those around him. The way we live shows others our strength of our commitment to serving God. Is God living in your home?[421]

In Genesis 28:16, *"Surely the Lord is in this place, and I did not know it."* Do you find yourself like Jacob, or wondering if God is in this place? God sets up a ladder for us to be in His presence. Yet, Satan wants us to be ignorant of God's promises for our lives and in our homes, to remain discouraged.

---

[419] Psalm 127:1
[420] Deuteronomy 10:18a
[421] Joshua 24:15, Nelson Study Bible, NKJV.

Begin Day 86:
Spiritual Walk

See your ladder that God has set up for you by following two provisions.

Number one: Faith in God's Word.[422] Sometimes, we are unable to see God's purpose. Are we seeking eternal life and operating in the perspective of God's Word? Alternatively, whoever contradicts the Word is living a lie, which is one of Satan's most powerful weapons used against unbelievers and believers. Only Jesus Christ can set you free.

Number two: Believe in God's Word and that Jesus Christ is the one standing at the top of that ladder.[423] Through the authority and power of God's Word, we can overcome any principalities, demonic spirits, or anything that one is facing. God can release His angels for protection, direction, and come to the rescue.

During our spiritual walk, we are to rely on God to change our attitudes. He wants us to have a godly character in our homes, in our lives, and for spiritual leadership. For example, Eli had spent his entire life in service to God. His responsibilities were to oversee all the worship in Israel. Consequently, in pursuing this great mission, he neglected the responsibilities within his own home. Do not let your desire to do God's work cause you to neglect your own family. If you do, your mission may degenerate into a quest for personal importance, and your family will suffer the consequences of your neglect.[424]

---

[422] Matthew 4:1-11
[423] John 1:51; Matthew 10:33
[424] 1 Samuel 3:13, Life Application Study Bible, NKJV, 1996.

Begin Day 87:
Temporary Home

On another note, no earthly city will ever give permanent peace to its inhabitants. Abraham realized that. Abraham left Ur, the great city of his day, and became a wanderer for God's sake. Although Abraham settled in Hebron, he realized that it could never be the fulfillment of his quest. He sought a holy city, where the Builder and the Maker is God. That city, the New Jerusalem, will be a place where all who love God can live together in lasting harmony. All physical death and sorrow will be done away with.

In the New Jerusalem, there will be neither church, nor mosque, nor temple, for God Himself will dwell there. The crystal river of life will flow from His throne, and the tree of life will feed and heal the nations. In that city, the family of God will be reunited for all eternity. Not just Jew, Gentile, and Arab, but people from 'every nation, tribe, people and language,' for we are all one family. Until then, neither the might of arms, nor the power of diplomacy, but only God's Spirit of lasting peace comes. Moreover, we all have a responsibility to bring about peace and reconciliation wherever we can. To that end, we can all pray for the peace of Jerusalem. We can pray that God's Spirit will soften hearts, and transform minds so that the killing will end, and even on this earth, Jerusalem can become the 'City of Peace.'[425]

In our household, we have to believe on the Lord Jesus Christ. When we recognize Jesus Christ as Lord, and trust in Him, our entire life and salvation are assured. If you have never trusted in Jesus to save you, whether it is in your household, church or public place, do it quickly. Your life can be filled with joy once you allow Jesus Christ in your home and life. The saying, 'Home, Sweet Home,' will be sweet to have our Holy Savior living in your home or where you reside.

---

[425] Ed Dickerson, "Signs of the Times," November 2004.

Begin Day 88:
<u>Eternal Home</u>

John 14:2: *"In My Father's house are many mansions; if it were not so, I would have told you. I go to prepare a place for you."*

Following Jesus' Word, illustrating that the way to eternal life is secure, is to trust in Jesus Christ. However, you may be unwilling to believe. This Scripture is describing *everlasting life,* also mentioned in *Matthew 19:29*, and is rich in His promises. Jesus is letting us know that He will prepare a place for us and will come again. We can look forward to eternal life because Jesus has promised it to all who believe in Him. Although the details of eternity are unknown, we need not fear since Jesus is preparing for us, and He will spend eternity with us.[426] God responds: "And the posts of the door were shaken by the voice of Him, who cried out, and the house was filled with smoke."[427] If the doorposts of the heavenly temple shook in response to God's holiness, how much more will the whole earth shake when the Lord visits it?[428]

---

[426] John 14:1-3, Life Application Study Bible, NKJV, 1996.
[427] Isaiah 6:4
[428] Isaiah 6:3; Matthew 24:29-30, Nelson Study Bible, NKJV

Begin Day 89:
Singleness

The Greek word *Haplous* means 'simple or single.'[429] 'Singleness' as a purpose keeps our eyes from the snare of having a double treasure and a divided heart. Another term for *singleness* is *aphelotes*, which denotes 'simplicity.' In *Acts 2:46*, the idea is an unalloyed benevolence expressed.[430] *Singleness* can refer to someone that is separated from his or her spouse through divorce or separation or those who have never been married.

What is the major problem being single? Most single people think that they have to mingle and date someone. No one wants to be alone. Bodies are craving to be with that someone to hold, cherish, admire, and to love. Are these cravings natural or lust? Whose standard are we following: God's or that of the world? In a dating relationship with the opposite sex, we tend to confuse the feelings of infatuation, lust, and love.

---

[429] Vine's Concise Dictionary re: Matthew 6:21-24
[430] See also Ephesians 6:5 and Colossians 3:22

Begin Day 90:
Infatuation

Infatuation is derived from the word, *infatuate*, meaning to make a fool of, to make foolish, cause to lose sound judgment, to inspire with foolish or shallow love or affection, infatuated—a person who is infatuated.[431] How many of us have been infatuated, or are willing to admit it?

For example, I was dating a young man at the age of fourteen, introduced through his close friend. His close friend was a couple of years older than I was. However, the young man I was dating was infatuated with me, making plans for marriage once he graduated from high school within a year or two. Consequently, we were only dating for a month when he announced the good news to me. At the age of fourteen, I knew in my heart and mind that I was not ready for marriage when asked this question. Instead of taking this question seriously, I laughed.

Later, I had feelings for and became interested in his best friend. My heart fluttered, pounded, and my fingers became clammy and sweaty whenever he was around us. The dating relationship started to digress.

One day, when my boyfriend left us alone together, I lost self-control. He shared his feelings right away, about wanting to be with me regardless of his friend dating me. We said the words 'I love you,' 'I have never felt this way for anyone before,' and 'you made my heart pound in your presence when I first laid eyes on you.' These were the same words that my boyfriend used when he announced his interest in marriage. I was foolish to think that I could truly know what love is.

In my foolishness, I ended up crushing their feelings altogether. Yes, my boyfriend caught his best friend and me in the act of kissing. Imagine the anger my boyfriend had towards me and/or his best friend, as his feelings and heart were being crushed all in one. Alternatively, I was lost for words, felt ashamed, and did not know what to do. My boyfriend's best friend tried to apologize, but he could not hear him because of his emotional state. Additionally, he wanted to ask his permission to date me and how we supposedly felt about each other. Then, a fight broke out. Overall, it was not worth all this commotion since I was only infatuated with both of them.

At the time, I thought that I loved one guy more than I loved the other, and then I had to choose. I confessed how I viewed both of their characteristics and personalities. I had to conclude what I liked most about them. Additionally, I had to admit how I thought I felt about them. What is even funnier, although years have passed, when I talk to either one of these guys, my heart still pounds heavily, or I'll get a case of sweaty palms? However, deep down inside, I know that it is still not a *love* for either of them.

Jesus had agape love for us.[432] The example allows us to see how we confuse the two terms, 'infatuation' and 'love,' once we find ourselves attracted to the opposite sex, usually for the

---
[431] Webster's New World College Dictionary.
[432] 1 Corinthians 10:13

wrong reason. The list of what can cause one to feel infatuated, to lust after, or even to love a person can go on endlessly. Some of the items on such a list would be a sudden attraction that you know shouldn't be pursued, cologne, appearance, or the sound of a soothing voice.

The best way to know the truth is from the Man himself, Jesus Christ. Ask God for spiritual discernment and insight to know if this person is the one for you that He has planned. If not, to remove this person from your life. Eventually, I concluded while living the single life, that I want to be more intimate with God.

Begin Day 91:
Spiritual Vision

The eye is the lamp of the body. If your vision is clear, your whole body will be full of light. But if your vision is poor, your whole body will be full of darkness. If then the light within you is darkness, how great is that darkness!

Matthew 6:22-23 Berean Study Bible

Spiritual vision is our capacity to see clearly what God wants us to do, and to see the world from His point of view.[433] Consequently, if we cloud spiritual insight with self-serving desires, interests, and goals, we may block God's vision for today. Serving God is the best way to restore our spiritual vision.

A *good eye* is one that is fixed on God. Furthermore, the *lamp* represents Christ, and the *eye* represents spiritual understanding and insight. Evil desires make the eye less sensitive and blots out the light of Christ's presence. If you have a hard time seeing God at work in your life, check your vision. Are there any sinful desires blinding you to Christ? [434]

---

[433] Matthew 6:22, 23; Luke 11:34
[434] Life Application Study Bible, NKJV, 1996.

Begin Day 92:
Single in Waiting

I have dated men in the past that were not for me. After prayer, I am thankful that God sent the signs and warnings that the person was not His choice. Furthermore, God spoke to me about who He has planned for me. He also let me know my blessings for a mate will not be delayed any longer once I follow His will.

I felt like I was stuck in a rut by allowing myself to be caught up in believing the worldview that we have to be matched with someone. Instead, I will wait on God's plan for me since I keep falling for the wrong men. If I am willing to wait on God, I will not end up being stuck with someone whom God sees unfit for me. Then a temptation to break the *Tenth Commandment* might occur by desiring to be with someone else. Do not spend all your energies on someone who is not in God's will. I will no longer view the world's reasons for being with someone, or point my finger at someone else by asking, 'why are you alone?' Yet, at the same time, we must acknowledge that some people are meant to be single.[435]

First, we are to know our purpose for being with someone. God wants us to focus on His purpose for our lives first. A partner comes second. Purpose puts you in a position to receive the right partner. Quit feeling sorry for yourself. God gives us the power to choose, so stop focusing on the loneliness and misery of not being with someone. \
For example, when I focused on being alone, longing to be with someone, it would lead to feelings of lust. I would lust after someone, which led to fantasizing about them on an intimate level. I know that according to God's standards that are written in the Bible, those actions are not in His plan for those who are single. Paul points out the instructions for those who are single, which details the difference between a heart for God and a heart for one's partner. We can easily see the heart for God in how Jesus was tempted.[436] Instructions on a Christian relationship and marriage --[437] are further discussed in my book, *Unleashing the Spirits*.

Nonetheless, some single people feel a tremendous pressure to be married. They think their lives can be complete only with a spouse. Nevertheless, Paul underlines one overarching advantage of being single, which is the potential of a greater focus on Christ and His work.

---

[435] Matthew 19:10-12
[436] 1 Corinthians 7:33-34 and Matthew 4:1
[437] 1 Corinthians 7

Begin Day 93:
Singles: Breaking the 7th Commandment

On another note, many singles break the *Seventh Commandment*.

Some may label unmarried persons who are having sex as 'adulterers or adulteresses,' claiming they are breaking God's law of adultery. Others may refer to unmarried couples engaging in any sexual acts as 'fornicators.' After the moment of pleasure, it stinks.

Some argue that the 'clothes' one wears creates a distraction and stirs thoughts of lust in the eye of the weak woman or man who stares too long at the seductive attire.

According to biblical principles, *clothes* refer to the 'old' man, before one was saved. Yet, sometimes, people are quick to make accusations about someone's outer appearance. They feel a woman's attempt at provocative dress can be seductive to a man's eye and lure him to her with wrong intentions.[438]

Furthermore, there are other things that can influence a person in a lustful state of mind. They may have a willingness to change their outward appearance and/or personality to fit in with the crowd. They may seek an approval or acceptance from a peer group. They aren't willing to seem different or an outcast among their peers.
Finally, they may not be concerned about death and/or sexual orientation.

Several possible solutions are to ask God for a new heart and mind. Seek God's purpose for your life and God will turn you into a 'spiritual creature searching for the truth.' We are always looking beyond the obvious since God is a miracle worker and healer.
Sherlock Holmes had to narrow down the facts or evidence at hand to solve the mystery and never was satisfied until he uncovered the truth.

Consequently, you cannot find answers by hanging out with the world, which will only encourage you to think and act like they do.

Jesus tells us that we are to be holy, which means to 'be set apart from those things of the world.' If you are caught in the web of the worldly ways, God cannot speak to your heart and mind. We are to open our souls to the Holy Spirit and dedicate our lives to Jesus Christ to hear from our Heavenly Father.

In the long haul, if you do not allow God in, you will find yourself unhappy, and you will not know your purpose. There will be no substantial joy in your life. You will be left with despair and depression unless you allow God in -- greater is He that is in you than he (satan) who is in the world.

---

[438] Harden, Michael. Sermon on 8.15.04 at New Testament Church (Milwaukee WI) and author emphasis.

Begin Day 94:
Lust

These are synonyms and descriptions of the word *lust. Pleasure, delight, appetite, sexual senses, a desire to gratify the senses in a bodily appetite or sexual desire, as seeking unrestrained gratification, inclination, overmastering desire, lust of power, and 'lusts of the flesh' as described in 1 John 2:16.*[439]

Lust is not *love*. It is an abnormal desire, so do not confuse it with love such as love for self, family, wife or husband. It is the desire of possession. This is why lust is a sin because it is a desire to own something that belongs to someone else. If you are lustful, you are willing to do anything to possess it. People have been known to lie, steal, and even kill for the object of their desire.

Jesus said we could be content with what God has provided, and lust not for our neighbor's wife or his possessions. Although it seems harder to be single than someone already married, we are to remain righteous and holy. The Bible makes it clear that men and women will never achieve such holiness, but can only continue to try to fight their human emotions caused by living in this world. Our responsibility is to confess our frailties to God and pray for forgiveness.

---

[439] Webster's New World College Dictionary.

Begin Day 95:
Lust: Perverse Sexualities

Lust can lead to relationships that God views as an abomination: 'homosexuality,' 'bi-sexuality,' and 'bestiality.' Because of the feelings of sexual lust, your flesh will never be satisfied, and desires grow stronger as the cravings take control over your senses, and lead you to sin that could have been avoided with the conviction of the Holy Spirit. If you would only take the time to listen to God's voice, any lustful emotions tugging at your heart or any sexual pressures will vanish, and you are able to resist sin with God's help. If you find yourself lusting in such a way, say, "I want to please God, not focus on myself."

Another form of lust is self-gratification, in which you may be turning to pleasing yourself instead of your partner. Homosexuality or bi-sexuality as a desire can be interpreted in many ways, but in a biblical sense, this is a direct contradiction of God's command to be fruitful and multiply, and science has proven the purpose of copulation to produce children is to have a healthy world population. Inbreeding studies, where people have had sex with close relatives, have shown that genetic disease gets stronger. Humans are the only species that practice these forms of sexuality. Medically speaking, it could be said that because of abnormal hormones during gestation, when the sex organ of the fetus is formed, causes one to be receptive to the same sexes. Some people are born as a male, but with an increased amount of female hormones and surgery, they are becoming women, and some women prefer to be males. Would you say that you were born this way?

Bi-sexuality is a desire for sex with both the same sex as well as with the opposite sex. In other words, God did not create people to be homosexuals or bisexuals.

Bestiality is an abnormal desire for sex with animals.[440]

Those who choose sexual abnormality may do so out of childhood trauma, or a belief that they are more comfortable in such a reality. If a relationship cannot produce children, it should be avoided.

Each of us chooses our reality, circumstances, and conditions of life before coming into the body of Christ. God granted us free will, where people are able to create their own experiences by their choices. God blessed us with sacred gifts. One of those gifts is our sexual identity, which is to be saved until marriage or union. However, we continue to misuse and abuse our bodies with our own sexual desires and lusts.

Moreover, God gave 'you' the authority and power to decide and declare for yourself, so why are you lustful? God expects us to practice 'celibacy' or 'preserve our virginity' until we are married. We may struggle with lustful desires by lusting with our eyes, minds, or even in our hearts -- 'in need of a relationship' to avoid loneliness. Join a supportive group, or speak with a family member or friend to help with the issues. Alternatively, you can join a singles fellowship class to hear other confessions and find solutions to your problems. Moreover, once you are convinced that sin is disgusting and grow to hate sin, and then you are able to

---

[440] Statement by Sonny J. Turner

conquer and overcome our feelings of lust.

God expects us to love Him first, others second—and ourselves? Last.

Begin Day 96:
Defining Love

Love has too many definitions in the *Webster's New World College Dictionary*. Here are a few: a deep and tender feeling of affection for or attachment or devotion to a person or persons; an expression of one's love or affection; and a strong liking for or interest in something or someone.

Love can also refer to God's tender regard and concern for humanity. Human's devotion to and desire for God as the supreme God is also *love*. Some believe *showing love* is evidenced by embracing, fondling, kissing, or some other physical form of affection towards another. Others argue that it is an emotion of love such as to be in love or to love someone. Delight in, or take pleasure in, is another meaning of *love*.

Begin Day 97:
Old Testament View of Love

Ahab, a Hebrew word, means to love; like, which is a strong emotional attachment to, and desire either to possess or to be in the presence of the object; familiar, romantic, or friendship.[441] In some references, it can signify sexual lust.[442] Making love usually is represented by *yada* -- to know, or by *shakab* – to lie with. Sometimes *ahab* depicts an overtone of family love; his master as a son loves his father.[443] [444]

Ahabah, which also means love (feminine form), has the same range of meanings as the term, *ahab*. It can refer to a family, friend, romantic, or sexual love, as a state of being or actions of strong affection and commitment.[445]

---

[441] Genesis 22:2; 24:67; 34:3; Ruth 4:15
[442] 2 Samuel 13:1
[443] Deuteronomy 15:16; 1 Samuel 16:21; 18:16; Exodus 21:5
[444] Vine's Concise Dictionary.
[445] Genesis 29:20; Deuteronomy 7:8; 1 Samuel 18:3; Hosea 3:1

Begin Day 98:
New Testament View on Love

Agape describes the attitude of God toward His Son,[446] those who believe on the Lord Jesus Christ,[447] to convey His will to His children concerning their attitude one toward another,[448] and toward all men,[449] who express the nature of God.[450] There are Scriptures on *agape love*, where God demonstrates His love for humanity by sending His Son, Jesus Christ to earth.

Moreover, Christian love, whether exercised towards men and women, generally is not an impulse from the feelings. It does not always run with natural inclinations, nor does it spend itself only on those for whom some affinity is discovered. Love seeks the welfare of all, and works no ill to any;[451] love seeks the opportunity to do well to all men, and especially toward them that are of the household of the faith.[452]

- *Phileo* represents tender affection. The words *agape* and *phileo* are used for the love of the Father for the Son.[453]
- *Philanthropia* denotes love for man, hence, kindness,[454] and His love towards man.[455]
- *Philotheos* -- a lover of God
- *Philoxenos* -- loving strangers; lover of hospitality
- *Philagathos* -- loving that which is good, lover of good
- *Philarguros* -- loving oneself
- *Philedonos* -- loving pleasure, lovers of pleasure

In a relationship, we are seeking *agape* love.

The best relationships start from a friendship (*phileo*). It is a period, if you are both single, that lets you get to know one another, share common goals in life, and share the love God has for you (*agape*). If it leads to a deeper relationship in accordance with God's desire that you watch for the best outcome (especially if either of you have children) then you may decide to marry.

Sometimes, relationships start with a physical attraction that catches our attention, also known as *Eros*. *Eros* can refer to *erotic*, another term for lust and physical stimulation that causes our heart to pump fast and hard, our hands to sweat, and want to know their name

---

[446] John 17:26; 3:16; Romans 5:8
[447] John 14:21
[448] John 13:34
[449] 1 Thessalonians 3:12; 1 Corinthians 16:14; 2 Peter 1:7
[450] 1 John 4:8
[451] Romans 15:2
[452] Galatians 6:10; 1 Corinthians 13 and Colossians 3:12-14
[453] John 3:35; 5:20 for the believer; 16:27 both refer to Christ's love, and the love for his disciples John 13:23; 20:2
[454] Acts 28:2
[455] Titus 3:4

and phone number. You want to see more of that person, and want to get to know them, hopefully avoiding the physical urges to be intimate. Then, if you are mature enough, it leads to *phileo*, which is having feelings or affection for that person. It can also refer to a close relationship or friendship.

Once you are engaged or married, hopefully, this affection can grow to *agape*, with an unconditional love for your spouse. Remember, to delight in someone and take pleasure in someone, is a form of *lust*.

Be careful not to confuse the two.

Begin Day 99:
Courtship

We tend to look at the styles of dating from the world's perspective. God's standard on dating is known as *courtship*. *Courtship* means the act, process, or period of courting or wooing. In layman terms, this is someone God has destined (chosen) for you. You take the time to date them for a period, get to know their character and your shared goals for life, and that leads to holy matrimony, should the Lord allow the relationship to mature.

As a youth leader at New Testament Church in Milwaukee, WI, I became familiar with a recommended book, entitled *I Kissed Dating Goodbye*. Some reviewers argue that his views are too strict and structured and that the ideas seem unlikely to be carried out by singles that are dating. The most valuable viewpoint shared is that we are no longer 'dating' but 'seeking' a lifelong companion through courtship. Once we decide to kiss dating goodbye, we are seeking God's will for our lives. We begin paying attention to a lifelong commitment to God, then to the one we are courting.

A marriage based on Him will survive, and you cannot know that for sure without courtship.

Begin Day 100:
Unmarried

If you are unmarried, use your special opportunity to serve Christ wholeheartedly.[456] When Paul says the unmarried person does even better, he is talking about the potential time available for the service to God. The single person lacks the responsibility of caring for a spouse and raising a family. Singleness, however, does not ensure service to God such as the involvement in service depends on the commitment of the individual.[457] Furthermore, Paul's advice comes from the Holy Spirit, who guides and equips both single and married people to fulfill their roles.[458]

'Virgins' is the classification given to the unmarried in the church, which included widows and those who had been married before. Though Paul is concerned with both celibate men and women, the attention we focus on here is the women.[459]

To the contrary, Paul saw turbulent days ahead for married believers because, in times of persecution, consideration for the family can make it difficult to live out Christian convictions fully. A virgin would have lesser family responsibilities and would not be deterred by the possibility of repercussions affected by her husband or children.[460] Consequently, Paul does not want to be understood as prohibiting marriage altogether. Paul is not saying to get married is a ticket out of sin, but married couples are to dedicate themselves to God's work.[461]

A second interpretation suggests that the fiancé carry out celibacy until marriage since his mate is still a virgin. If a man has difficulty in controlling his sex drive or his will is weak, he ought to marry. On the other hand, if the man can control himself and keep himself from immoral action, he can remain single.[462]

---

[456] 1 Corinthians 7:32-34, Life Application Study Bible, NKJV, 1996.
[457] 1 Corinthians 7:38, Life Application Study Bible, NKJV, 1996.
[458] 1 Corinthians 7:40, Life Application Study Bible, NKJV, 1996.
[459] 1 Corinthians 7:25-40, Nelson Study Bible, NKJV.
[460] 1 Corinthians 7:26, 27, Nelson Study Bible, NKJV.
[461] 1 Corinthians 7:28-29, Nelson Study Bible, NKJV.
[462] 1 Corinthians 7:8, 36-38; Life Application Study Bible, NKJV, 1996.

Begin Day 101:
Boundaries For Singles

Nathan Bailey, in an online book on Courtship,[463] views the dating scene as an outlet to hide one's true feelings and all their faults, presenting a false impression to keep their partner interested. For example, women are wearing fake eyelashes, falsies (silicon breasts), weave, bootie busters (extra padding), etc., to attract men. Then again, men are willing to lie about their financial income, status, and drive rent-a-cars, rent-a-suits, and whatever it takes to impress a woman. Some men believe a woman is only seeking a man with fame and/or wealth. There are many men are willing to impress a woman to the extreme to have a one-night stand. Increasingly, our society gives some women the impression they can attempt to attract a man for sexual gratification.

The movie *Jersey Girl,* with Ben Affleck and Jennifer Lopez, displays a story of a man who marries the woman he loves. Jennifer Lopez, Ben Affleck's wife in the movie, dies after giving birth to a baby girl. Later, we see a woman in a video store flaunting her sexual appetite on him. She is, once she realizes that he is a single parent raising his child on his own, overtly throwing herself at him. When they meet at a local restaurant, and she finds out that he has not had sex for several years, she feels that she can encourage him to make out. She states her opinion that a man should get laid and not to deprive himself of sexual gratification after so many years. Here, Ben Affleck's character, while not willing to have sex after his wife's death, allowed her flattery and enticement to meet his sexual appetite.

There are believers of Jesus Christ hanging out in bars and other un-Christian places to meet their mate, including online dating services.

Some boundaries one would cross to appeal sexually to the opposite gender are: spraying on cologne or perfume to arouse their senses, wearing a provocative wardrobe, engaging in phone sex, cybersex (online interaction), and participating in a virtual fantasy on online dating services to appear as a 'good catch.'[464]

Romans 5:3-5, NKJV: *"And not only that, but we also glory in tribulations, knowing that tribulation produces perseverance; and perseverance, character; and character, hope. Now hope does not disappoint, because the love of God has been poured out in our hearts by the Holy Spirit who was given to us."*

Our actions reveal our strengths or weaknesses.[465] One has to beware of impulse decisions. Most singles fight emotional storms within their souls and concerns, wondering if God will keep His promises. God will restore our weary souls through His Word. His Word will nourish us, replenish us, and rejuvenate us again to believe in the invisible God through our 'faith.' Do not sink into repeating sins, continually praying for forgiveness to God, only to find yourself returning to the same sin. This cycle can be broken once we turn away from our sins. Jesus

---

[463] http://polynate.net/books/courtship/
[464] Viden, Holly and Michelle McKinley Hammond. *If Singleness is a Gift What's the Return Policy?* (emphasis added by author).
[465] 2 Corinthians 10:3-4

said to the adulterous woman brought to Him by the scribes and Pharisees, "Go, and sin no more." We can follow that command by no longer giving in to fleshly desires. Another instance of staying pure is the story of Joseph, who fled from his master's house when Potiphar's wife wanted to lie down with him. Joseph escaped from the temptation to commit adultery.[466]

Flee means to run from. *Loneliness* is the absence of intimacy.

In our minds, '*Purpose*' comes first. '*Partner*' must be second. *Purpose* puts you in position to receive the *right partner*.

Quit feeling sorry for you. God will grant you the power to choose. Stop focusing on loneliness and misery.[467]

---

[466] Genesis 39 and 2 Timothy 2:22.
[467] Viden Holly and Michelle McKinney Hammond. *If Singleness is a Gift What's the Return Policy?* p 200.

Begin Day 102:
Singles Face Temptation

Singleness, as a mental burden, can destroy individual lives.[468] The main destructive force is temptation by giving in to, or engaging in, the thought of sexual pleasure, or putting those lustful ideas into action. The Devil's best weapon against us is enticement.[469] If we revert to sin, it can tempt us in another direction, distracting us from Christ. Satan has people believing that they are "good enough" to enter the Kingdom of Heaven.[470]

1 Thessalonians 4:3-8: The temptation to engage in sexual intercourse outside the marriage relationship has always been powerful. We find that giving in to temptation can have disastrous results. Sexual sins always hurt someone. Consider the other people that are affected by your behavior. Individuals, families, businesses, and churches all experience the adverse effects of an illicit relationship. Managers find themselves dealing with the consequences of employees sneaking off during work hours. Spouses or other family members are left to handle family issues alone. Singles, instead of focusing on God, begin to trade their time with Him (or avoid Him altogether because of their wrongheadedness) for time with the object of their desire. If you wish to understand why sexual sins are more harmful, look at *1 Corinthians 6:18*. Sexual desires and activities must be placed under Christ's control. God has created sex as an expression of love between a husband and wife, meant for procreation and pleasure. The sexual experience is limited to the marriage because such behavior outside the holy union has consequences. The Holy Spirit works in us and conforms us to the image of Christ.[471]

---

[468] 1 Peter 5:8
[469] 1 Thessalonians 2:17-18; James 3:13-16
[470] Evans, p. 217.
[471] Romans 8:29

Begin Day 103:
Woman's Perspective On Dating

If a man appears 'needy,' and sees you as a 'motherly image,' it is a turn-off for most women. An insecure man needs some reassurances from a woman. Women are usually attracted to men who are confident, not arrogant. Most women, whether they know it or not, are looking for an *agape* type of relationship: someone who is intimate, open to communication, a good listener, intellectual, and romantic. Why *agape*? Because that is exactly "Who" God is!

Today, too many women are approaching men, and not waiting to be approached. Younger women (puberty to mid-twenties) often do not know what they want in a relationship, only seeking for the "now experience," and don't worry about what may happen later, in which they must deal with consequences. Women do not realize that men are viewing those flirtatious women as easy pickings. Men see these women through lustful eyes with sexual images overcoming their thoughts. Furthermore, these sorts of women worry about getting a man, instead of keeping him.[472] Moreover, when a woman pursues a man, he will relax more and be more passive about the relationship.

Again, a woman who pursues a man will likely succeed in getting him in bed, but not succeed in getting what she hoped for since he will likely lose interest. When a woman decides to end the relationship, a man may be suddenly attracted to her and become more interested. He likes a challenge, something to fight for, and go after it. Once he loses it, he realizes that maybe she was the one for him after all, or trying to prove to his 'ego' that "I can get her back."[473]

A woman is excited by the thought of being seen, heard and desired, and reassured by the possibility of getting what she needs and wants. When a man makes a woman feel feminine, her mind is stimulated and intrigued, possibly generating feelings of warmness, tenderness, and vulnerability. Her heart begins to open as she remembers that she is special. What allows a woman to bring the best out in a man could be summarized as 'feminine radiance.' A woman expresses her feminine radiance, embodying the three basic characteristics of femininity: she is self-assured, receptive, and responsive. These three qualities in a woman make a man more attracted to her.[474]

---

[472] Mars & Venus On A Date: A Guide For Navigating The 5 Stages Of Dating To Create A Loving & Lasting Relationships.
[473] Mars & Venus On A Date: A Guide For Navigating The 5 Stages Of Dating To Create A Loving & Lasting Relationships.
[474] Mars & Venus On A Date: A Guide For Navigating The 5 Stages Of Dating To Create A Loving & Lasting Relationships.

Begin Day 104:
Woman's Perspective On Self-Assurance

Self-assurance will always get you what you need. *Webster's College Dictionary* defines *self-assurance* as someone confident in oneself, or in one's ability, talent, etc. When a woman shifts from her self-assurance to chasing a man's affection, she becomes less attractive. When a man pulls away, a woman tends to blame him and does not realize how she can be part of the equation. Sometimes we should not put the blame on the other party. Instead, do not point the finger at someone else; we need to check our own shortcomings. The Bible is very clear on this point.[475]

Examine the person you see in the mirror, inside and out. Notice what you are dishing out in your relationship first, before jumping to conclusions, such as assuming he is cheating. He may have mental, emotional, or social issues can diffuse the dating relationship. Review your behavior around him. What you carelessly say or do can be a part of the relationship ending in turmoil, or lead to the point of breaking up. A good man will respect your decision, but you are most likely assuming that he wants to hear what you have to say.

Self-assurance draws and keeps a man's interest.

---

[475] Matthew 7:3-5

Begin Day 105:
Women are Jewels

A woman needs to remember that she is the 'jewel,' and he is providing the setting for her to 'shine.' A woman should not only have a high self-esteem but also appear confident in her dealings with other people. Do not allow any man to bring you down in the gutter. Open your heart only if he is respecting and treating you with respect beforehand. If the relationship does not feel right, and you see red flags, don't allow the relationship to progress since, in the end, you will end up hurt and torn apart.

A *receptive woman* is able to receive what she gets, as well as not being resentful if she gets less. *Receptivity* is being able to receive whatever can be received in a circumstance and the ability to benefit something good in every situation. *Webster College Dictionary* defines *receptive* as receiving or tending to receive, take in, admit, or contain, able or ready to receive new ideas, inclined to the favorable reception of the suggestion. Therefore, when a woman displays her sexual side before she is ready, she has stopped being *receptive* (allowing the man to please her, treating her as a jewel) and becomes *accommodating* (attempting to please the man).

When a woman gives more in a relationship, she loses her sense of receptivity. She expects more than a man has been giving, and assumes that he will support her because he *owes* her. A woman being receptive to a man does not mean she agrees with him all the time.

A woman's responsiveness is most attractive when it is authentic and not exaggerated. It is not so much what a woman does for a man who makes him happy, but the way she responds. Each time a woman chooses to find and express her positive responses to a man's attempts to fulfill her, he feels encouraged to pursue her. A woman responding to a man with the three attributes of femininity: being assured, receptive, and responsive, will find him treating her like a jewel.

Begin Day 106:
Desperation when seeking the Perfect Man

Sadly, too many women are so desperate to have the *'perfect man,'* they do not ask questions, they do not do their homework, and they do not think about the fact that they are putting their lives in jeopardy by engaging in unprotected sex. Furthermore, society puts so much pressure on women to be in a relationship. Even if women have furthered their education and have a Ph.D., own a home, and have mastered in success and/or wealth, she is viewed as a failure without a mate. People tend to question a woman who has so much going on in her life but is without a significant other.

Additionally, mothers and grandmothers may tend to pressure women and young girls to have a man, always saying things like, 'When are you going to bring a man home?' or, 'You're so pretty, why don't you have a man?' This may be because motherhood is so pleasant that they wish their daughters to be mothers as well.

Many people may focus on a woman's age because she is in her prime, and once she is over forty and still not married, they might denigrate the woman as an 'old maid.' Many harbor the erroneous belief that if you want a man, you must please him sexually. It appears to you that you must change everything about yourself to keep him. Evidently, societal expectations are highly focused on women in a relationship.

Women have tremendous power inherent in their choices. If a woman chooses a platonic (non-sexual) relationship, she'll learn to listen to him, watch his habits, and get to know his friends and family.
A woman who reacts too quickly, out of desperation to be married, may find herself in an uncomfortable relationship with her quick reaction. Too often women ignore the inner voice that tries to give them an early warning signal, and the intuitive voice will continue to let them know, throughout the relationship.

Women, do not fall for the Devil's deception, believing that you have finally found your soul mate, and discover that you have married the wrong person. God also expects us to honor the covenant He set for married couples. Although you married the wrong person, the Bible instructs you to maintain that difficult marriage relationship until he dies, or infidelity is proven and can file for a divorce under the Mosaic Law. Paul expands on this, stating that you also should remain in a relationship with a non-believer until that person leaves the relationship. There may be other reasons to divorce your mate, but not primarily because you married the wrong person. God does not want to see you miserable. Yet, He wants you to turn to Him before making this covenant with the person you plan to marry in the beginning. This is how God views marriage.

Begin Day 107:
Desiring a Soul Mate or another Man to Date?

God will bless us with our soul mates. We are to flee from any covetous activity, which is to desire what belongs to someone else. You cannot focus on desiring and wishing to be joined with a man you hope will become your husband someday. Instead, seek confirmation from the Lord. Do not settle for less than God's ideal person for you. God cannot bless a mess when your heart is based on covetousness, envy, and jealousy since these character flaws will always cause us to lose.[476]

Have you forgotten who you are? What is love? How do we love someone? If we love someone, it must be unconditional, from the depths of our heart and soul, not expecting any appreciation from our companion.[477] According to the book, *The Unspoken Love: What Women Don't Know and Men Don't Tell You*, while you wait for a godly man, you are to remain a well-kept woman. In other words, we are to keep our hair done up, dress elegantly, and maintain a hygienic existence.

As women, we are to support our men spiritually and emotionally, and recognize we are feminine creatures created to help our mates. Yet, this does not mean that we have to go out on a limb and support him financially. We must avoid being involved with anyone that cannot improve the quality of his own life. Ideally, the man is the breadwinner and must provide for his home. However, we can review all the finances and make sure the checkbook is intact. Sometimes, we may have to work to help take care of the household and bills, but not capitulate to doing it all. God knows your needs, and when the right person comes along, God will lead them to your door.

---

[476] James 3:14-16

Begin Day 108:
Men's Classification of Women

Men classify women in these categories: freak, friend, or forever.

Freak is the attraction, sex appeal, and sexual gratification he gets from her. Some women believe that if they are having sex with a potential mate, he will marry her, except he is never thinking about a serious relationship that leads to engagement or marriage. He gets what he wants since she is giving it up. He likes her and may feel love for her, continue to have sex over a period until he meets someone he values, and then he will drop the freak and marry the woman he values.

Friend is viewed as a platonic friendship. Women may see things in a different light leading up to marriage. He may be pleasant to you and say wonderful things about you, but he never forms an intention to marry. Friendship sometimes confuses women. You may share deep secrets and other feelings with him, causing you to think it is love since you never shared this information with anyone else. Even if the courtship starts as friends, then leads or ends in matrimony, learn to listen to what your friend says. Sometimes women deceive themselves into believing he is the one. Men are usually committed to their words: friendly, caring and helpful, but it does not mean that he loves you or desires to marry you.

A Forever relationship:
1. Pursuit of you
2. Does not leave anything to the imagination
3. Deeper relationship than a friendship
4. Dynamics of romance and prospects of marriage surface in your conversations
5. Dreams about future with you
6. Conversations are filled with 'us' not 'I' or 'me'
7. Markets himself as potential husband by painting a picture of what life would be like with him
8. Asks you to meet important people in his life
9. Purges activities or people from his life to make room for you
10. Relationship intensifies
11. Seeks out your presence either by phone or in person frequently and acknowledges when he misses you
12. Consistency to his interactions with you
13. Day-to-day details of your life integrate into a partnership
14. Backed up by actions confirming his intentions

Begin Day 109:
Women, Protect your Hearts

Protect your heart and take heed to what the man is conveying to you. Likewise, please try not to imagine yourself with this person. Do not underestimate the power of imagination. You may see a future with your best friend by projecting lustful desires and playing out the scene in your mind, or you may visualize and fantasize a lifelong relationship with him. The expectations of that relationship may die before it starts because you lose hope, setting unrealistic goals your future. You will only break your heart, and maybe his, leaving you with great disappointment. Therefore, it takes discipline to be with someone who is wonderful, and you enjoy being in their company.

God also wants to protect our hearts from heartbreak and disappointments.[478] We are unable to change our past, but our past affects our present actions. We are to move forward, and not dwell on our past or past relationships. We are expected to learn, not repeating the same mistakes of our past, and accepting what the present offers us. God wants to give us a future. Protect your heart by not allowing a man to compromise your commitment to God.

If your man is not saying anything about commitment, then do not move in that direction. Listen to his words and watch for confirming actions. If a man wants sex or is seeking a "brief good time," it proves to you that 'any woman will do.' If a man wants you and honors your commitment to God, please be aware that *only you* will do.

Women possess the power of sexuality. We must hold the goodies (sex) until marriage. If he is willing to wait, usually, it will fully prove he is committed.[479] It is important when qualifying a man for potential marriage that we recognize the intentions of his heart. Then, articulate your standards, and if he opposes your values, then he does not value you and probably never will. Listen carefully to what he is saying, and determine how he views your value, which will give you a picture of his ideal relationship.

---

[478] Jeremiah 29:11-13
[479] The Unspoken Love: What Women Don't Know and Men Don't Tell You (emphasis added by author).

Begin Day 110:
Men's Attraction

Men are attracted to success. He feels that he is a success in fulfilling a woman's desires and wants; this is when he finds himself more attracted to her. What allows a man to bring the best out in a woman is his masculine presence, embodying the three basic characteristics of masculinity. He is confident, purposeful, and responsible, which makes a woman more attracted to him.

Men know when women are attracted to them. But too many women are willing to commit to a man who will not commit to her. Waiting for the man to commit does not make her feel the indication of true love. If he tells you that marriage is not his immediate plans, but later he asks you to marry him—believe him. Men decide when it is time for them to get married, and then search for a mate. Women, on the other hand, fall in love with their feelings, in which they come to their decision to marry. Consider and enjoy other options if you are in a relationship that is not mutual in purpose.

If you are trying not to lust, do not entertain yourself with pornographic activities, and be careful what dating sites you go to online when surfing the Internet, or accept pop-ups going to pornographic sites. Chat lines are not the answer either. Most people are looking for fun and a quick way to meet someone to have sexual relations. Do not behave as if you are in a committed relationship when you are not. If so, this leads to disappointment, especially if he chooses not to be in a committed relationship. Just view him as a friend or remove him from your life. On the other hand, most men do not want a woman to say, "let's be friends," when she thinks about a serious long-term relationship. It is best to be honest and not lead a man on.

Lastly, women think they can change a man after they are married. Men are highly motivated to win you, but change only occurs with the Holy Spirit. Women tend to forget the broad range of abilities and talents that we possess. We can take a vision, refine it, advance it, and complete it. Good women are a stabilizing and blazing force in the life of a man. To encourage a man, you must first hear him.[480] *Empathetic listening* is to comprehend where he is coming from, to be alert to his feelings, and to listen without talking, nagging, complaining, or giving advice.

---

[480] Proverbs 20:5

Begin Day 111:
Man's Prerogative when Dating

When a man makes a woman feel feminine, she is turned on by his unique talents, traits, interests, or characteristics. If a man does not turn a woman on, it does not matter how funny, rich or successful he is. A man tends to bring out the best in a woman through his masculine presence. The most attractive attribute of masculine presence is confidence. Confidence in a man makes a woman breathe deeper, relax, and open up to receive the support he has to offer. When a man has a can-do attitude, even if he doesn't have all the answers, a woman can relax.

A confident man contains his feelings until he has figured out what to do. A confident attitude reassures a woman and lets her believe everything will work out as it should. When a man is confident, he is able to come up with a plan. Women love a man with a plan. Women do not like it when a man is too dependent on her for direction. A woman is happy to do some of the planning, but she wants the man to lead the way confidently.

On the other hand, if a woman is a sympathetic listener, a man can transform even a disappointing date into an intimate and rewarding experience for the woman. A man with a purpose is most likely to have a sense of direction or vision, provide his interests, and a sense of concern for his significant other. It does not matter how great the plan or purpose is, a woman will find him to be attractive since he is passionate about achieving his purpose. When he focuses his purposefulness on her by focusing on making her happy, then he succeeds at sweeping her off her feet. However, a smart woman knows that she cannot fulfill all his needs if there seems to be too much pressure on her and their relationship. A woman should not expect a man to give up his Godly goals or dreams to make her happy.

A man seeks love, food, and appreciation. You will hear men say, 'a way to a man's heart is through his stomach.' Most men love a woman who knows how to cook and caters to her man. Second, man desires to be loved and wants a woman who can meet his needs sexually, emotionally, and mentally. She not only pleases him in the bedroom, but also is willing to listen to his problems at work, at school, and handle his diverse temperaments. Furthermore, a man seeks a best friend or motherly love, including someone that is a good girl with a freaky side. Lastly, a man wants to feel appreciated for all that he does.

Begin Day 112:
A Man's Expectation of A Mate

Most men expect their mates to work, whether as a homemaker, a small businesswoman, or in the employ of a large corporation. Women sometimes take for granted that he pays the bills, buys all necessities, and financially takes care of the household. Women, if the man is the primary breadwinner, can shower their husband with small gifts, cards, hot baths, and other things they would enjoy most. To say "I love you," and "Thank you for everything you do," is a small token of showing your appreciation.

Another way to show how much you care is to take him out to dinner or a movie; or to wear sexy lingerie, play his favorite song, and dance for him in the privacy of your home. Whisper sweet love words in his ear, and kisses that are soft and delicate, as you give him a massage. Be willing to listen or to be silent, while he is speaking, and ignore how your day went unless he asks.

On the other hand, women can make life miserable for men. Constant complaints or nagging about how things could be, or wishing things were different will be a definite turn off for the relationship. A woman's words can crush a man's self-esteem and cause them to lose their motivation and drive. A negative attitude can eat up a man, and destroy him mentally, emotionally, and spiritually. A woman sets the tone in her household. A man's honor is to be your protection and provider, and a woman's purpose is to protect his heart as his helper, allowing him pride in all he does. Learn how to build your house and perfect your gifts now while you are single.

Gossip is not something you want to have come from your home. Neither of you should be discussing the part of yourselves that creates your professions, your finances, your home, your children, or your health with others without your mate's permission. Consider how, especially in today's social media world, you can keep things appropriately private. This includes the issue that comes up with many married women. Men sometimes expect their wives to be like their mothers (after all, she was their model for women when they were growing up), and you must hold your own personality when dealing with your mate. If that should come up, discuss the issue quietly with him so that you each know where maturity lies.

Begin Day 113:
Man's Sense of Direction

A man needs to have a sense of direction first, and then he is ready to create a relationship to support him in making his dreams come true. When a man is passionate about his work, his interests, his goals, and his future, a woman's desire to be with him becomes greater. When he is self-directed and self-motivated, a woman feels very relaxed and comfortable with him. Rather than feeling she needs to take care of him, she feels he has the energy and motivation to take care of her. A man's sense of responsibility allows her to chill. However, a way to kill any relationship is for one to tell the other all their problems. Before sharing his vulnerable side, a man should clearly demonstrate that he could be responsible for himself and for her. Independent women are accustomed to taking care of themselves, to where she no longer requests a man to meet her needs.

Instead of needing a man primarily for survival and security, a woman needs a man for emotional comfort and nurturing. Then, she feels a natural chemistry on all levels: physical, emotional, mental, and spiritual. Moreover, a man's gift is to be responsible for a woman's fulfillment, while a woman's gift is to be responsive and receptive to his gift. Giving is an expression of love. The problem comes up when women cannot get back the support they need and deserve.

Begin Day 114:
Man's Perspective On a Needy Woman

From a man's point of view, there is a world of difference between a needy woman and a woman who needs him. When a woman is needy, she demands more than a man is offering. It is her lack of appreciation for what he is offering that makes her 'needy.' Instead of appreciating what a man offers, she can start cultivating the attitudes of self-assurance, receptiveness, and responsiveness.

Alternatively, a woman may feel she requires more. However, she should still appreciate what a man has to offer. This does not mean that a woman has to be helpless. From a man's perspective, a woman is most attractive when he understands her needs, and she feels self-assured that her needs will be fulfilled. When a woman denies the fulfillment of her needs for a man, it sabotages the dating process.[481] [482]

---

[482] Mars & Venus On A Date: A Guide For Navigating The 5 Stages Of Dating To Create A Loving & Lasting Relationships (emphasis added by author).

Begin Day 115:
Ministers Must Speak About Relationships

Ministers have an excellent opportunity to provide education, compassion, and understanding. The church must preach the truth and become a place where everyone can come to hear the Word, without feeling they will be ostracized, regardless of their sexual orientation. If we cannot turn to our churches, where many of us grew up and to which many of us look upon as an extension of our families, then we will continue to live in denial.

Therefore, ministers should have sessions, seminars, conferences, or teachings on how the Bible views singleness, courtship, dating, and even marriage as a whole. Godly parents will guide their children in proper courtship and behavior through their teen years. Many people do have to learn on their own, but can, in Christ, turn their minds to His will. But now as believers, we have to renew our minds and hearts on how God views marriage—adapt to this as new creatures in Christ.

Begin Day 116:
Courtship

Courtship is a biblical process in finding and choosing a mate while glorifying God. *Courtship* is also honoring and respecting each other. Moreover, the process of courtship leads to honoring the Lord in the matrimony of marriage, which is a *sacred covenant*. Without God's consent on a future mate, there may be some heartbreaks as a result. There can be emotional and/or mental distress from broken relationships, in which someone was caught cheating or simply walking out of your life when things do not work out. This is a form of dating, not courtship. Overall, courtship is focused on a loving and lasting relationship. As for dating, it is a combination of broken hearts and emotional or mental baggage, including sexual insecurities.

During courtship, many couples see their personality differences as complementary. We have to be alert to ways your personality type may be a source of irritation to your mate. Furthermore, Nathan Bailey explains on his website: www.polynate.net/books/courtship/part1.html,
Our teen years are meant to build interpersonal, social, financial and character skills. Teens today are distracted by the quagmire of relationships and dating. We are to be focusing on developing a deep, intimate and personal walk with God, as young warriors in this world today, to overcome the Evil One.[483] Moreover, our culture teaches singles to engage in multiple dating relationships, as if it is a normal and useful practice. Modern dating has been around less than a century. Modern dating is also far away from God's original plan. Ideally, our primary purpose in life is to seek and serve God and fulfill our destiny with Him.

Courtship is God-centered and biblically based. An endless series of temptations exists; guilt, disappointment, frustration, and heartbreak. Open communication and honesty during your courtship, while exploring their career goals, expectations, and daily lives, including meeting their families afterward, can give you an inclination if you can see a future with this person. Before marriage, it's a good thing to check out their family and friends. The old saying, 'the apple doesn't fall too far from the tree,' is sound advice.

Learning how to build solid friendships is a way of preparing us for marriage. Friendships and non-romantic relationships are showing a mutual interest by building an atmosphere of trust and understanding. There is a difference between *'quick fix'* and intimacy with God. A relationship with God is to be able to hear His voice when God speaks to you. Develop oneness. Prayer is intimacy with God, not quick answers.[484]

Courtship is like looking through the rearview mirror, the pathway to marriage at the end of the road. Enjoy the *season of singleness* since God is preparing us for our ultimate soul mate and for the foundation for His blessing. Courtship is to have full of knowledge and approval from either or both parents, and moreover, to succumb to spiritual accountability as a couple. Godly couples provide protection, correction, and direction. While courting, one is able to determine if this person is marriage material. Most believe, while courting, there are no

---

[483] 1 John 2:13
[484] John 15:5

romantic interactions until after a commitment to marriage. (www.polynate.net/books/courtship/part1/html)

Early stages of courtship are limited amounts of time together or very little one-on-one time alone. *Dating* equates to possessiveness about being together, isolated locations, and approval addictions. *Courtship* equates to a conscious fostering of the relationship, where one's spirit seeks for emotional oneness such as an engagement period, and a physical oneness can ensue once the couple is married.

Courtship can fail by not establishing a relationship with a godly person who is held 'accountable' for their actions. Courtship can fail by not receiving blessings from parents or a godly couple. It can also fail by not listening to God and waiting for His direction. A couple who fails to complete the preparation steps can be viewed as a *dating couple*.

How courtship leads to a lifetime with God's chosen, is by focusing on Christ, not each other or the relationship itself. Avoiding warning signals or dangers such as physical, emotional, and spiritual oneness, which are usually involved in dating relationships. One is willing to establish and enhance communication. See the virtues and faults in a future mate, and encourage and correct them. Courtship preparation before *courtship* begins, which is a commitment, and is the main focus -- building a solid foundation for a lifelong marriage and preventing divorce.

Begin Day 117:
Courtship Processes

1. Identity in Christ
2. Ministry involvement
3. Foundation building
4. Friendship levels: acquaintance, casual, close, and intimate
5. Courtship and accountability
6. Engagement
7. Marriage

It is God's job to appoint you a mate and reveal him or her to you His choice in His time. Prepare yourself to be someone's mate while you wait for God's revelation. However, what you hunger for, you will attract. The type of man or woman you want will be attracted to the type of woman or man you are. God created us to have these desires, but also gave us the power to learn how to master them. We do so by bringing our minds, will, emotions, and body under control of the Holy Spirit and by living a Spirit-led life.

Begin Day 118:
Dating

The Bible never mentions the words *dating* or *courtship*. However, it gives principles and guidelines for male and female relationships. Therefore, we are to save ourselves physically, emotionally and spiritually for the one person God would have us marry. When we put our needs aside, it demonstrates faith in God's will. Wait for God to reveal His choice of a mate. Concentrate on *being* with the right person, instead of *finding* the right person. Intimate friendship with the intended person can lead to marriage as its result. There is no need to 'try out' people.

Dating is man-centered. *Dating* is a modern socio-cultural way of meeting new people who you can imagine yourself in a relationship with, either intimately or permanently. However, dating only leads to a 'disaster,' since most couples are seeking self-gratification, instead of 'happily ever after' marriage. Primarily, dating leads to intimacy, but not necessarily to commitment. Many dating relationships skip the 'friendship' stage of a relationship, and one often mistakes a physical relationship for love.

Additionally, dating often isolates a couple from other vital relationships. Often, it distracts young adults from their primary responsibility of preparing for the future, which can cause discontentment with God's gift of singleness and creates an artificial environment for evaluating another person's character. Usually, the scope of dating develops a self-centered, feeling-oriented, concept of love.

Dating also teaches people to break off difficult relationships, conditioning them towards divorce rather than marriage.

Begin Day 119:
Dating Appetites

Some of us develop an appetite for variety and change, leaving more time for falling into sins associated with singleness.

Simply, the more time one spends with their significant other promotes lust and moderate sexual activity. Opening the door for fornication instead of practicing celibacy (remaining a virgin until marriage) creates a permanent endorphin-bond between two people who are not likely to spend their lives together.

Casual dating lacks the protection and guidance afforded by parental approval of courtship. Parental guidance prepares children to face life's realities. Good parents recognize that children need a good discussion of sexual closeness, disease, and emotional entanglements. Yes, schools teach sex education, but parents still have good advice. Generally, dating devalues sex and marriage. Furthermore, it embarks on a romantic progression before people are ready to follow through and commit to marriage. Overall, dating encourages short-term relationships over long-term friendships.[485]

---

[485] Extracted from *Dating: Is It Worth the Risk?* by Reb Bradley; *I Kissed Dating Goodbye* by Joshua Harris; *Dating, Betrothal and Courtship* by Dr S. M. Davis; *Dating vs. Courtship* by Paul Jehle and various posts to the "Courtship Ring" mailing list.

Begin Day 120:
Reasons for Breakup(s)

Dating is a self-centered focus. Here are some reasons for breaking up:
1. Excitement is gone; the relationship is boring and/or demanding
2. Someone more attractive or better comes along
3. Dating other people
4. One is ready for marriage, and the other is not
5. Arguments and constant fighting or debates
6. The romance is gone, or the parties do not care anymore
7. Someone does not meet the other's needs
8. Never involved seriously in the first place.

Begin Day 121:
Dating for Women

Dating for women is usually fantasy-based. For example, young women see themselves as Cinderella, where she gets her prince and lives happily ever after. It is similar to lustful feelings and thoughts. Women can have trouble controlling the lustful closeness that a man's attention brings. Once it starts in the mind, it can lead to sexual activity or masturbation, and continue to fantasize on these lustful thoughts.

Begin Day 122:
Dating from a Man's Perspective

For men, dating is physical. They react with their eyes, gazing at a woman's physical or physique, how she wears those jeans or tight outfit or a flirty, sexy dress, and how she walks. He imagines what she looks like with her clothes off, naked, and what she would be like in the bed. After speaking to my closest and longtime friend, he mentioned that men could simply view a woman and want to marry her!

If a man is serious about a woman, he will show his respect for her. While physical urges are difficult for men to control, they need to understand that a Godly relationship includes a desire to treat all of God's creation, including women, gently and without emotional pain.

Begin Day 123:
Sex During a Dating Relationship

Once a dating woman is ready, after her one- to six-month rule, she wants it steady and all the time. He has trained himself not to have sex all the time or every day as she wishes, especially if he's heard from other men who have cohabited with women or has done so himself. When he desired to sex with his woman, she was not ready. A "no" response lets a woman assume he has to be cheating and respond, "You must be cheating on me." After hearing this, some men will go ahead and cheat.
Women need to be careful to ask questions and decide if they want to explore a physical relationship.

On the other hand, a woman thinks if she does give into a sexual relationship right away, a man will call her a 'hoe' and other degrading names. She may not be so willing to find herself in the category of "easy to get."

Some women are loose and simply are in the dating scene for sex. If a man doesn't satisfy her, she dumps him. He will be left wondering what just happened, and hurt in the process. Men also have to be careful what they ask for.

Begin Day 124:
Dating mimics Oneness

Dating can mimic a oneness similar to marriage but lack commitment and responsibility. One usually dates for intimacy, wanting to be loved or seeking for love, and feel accepted. A woman is viewed by a man as a suitable helper, completeness, and oneness. A man is viewed by a woman as a suitable mate, supportive, and companionable.

Male's view: physical→emotional→commitment→spiritual

Female's view: emotional→physical→commitment→spiritual

Begin Day 125:
Engagement

Engagement is the shortest period when choosing a mate, but a start to laying a good foundation for marriage. *Engagement* is the time to prepare for your wedding and final preparation for marriage. Courtship becomes as sacred to you and your partner as is co-habilitation, kissing, intimate hugging, sex, and raising children. These topics should be thoroughly discussed to determine if this person is the ideal person to join in marriage. Recognize not only your physical bodily desires but also your emotions within your spirit, which will be dedicated to that one partner for the rest of your lives in your sacred vows.

Each of you should check with your Heavenly Father for confirmation that this person is the ideal partner for the rest of your days together.

Begin Day 126:
God's Yoke

Two people physically involved with each other will have trouble discerning God's will by disregarding His rules for a godly relationship.[486] God also informs us in the Scriptures, not to be unequally yoked.[487]

2 Corinthians 6:14, NKJV: *"Do not be unequally yoked together with unbelievers. For what fellowship has righteousness with lawlessness? And what communion has light with darkness?"*

Paul urges believers not to form binding relationships with non-believers because this might weaken their commitment, integrity, or standards. He also explained that this did not mean isolating oneself from non-believers.[488] Paul even tells Christians to stay with their non-believing spouses.[489] He wants believers to be active in their witness for Christ to non-believers, but not to lock themselves into personal or business relationships that could cause them to compromise their faith. Believers are to avoid situations that could force them to divide their loyalties.

Moreover, it takes faith and courage to wait on God.[490] Patience and waiting for God is not easy. Often it seems that He is not answering our prayers, or does not understand the urgency of our situation. This type of thinking implies that God is not in control, or God is not fair. Lamentations 3:24-26 calls us to hope and wait for the Lord because often God uses waiting to refresh, renew, and teach us. Make good use of your waiting times by discovering what God may be trying to teach you. We are to pause for further instructions because impulsive decisions made without waiting on God's direction or timing can lead to a disaster. Prayer for purity—God saves His best for those who are willing to wait.

Spiritual maturity is inner faith and a deep belief that you have intimacy with God. A Godly character displays the *Fruits of the Spirit*.[491] God would not allow you to marry someone that you are not attracted to. This attraction is not only based on his physical appearance or facial looks. The attraction can also be their intelligence, compassion for you and the Lord, their love of spontaneity or adventure, well-spoken, and desire for you. God loves you.

You are to love and celebrate the person He chooses for you to spend the rest of your life with. However, there is a difference between attraction and respect such as being attracted to someone you do not respect.

Moreover, as followers of Jesus Christ, are told not to be with someone who is an unbeliever. We are to be equally yoked in relationships. We must begin with the passion for God's view of relationships. We must discuss the giving of our time and energy in the relationship; politics;

---

[486] Luke 16:10
[487] 2 Corinthians 6:14
[488] 1 Corinthians 5:9, 10
[489] 1 Corinthians 7:12-13
[490] Psalm 27:14
[491] Galatians 5:22-26

money; how to raise children; standards of living; how men and women relate; the role of a man; the role of a woman; and so forth.[492] Once God gives you a revelation, write it in a journal or on paper, and write down your dreams or visions. Establish your future in your mind[493] so that it may be difficult to stray from your standards. Your vision will also help you set boundaries, dictating to you where you will go and keep you from unsavory ventures.[494]

---

[492] The Unspoken Love: What Women Don't Know and Men Don't Tell You.
[493] Habakkuk 2:2
[494] Proverbs 29:18

Begin Day 127:
Courtship & Commitment

Courtship is a definite direction. Commitment is trust. Not even love will hold or save a marriage when trust is broken. On the other hand, many single people may have a fear of commitment. The Bible talks about the 'spirit of fear' in 2 Timothy 1:7. Here, Paul speaks of three characteristics of the effective Christian, of which are power, love and a sound mind (wisdom). These are available to us through the Holy Spirit that lives in us. Follow God's lead each day so that your life will move fully to exhibit these characteristics. We cannot live in fear and trust God at the same time. Fear is from Satan and not of God.

Begin Day 128:
Single, Set Yourself Apart

As believers of Jesus Christ, we are 'set apart,' by which a biblically appropriate behavior would not compromise our integrity or defraud another person. Singles tend to view dating as 'looking for a marriage partner.' Furthermore, online dating sites and phone services are a tool to meet and know other available singles.

Yet, *courtship* is allowing God to do the seeking and searching. He will bring the right person into your life and reveal that choice to you. If a man is willing to make it through the waiting period, he is a serious contender. If you choose to marry him, remain steady. The follower of Jesus who has a willing heart and wisdom to discern God's choice will know when the time is right.

Isaiah 55:9: *"For as the heavens are higher than the earth, so are My ways higher than your ways, and My thoughts than your thoughts."*

Just like the Israelites, we can foolishly believe we know what God is thinking and planning. We need to get away from thinking we are 'in control.' At times, it may appear as though we are, but God is our creator and knows us better than we know ourselves. God's knowledge and wisdom are far greater than that of man. We are foolish to try to fit God into our mold -- to make His plans and purposes conform to ours, but instead, we must strive to fit into His plans. We usually do not turn to Him until we are down and out, and have nowhere else to turn to or no one else to call. We can seek God sooner and allow God always in our lives.

Begin Day 129:
Patience is a Virtue While Waiting for Your Mate

Patience is a desire to benefit from one another at your own expense and to let *Love* become the preeminent force in the relationship. Love holds a relationship together, not infatuation, attraction, or even desire. Love will allow a couple to endure through the hard times, even when things threaten the long-term relationship. Love is worth waiting for. There are three sides to a story: his side, her side, and God's point of view.

Prayerfully ask God to reveal this man or woman to you. Do not ask unless you are willing to accept God's answer. Be prepared to act on it and desire to know all, and do all to complete the will of God. God is willing to make his purpose known – do not show it unless you are considering doing it. God will shape and mold you into the person He called you to be, and will speak His plans in your life. Submit your situation to Jesus. God does not shout or shake you up. God whispers, and we are able to hear His voice when we are quiet, without any distractions.[495] God desires a spiritual, unconditional commitment to Him before matching you with one of His sons or daughters.

---

[495] Psalm 46:10

Begin Day 130:
12 Steps to Recognize God's Chosen Mate

There are **twelve steps** to recognizing God's mate:

1. *The Test of the Word.*[496] *Many answers we seek about relationship choices have already been provided in the Bible.* You should carefully and prayerfully search the Word with the faith and expectation that God will reveal His will. There are wise and unwise choices for marriage mentioned in the Bible. Some of these wise choices are a suitable mate, which is one who pleases God.[497] A *suitable mate* is one who can experience anger without being controlled by it and prevents harsh feelings to continue.[498] A *carefully selected mate* is one who has a job. Love is a wonderful thing, but love alone will not buy groceries. A lazy mate is a burden, but an industrious mate is a blessing.[499] On the other hand, *unwise choices* are an ill-chosen mate who is sexually promiscuous. Marriage alone will not automatically reform a loose person's ways. Although behavior changes are possible, they must be demonstrated before marriage.[500] A *tactless mate* is one who has an argumentative and complaining spirit. A person who always has something negative to say will be a pain to live with for the rest of one's life.[501] An *insensitive mate* is one who is not compassionate and does not strive to understand one's partner. Understanding is mandatory for an effective marriage.[502]

2. *The Test of Prayers.*[503] *Have I immersed myself in a serious labor of prayer to understand God's direction?* God desires to provide us with answers to life's questions, even more than we desire to receive those answers. For us to hear from God, we must throw aside our worldly weapons of selfishness and pride, so that we can come out with hands raised high in sweet surrender to the authority of God's love.

3. *The Test of Peace.*[504] *Is there a serene flow of peace, trust, and contentment about the relationship and its circumstances?* Each person has a built-in 'early warning system' for relationships. The purpose of this system is to alert us to any dangers lurking within our decision-making process. If we consistently heed the prompting of this system, it becomes even more sensitive and accurate. If we ignore our inner warnings, the system becomes weaker, less accurate, and eventually mute.

4. *The Test of Communication.*[505] *Is it easy to discuss both tough and tender topics, and to address problems together through open discussions in a grudge-free atmosphere?* Every relationship encounters those 'hot potato' topics that instantly raise the pressure. The question is not whether a relationship will encounter these threats to good

---

[496] Psalm 119:105
[497] Ecclesiastes 2:26
[498] Ephesians 4:26
[499] Proverbs 13:4; 2 Thessalonians 3:10
[500] Proverbs 6:25-35
[501] Proverbs 21:9; 27:15-17
[502] 1 Peter 3:7-9
[503] Matthew 7:7
[504] Philippians 4:6-7
[505] James 1:19-20

communication, but how they will be handled when they arise. Good communication is crucial to a healthy relationship. Stifled communication hinders growth.

5. *The Test of Complimentary Value.[506] Are we compatible with each other? Do we regard each other with a sense of value and worth?* No more thinking about is he or she as Mr. or Mrs. Right: it is all about our future and long-term goals. Can we compromise our issues, can we get along, and are we able to work the differences out together as a couple? Do not just look at their physical appearance; it is what lies beneath or on the inside.

6. *The Test of Gain or Drain.[507] Does this person to build me up. Do I have neutral feelings towards them? Do I feel as if I am always giving or always getting? Do I leave this person's presence edified or petrified?* We are to look for how they bring the best out of us, to edify and encourage one another. Someone who is negative, thinks negatively, and speaks negatively will only bring out the negative side in us. God wants us to have unspeakable joy.

7. *The Test of Commitment.[508] Is my partner at the very top of my priority list, above my parents, siblings, friends, former lovers, and possessions? Am I willing, without reservation, to commit myself wholeheartedly to this person, and to wake up next to him or her every morning for the next fifty to eighty years?* It may seem hard at first, or the thought may seem devastating, but we have to trust in God to choose our mate for us and lead us in the right direction to them.

8. *The Test of Time.[509] The relationship may seem 'right' for me, but is it also 'ripe' for me?* Timing is important. Being at peace with God is to discover, accept, and appreciate God's perfect timing. The danger is to doubt or resent God's timing. This dangerous thought pattern can lead to despair, rebellion, or moving ahead without His advice.

9. *The Test of Finance.[510] Have both of us lived within our financial means and handled money well during our life as singles? Are we financially prepared for the expenses involved in marriage?* We should look at these questions before jumping into marriage. Once you are married, you may have a joint account and will have to learn how to take care of you, your spouse, and soon to be family. If one is unable to get their bills under control, this is something that you will bring in the marriage, which can cause much frustration and stress that can be eliminated at an early stage. Take charge and learn to handle your money efficiently. You may consider getting financial counseling or advice from a financial advisor or take a course or godly counsel from seminars. Be willing to be open to life's challenges and be able to change things for a financially secured future.

10. *The Test of Chemistry.[511] Do we click? Do I feel physically and emotionally drawn to my partner, and am I pleased by his or her presence and touch? Would I be easily motivated to satisfy my partner unselfishly? Would I hold back from any sexual activity because of emotions? It is one thing to click, but what does it take to make this*

---

[506] I Corinthians 12:14-23
[507] 2 Corinthians 6:14-18
[508] Matthew 19:4-6
[509] Ecclesiastes 3:1-8
[510] Luke 14:28-30
[511] Proverbs 30:18-19

relationship work? Most people believe restoring a relationship is through compromise instead of argument. Moreover, it is more than a physical and sexual chemistry that is required. One must be able to work things out by learning when to listen instead of talking, to be able to read your partner's emotions without causing conflict, how to have intimacy with God and to be filled spiritually, and relate to each other intellectually.

11. *The Test of Godly Counsel.*[512] *Have I taken the time to expose my relationship and marriage plans to the caring examination of a trusted and competent counselor? In this relationship, are we able to be real with one another? Are we able to share our future goals, plans, and ambitions with one another?* We can support each other, and come to some agreement in the relationship. We could be in love blindly, however, still being careful on who we choose. They can be jealous, envious, and wish they were in your shoes. If you think about separation, the best counselor to ask for advice is from God. Be able to hear His voice, see His signs or visions for our lives, or feel God's presence when this person is around us.

12. *The Test of Agape Love.*[513] *Am I a selfish person? Would I rather please my partner more than I would like to please myself? Am I willing to do all I can to help my mate reach his or her potential? Do we love each other just as we are, without expecting each other to change?* Think about that person or parent that loved you unconditionally. The day you were born, how they nurtured you, talked to you in a soft sweet voice, singing lullabies in your ear, and holding you so close. Kissing on your cheek, whispering *'I love you'* in your ear, and praying that God will have his Guardian Angels to watch over their baby. Imagine how much they loved you and wanted the best for you. Imagine how much Jesus loved all of us, no matter what we did or what we said or how we lived, He died for us on the Cross. Suffered and gave His life up for you and me…this is unconditional love. We may not be expected to lay down our lives or to be nurtured in a relationship, but hope that our love will be treasured forever.

---

[512] Proverbs 11:14
[513] I Corinthians 13

Begin Day 131:
Singles, Build A Healthy Dating Relationship

Do not let a relationship move too fast in its infancy. Romantic affairs that begin frenetically frequently burn themselves out. Take it one step at a time. Do not discuss your personal inadequacies and flaws in detail when the relationship is new. No matter how warm and accepting your friend may be, any great revelation of low self-esteem or embarrassing weaknesses can be fatal when interpersonal valleys occur. Remember that respect precedes love. Do not call too often on the phone, or give the other person an opportunity to be tired of you. Do not be quick to reveal your desire to get married, or that you think you have found Mr. Wonderful or Miss Marvelous. If your partner has not arrived at the same conclusion, you will throw him or her into a panic.

Begin Day 132:
Cautious Lovers

Cautious lovers who like to nibble at the bait before swallowing the hook are constantly testing relationships. This testing procedure takes many forms, but it usually involves pulling back from the other person to see what will happen. Many weeks pass without a phone call. Sometimes flirtation occurs with a rival. The question, "How important I am to you, and what would you do if you lost me?" The person wants to know, "How free am I to leave if I want to?" It is a form of abuse, and if you should decide to let that person control you, you will find yourself spending a lot of time thinking of that person rather than God. Do not grasp the other person and beg for mercy. Some people remain single throughout life because they cannot resist the temptation to grovel when the test occurs.

Extending the same concept, keep in mind that some dating relationships that continue for a year or more, and seem to be moving towards marriage, may be given the ultimate test. A breakup may occur, initiated by one of the lovers. The rejected individual knows that their future together depends on the skill of how he or she handles that crisis. If the hurting individual can remain calm, the next two steps may be reconciliation and marriage. If not, then no amount of pleading will change anything. Do not depend entirely on one another for the satisfaction of every emotional need. Maintain interests and activities outside that romantic relationship, even after marriage. Guard against selfishness in your love affair.

Abusive people will want to make sure the person they are seeing will not give them up. Their attitudes will be possessive, keeping you separate from other people and the wisdom of your friends. They'll put your friends down, and convince you that you need to listen to them. They will eventually demand that you give God up for them. Recognize the behavior, and talk to the people they're trying to separate you from. Leave that relationship behind. It is not of God.

Neither the man nor the woman does all the giving. Beware of blindness to obvious warning signs that tell you that your potential husband or wife is disloyal, hateful, abusive, spiritually uncommitted, hooked on drugs or alcohol, given to selfishness, etc. Marriage to someone who does not commit to God is a far worse existence than the loneliest single experiences.

Begin Day 133:
Early in the Dating Relationship

Beginning early in the dating relationship, treat the other person with respect and expect the same in return. A man can open doors for a woman on a formal evening without gaining contempt, and a woman can speak respectfully of her escort when in public. If you do not preserve this respectful attitude when the foundations of courtship are being laid, it will be virtually impossible to construct them later.

Do not equate human worth with flawless appearances. If you require physical perfection in your mate, he or she may make the same demands of you. Neither of you will keep it for long. Do not let love escape you because of the false suppositions. If genuine love has escaped you thus far, do not begin believing 'no one would ever want me.' That deadly trap can destroy you emotionally. Millions of people are looking for someone to love. Most of those have unrealistic expectations of the person they are dating. Holding someone to an image of perfection is not what God does, and is not part of His plan.

Regardless of how brilliant the love affair has been, take time to 'check your assumptions' with your partner before committing yourself to marriage. It is surprising how often men and women plunge toward matrimony without ever becoming aware of major differences in expectation between them. Sexual familiarity can be deadly to a relationship. Besides the many moral, spiritual, and physical reasons for remaining celibate until marriage, there are numerous psychological and interpersonal advantages as well. Both men and women lack respect for those who are 'easy,' and often become bored with those who have held nothing in reserve. Likewise, women often disrespect men who have only one thing on their minds. Both sexes need to remember how to use the word, 'No.'

Begin Day 134:
Commitment Between Couples

If the commitment between a man and a woman is given insufficient attention, the relationship will wither like a plant without water. Few lovers seem to realize that extreme dependency can be just as deadly to a love affair as a lack of commitment. It has been said that the person who is needy toward the other will normally be in control of the relationship.

Marriage does not eliminate one's need for freedom and respect. Choose to keep the mystery and the dignity in your relationship. If the other partner begins to feel trapped and withdraws for a time, grant him or her some space, and let yourself pull back as well. Do not build a cage around that person, because you will trap yourself in it. Instead, release your grip, with confidence in God's providence, while never appeasing immorality or destructive behavior.

Whether we are dating by abiding by courtship rules, we must follow God's model of relationships. Courting happens only once and ends in a lifelong covenant relationship. On the other hand, dating happens many times, and if handled inappropriately, resulting in heartbreaks, hurt feelings, and can leave emotional scars. Also, be attentive to emotional attachments that appear to be acceptable in dating. People willingly create rampant emotional promiscuity, giving pieces of their heart, and sometimes engage in sexual activities. One might wonder what is left for our lifelong partners.

Begin Day 135:
Sex or Abstinence?

Biblical reasons to wait for *sexual fulfillment*:[514]

"Marriage should be honored by all, and the marriage bed kept pure, for God will judge the adulterer and all the sexually immoral."[515]

"And don't you realize that if a man joins himself to a prostitute, he becomes one body with her? For the Scriptures say, "The two are united into one..."[516]

Some people promise to marry just to 'get with you,' but they never fulfill that promise.[517] You cannot have sex outside of marriage and grow as a Christian. Do not let anyone pressure you to have sex. Moreover, some of us have engaged in sexual activities, but we can be forgiven and choose to remain celibate until marriage.[518]

Jesus loved and ministered to sexually immoral people, and told them to "stop sinning." Regardless of our sinful nature, we can allow the Holy Spirit to give us peace.[519] If we love and obey God, we will have life, peace, and find that even our troubles turn out for good. Fornication and adultery are a sin. You hurt people you love, and you bring emotional turmoil and unrest into your spirit.[520]

If we focus on courtship leading to marriage, instead of engaging in sexual relationships first, we will avoid risking our health, our future, and our ability to serve God. Our children will have a solid and mature set of parents. There are nearly one million teen pregnancies reported annually. There are many venereal diseases (STDs.) Some STDs have been identified as incurable. There are over 16,000 deaths in a year caused by diseases or the complications of diseases like AIDS. You will also avoid cervical cancer, pelvic, inflammatory disease, and infertility by not having sexual intercourse. However, if you decide to be intimate with your partner, it is best to both go to the clinic or doctor's office to receive advice on avoiding sexually transmitted diseases.[521]

---

[514] Whitelaw, Daniel. *Health and Emotional Reasons for Waiting for Sexual Fulfillment.* Sermon at Family Conference in 2001, emphasis added by author.
[515] Hebrews 13:4, NIV
[516] 1 Corinthians 6:16 NLT, also review verses 18-20
[517] Refer to other Scriptures Acts 15:20; Proverbs 5:3-13; 6:32
[518] John 8:11; Luke 7:48; Hebrews 4:15
[519] Psalm 37:3-9 and Romans 8:6, 28
[520] Ephesians 5:3
[521] Whitelaw, Daniel. *Health and Emotional Reasons for Waiting for Sexual Fulfillment.* Sermon at Family Conference in 2001, emphasis added by author.

Begin Day 136:
Abstinence

Abstinence is the only 100% reliable method of prevention since no birth control method, not even condoms, will guarantee you safety from pregnancy or disease. Abstinence is becoming increasingly popular. More than 50% of high school students have never had sex. Celibacy is increasing, even among those with previous sexual experience.

People who have sex before marriage, and those who live with their partners before marriage, have a greater chance of being separated or divorced. Waiting on marriage can avoid the heartbreak, regret, and anger that sex outside of marriage brings. Many people regret it. They feel used and worthless because they gave away something precious, or they end up hurting someone else, even though they didn't realize they would.

Remember, even though you may feel 'grown,' sex is very serious in the Bible. Every out-of-wedlock sexual encounter leads to a painful result or memory. You will remember that sexual moment as something you learned from, but you will forever regret the pain it caused.

To maintain healthier dating relationships, take the advice of others (if you are celibate) and admit that having sex ruins the relationship. The couple stopped getting to know each other and focused on the pleasure of the moment instead.

You can make better decisions about a marriage partner, It is harder to break up with someone, even if he or she is not right for you, if you have had sex. Furthermore, you can grow in emotional maturity. Do not use sex as an escape from life's problems.

Begin Day 137:
Unmarried

Paul gave instructions to 'unmarried and widows,' and discussed aspects of singleness and marriage.[522] For instance, Paul foresaw the impending persecution that the Roman government would soon bring on Christians. He gave this practical advice because being unmarried would mean less suffering and more freedom to throw one's life into the cause of Christ, even to the point of fearlessly dying for Him. Paul's advice reveals his single-minded devotion to spreading the good news.[523] Many people naively think that marriage will solve all their problems. Here are some problems marriage will not solve:[524] loneliness; sexual temptation; satisfaction of one's deepest emotional needs; and/or elimination of life's difficulties.

Marriage alone does not hold two people together, but commitment does. A commitment to Christ and then to each other, despite conflicts and problems, will survive the temporary difficulties and heartaches of this world. As wonderful as it is, marriage does not automatically solve every problem. Whether married or single, we must be content with our situation and focus on Christ, not on loved ones, to help address our problems.

On the other hand, Paul urges all believers to make the most of their time before Christ's return. Every person in every generation should have this sense of urgency about telling the Good News to others.[525] Life is short – there is not much time. Jesus was very clear about life's short timespan when he spoke the Parable of the Rich Fool.[526] Additionally, Paul urges believers not to regard marriage, home, or financial security as the goal of life. As much as possible, we are to live unhindered by the cares of this world, not getting involved with burdensome mortgages, budgets, investments, or debts that might keep us from doing God's work.

---

[522] 1 Corinthians 7:25-40
[523] 1 Corinthians 7:26, 29; Life Application Study Bible, NKJV, 1996.
[524] 1 Corinthians 7:28
[525] 1 Corinthians 7:29, Life Application Study Bible, NKJV, 1996.
[526] Luke 12:21-22

Begin Day 138:
Marriage

A married man or woman, Paul points out, must take care of earthly responsibilities, but also make every effort to keep them modest and manageable.[527]

Moreover, Paul used marriage as a tool to illustrate our obligation to the law.[528] Paul also emphasizes that marriage is to be lifelong. Where a marriage partner has died, the only restriction concerning remarriage is for the person to marry a fellow Christian. Even though some people think that remarriage is permitted, Paul emphasized that it is wiser to remain unmarried. The Holy Spirit enabled Paul to speak with apostolic authority and with spiritual wisdom.

---

[527] 1 Corinthians 7:29-31; 33-34, Life Application Study Bible, NKJV, 1996.
[528] 1 Corinthians 7:39, 40: bound by law: Paul states something similar in Romans 7:2

Begin Day 139:
Soul Mates

You thought you met the man or woman of your dreams. However, the romance blew up in your face. Then, you discovered things about the person you never realized while in the relationship. God requires us to stay in the relationship once married, and change comes as both of you deal with life together.[529] Moreover, people believe that the way to finding their soul mate is solely by chance, fate, luck, magic, or good fortune. Everything happens with God's help, but God helps those who help themselves. Without knowing, we find ourselves in the right place at the right time, and it miraculously happens. We can feel an immediate chemistry. Two errors many make at this point are: first, they fail to let a time of courtship occur, and second if they're getting along, they begin to miss that 'chemistry.' Life is not all be butterflies and flowers, instead of maturing into the relationship.

There are different elements creating chemistry. If you are seeking a potential soul mate, and not finding 'the one,' keep in mind that while you may have many shared interests, you both are also interested in other things. Are there things you don't do that fits the character of the person you seek? Consider expanding your field of interests into those areas. Another element of chemistry is maturity. Soul mates have similar levels of maturity. Maturity does not necessarily mean age similarities. We cannot fully recognize our soul mate until we are ready. We need to know ourselves before recognizing this compatible person for us. Each time we decide to terminate a courting relationship (whether it's the first date or several), our maturity and discernment increases. As we mature, we gain greater wisdom and self-control.

Chemistry equals resonance. When you discover your soul mate's (partner's) values concerning God, family, work, and marriage, meet your own, they resonate within you and inspire you. Effective discussion allows both of you to understand and meet your shared goals for the future. Being different people will undoubtedly have some issues that have a different viewpoint. You should not be so far apart on the issues that you, together, cannot meet God's greatest Commandments.

Resonance creates soul chemistry, which is a combination of different interests, complementary needs, maturity, and resonance values you share as a couple. However, when resentment builds, then different interests become extreme. When we love our partners, we actually start learning about their interests. Resonance of values creates a base from where we can work through the differences and find fair compromises, helping harmonize differences. We are attracted to someone who is different because our soul yearns to expand and embrace that which is beyond ourselves. An unhealthy chemistry is where one, or both, is only interested in what they can get out of the relationship. True love is giving, and seeking the growth of the soul.

Although some of us have faced loneliness and struggles in past relationships, we can overcome our differences and challenges when we desire and seek a quality relationship with God's help. We must determine to use thorough communication, honesty, and commitment.

---

[529] Ephesians 6:14-15

Originally, God created woman for man, Adam knew her.[530] He knew that Eve was not only his woman but also his other half, his soul mate for life. She was what he was missing in Paradise, and God knew that. Adam called her 'woman' since she was created from his rib. For Adam, Eve added happiness to Paradise. Remember that marriage is not for your pleasure, but to serve God. Yes, God wants us to be happy. Furthermore, God created Eve as a helpmate to help Adam perform his duties and taking partnership in dominion over the earth.[531] God's purpose for marriage is a team, fulfilling His call together, not only to be pleased with each other. There is, from the experience of many, a firm conviction that the recreational dating scene is not in God's plan for finding a mate. [532]

---

[530] Genesis 2:25
[531] Genesis 1:27-30
[532] http://www.polynate.net/courtship/part1.html and emphasis added by author.

Begin Day 140:
A Place called *Home*

The home is a primary setting for the restoration of the image of God. The home is also a place where the principles of real Christianity are put into practice, and its values transmitted from one generation to the next. In forming the first humans, and ultimately the first family, God established the basic social unity for humanity, to have a sense of belonging, and providing them with an opportunity to serve God. Therefore, God created man in His own image and in His likeness.

Begin Day 141:
One Flesh

After God created Adam and Eve, God gave them dominion over the Garden of Eden and all living creatures that roamed the earth.[533] Adam was allowed to name every creature and animal that lived, but none was compatible with him. Yet, God's work was not completed until He created woman. Adam further realized since the woman was created from his bones and flesh, she was called 'woman.' Adam, after seeing the woman God had made from his rib, declared what is considered 'marriage.' In *Genesis 2:24*, Adam states: *"For this reason, a man will leave his father and mother and be united to his wife, and they will become one flesh."*

God created the pair as one flesh to be stewards of the earth, to care for it, keep it under control, and to bring forth others who would do likewise. In *Genesis 2:21-23*, God formed and equipped Adam and Eve for various tasks, but the entire task leads to one goal—for all of us, and that is honoring God the Father. Man gives life to woman (rib taken from Adam's flesh – half of the genome), and woman gives life to the world (offering the other half of the genome and bearing the child until birth).

There is no room for thinking that one sex is superior to the other. God could easily have made a woman just as he made the other creatures. He chose to use part of Adam, giving 'oneness' or 'completeness' as a gift to Adam and Eve. They were created perfectly for each other. Marriage was not for convenience—God established it. There are three basic aspects. First, man recognizes his mate as a part of him. He leaves his parents and vows himself to her.[534] Second, man and woman are joined, also taking responsibility for each other's welfare, and vowing together to love their mate above all others. Third, two become *one flesh* in the sense of intimacy and commitment of the sexual union, in which is reserved for marriage, since they have recognized that responsibility.[535] *One flesh* means that any physical or sexual bonding is a lifelong relationship between two people.[536]

---

[533] Genesis 1:18-26; 2:15
[534] Genesis 2:24
[535] Life Application Study Bible, NKJV on Genesis 2:24-26.
[536] Ephesians 5:31

Begin Day 142:
Marriage Foundation

The foundation of marriage can be found in Matthew 19:5 and 1 Corinthians 6:16. Some people will confuse Genesis 4:1 as the first sexual experience between Adam and Eve. It is referring to the conception of Cain and does not state that it was their first sexual experience. Furthermore, Adam and Eve were the only human inhabitants on the earth, and God commanded them to be fruitful and multiply very early in their journey through Eden.[537]

We are to be comfortable with our soul mates. For example, Adam and Eve were naked and not ashamed of each other, as the verse in Genesis 2:25 states. As a married couple, we are to love each other unconditionally, and not focus on downfalls or shortcomings, changes in weight, other physical changes, faults, or any other negative aspect concerning our mate. Moreover, we will see how Adam and Eve handled labor, family, and relationships. Furthermore, we will look at other characters in the Bible to understand their gifts, family, and how they handled relationships under a sovereign God.

---

[537] Genesis 1:28

Begin Day 143:
Foundation: **Adam**

Adam was the first and only person on earth. Adam was lonely and never knew another living being. He had no childhood, no parents, no family, or friends. He had to learn to be human on his own. Fortunately, God did not let him struggle too long before presenting him with an ideal companion and mate…Eve. Adam and Eve's love was complete, innocent, and open to oneness, without a hint of shame.

His strengths and accomplishments were to name all the animals in the Garden of Eden, the first zoologist, and first landscape architect since he had to tend to the garden. He is the father of our human race and the first person made in the image of God—sharing an intimate relationship with God.

Alternatively, his weaknesses and mistakes were avoiding responsibility for his own actions, and he blamed his wife, Eve. He chose to hide rather than to confront the issue at hand with God. He made excuses, rather than admitting to the truth. Our human race would not be in this situation if he did not touch the forbidden fruit, or told God the truth instead of covering it up. These greatest mistakes, teamed up with his wife, Eve, brought sin into the world, and we are all born into a sinful nature. Only Jesus Christ can save us from death, and give us life. Yet, as Adam's descendants, we all reflect in the image of God and His likeness. We cannot blame others for our faults, and we cannot hide from God.

Adam's livelihood was a caretaker, gardener, and a farmer. His relatives were Eve, his wife, sons, Cain, Abel, and Seth, and numerous children not mentioned in the Bible, and the only man who did not have an earthly mother and father.[538]

Genesis 3:12, NLT: *"[Adam said], 'It was the woman you gave me who gave me the fruit, and I ate it.'"*

1 Corinthians 15:22, NLT: *"Just as everyone dies because we all belong to Adam, everyone who belongs to Christ will be given new life."*

---

[538] Life Application Study Bible, commentary, Read Adam's story in Genesis 1:26-5:5; 1 Chronicles 1:1; Luke 3:38; Romans 5:14; 1 Corinthians 15:22, 45; and 1 Timothy 2:13, 14. Moreover, men can learn from women and how to treat women with respect and love in Romans 12:9, 10, 16; Philippians 2:1-15 (NIV); I John 4: 20, 21 (NIV); and I Thessalonians 5:11, 13 (NIV).

Begin Day 144:
Foundation: Eve

Eve is the first woman in the world; also she is the mother of us all. She was the final piece in the intricate and amazing puzzle of God's creation. Adam had another human being with whom to fellowship with, an equal to share in God's image.

Satan approached Eve, where she and Adam lived. He questioned her contentment. How could she be happy, when she was not allowed to eat from one of the trees? Satan helped Eve shift her focus from all that God had done and gave in to the one thing God had withheld. Eve was willing to accept Satan's viewpoint, as Satan was speaking through the serpent, without checking with God first.

Do we check with God first? We get that, 'I've got to have it' feeling. Eve was typical of us all. We consistently display that we are her descendants by repeating her mistakes. Our desires, like Eve's, can be easily manipulated. They are not the best basis for action. We need to constantly keep God in our decision-making process. His Word, the Bible, is our guidebook in decision-making.

Eve's strength and accomplishment were being the first mother and wife. Additionally, she was the first woman alive on earth. She shared a special relationship with God, had co-responsibility with Adam over creation and displayed certain characteristics of God. Her weaknesses and mistakes allowed her contentment to be undermined by Satan, in which she acted impulsively without talking to God or to Adam. Not only did she sin, but shared her sin with Adam, and when confronted, she blamed the serpent.

The necessary ingredients for a strong marriage are a commitment to God, a commitment to each other, companionship with each other, complete oneness, and absence of shame.[539] The basic human tendency to sin goes back to the beginning of the human. However, Eve's occupation was as Adam's wife, helper, companion, and co-manager of the Garden of Eden.[540]

Genesis 2:18, NIV: *"The Lord God said, 'It is not good that man should be alone; I will make him a helper comparable to him.'"*

---

[539] Genesis 2:24-25
[540] Adapted from Life Application Study Bible, commentary, Eve's story can be found in Genesis 2:19-4:26 except her death is not mentioned in Scripture. *Wife Roles:* Proverbs 11:22; 12:4; 21:9; 27:15 (NIV); Proverbs 9:13; 14:1; 30:21, 23 (NJKV).

Begin Day 145:
Foundation: **Abel**

Abel was the second child born into the world, but the first one to obey God. Abel was a shepherd. He presented pleasing sacrifices to God, and his short life was ended at the hands of his jealous older brother, Cain. However, the Bible does not tell us why God liked Abel's gift and disliked Cain's, but both Cain and Abel knew what God expected. Only Abel obeyed. Throughout history, Abel is remembered for his obedience and faith, and he is called *'righteous.'*[541] Like Abel, we obey, regardless of the cost, and trust God to make things right.

Abel's strengths and accomplishments made him the first member of the 'Hall of Faith.' He was the first shepherd and first martyr for truth. Lessons we can learn from his life, God hears those who come to Him and recognizes the innocent person—and eventually punishes the guilty. He resided outside of the Garden of Eden. His parents were Adam and Eve; his twin brother is Cain, including numerous siblings not mentioned in the Bible.[542]

Hebrews 11:4, NLT: *"It was by faith that Abel brought a more acceptable offering to God than Cain did. Abel's offering gave evidence that he was a righteous man, and God showed his approval of his gifts. Although Abel is long dead, he still speaks to us by his example of faith."*

---

[541] Hebrews 11:4
[542] Life Application Study Bible, commentary. Abel is mentioned in in Genesis 4:1-8; Matthew 23:35; Luke 11:51; Hebrews 11:4; 12:24.

Begin Day 146:
Foundation: **Cain**

While we do not know many details of this first-born child's life, his story can still teach us. Cain got angry. Both Cain and his brother, Abel, had made sacrifices to God, except his offerings had been rejected. Cain's reaction gives us a clue that his attitude was probably wrong from the start. Cain had a choice to make. He could correct his attitude about his sacrifice to God. His decision is a clear reminder of how often we understand opposite choices. We may not be choosing to murder, but we are still intentionally choosing what we should not. The feelings motivating our behavior cannot always be changed by simple thought-power. However, we can experience God's willingness to help by asking for His help to do what is right, which can prevent us from setting into motion actions that we will later regret.

Cain was the first-born human child, following his father's profession–farming. However, when he was disappointed, he reacted in anger, taking the negative approach instead of the positive one that was offered. His anger is not necessarily a sin, but actions motivated by anger can be sinful. Anger can be the energy behind a good action, not evil. What we offer to God must be from a loving heart, and consisting of the best we are and have. The consequences of sin can last a lifetime. Cain was the first murderer recorded in the Bible and history. For some, it is hard to believe that he killed his very own brother. He lived near Eden (in the present day this is Iraq or Iran), and after the murder of his brother, he became a wanderer.[543]

Genesis 4:7: *"If you do well, will you not be accepted? And if you do not do well, sin lies at the door. And its desire is for you, but you should rule over it."*

---

[543] Life Application Study Bible, NIV, commentary. You can read more about Cain in Genesis 4:1-17; Hebrews 11:4; 1 John 3:12; and Jude 1:11.

Begin Day 147:
Foundation: **Noah**

The story of Noah's life involves not one, but two great and tragic floods. The world in Noah's day was flooded with evil. The number of those who remembered the God of creation, perfection, and love had dwindled to one. Of God's people, only Noah was left. God's response to the severe situation was a 120-year long change, during which he had Noah build a graphic illustration of the message of his life -- nothing like a huge boat on dry land to make a point. For Noah, obedience meant a long-term commitment to a project. Many of us have trouble sticking to any project, even if God directs it. It is interesting that the length of Noah's obedience was greater than the lifespan of people today. The only comparable long-term project is our very lives. Nevertheless, the great challenge Noah's life gives us—to live in acceptance of God's grace, an entire lifetime of obedience and gratitude.

Apparently, Noah was the only follower of God left before the flood. He was the second father of God's human race--a man of patience, consistency, and obedience. He was the first major shipbuilder, an amateur, who created the ark that did not crash into a disaster like one famous ship built by professionals, The Titanic. However, his weakness was getting drunk, and it embarrassed him in front of his sons. Furthermore, we can learn from his life that God is faithful to those who obey Him. God does not always protect us from trouble but cares for us despite trouble. Obedience is a long-term commitment. A man may be faithful, but his sinful nature always travels with him.

Noah was a farmer, shipbuilder, and preacher. He was the grandfather was Methuselah, his father was Lamech. Noah's sons were Ham, Shem, and Japheth.[544]

Genesis 6:2, NLT: *"So Noah did everything exactly as God had commanded him."*

---

[544] Life Application Study Bible, commentary. Noah's story is told in Genesis 5:29-10:32; 1 Chronicles 1:4; Isaiah 54:9; Ezekiel 14:14, 20; Matthew 24:37, 38; Luke 3:36; 17:26, 27; Hebrews 11:7; 1 Peter 3:20; and 2 Peter 2:5.

Begin Day 148:
Foundation: Lot

Some people simply drift through life. Their choices, when they can muster the will to choose, tend to follow the course of least resistance, which is following the way of the world. Lot, Abram's nephew, was such a person.

In his youth, Lot lost his father. Although this must have been hard on him, he was not left without strong role models—his grandfather, Terah, and his uncle, Abraham, who raised him. Still, Lot did not develop their sense of purpose. Throughout his life, he was so caught up in the present moment that he seemed incapable of seeing the consequences of his actions. It is hard to imagine what his life would have been like without Abraham's careful attention and God's intervention. Later, Lot drifted out of the picture because his life had taken an ugly turn. He had so blended into the sinful culture of his day that he did not want to leave it. Then, his daughters committed incest with him. His drifting finally took him in a very specific direction—destruction.

Lot, however, is called 'righteous' in the New Testament by Peter.[545] Ruth, a descendant of Moab, was an ancestor of Jesus, even though Moab was born because of Lot's incestuous relationship with one of his daughters. Lot's story gives hope to us that God forgives, and often brings about positive results from evil. For example, he was a successful businessman. However, when faced with decisions, he tended to put off deciding and then chose the easiest course of action. When given a choice, his first reaction was to think of himself.

Lot lived first in UR of the Chaldeans and then moved to Canaan with Abram. Eventually, he moved to the wicked city of Sodom. His worked as a wealthy sheep and cattle rancher, and city official in Sodom. His parent was Haran, as mentioned in the Bible, who was later adopted by Abraham after his father passed. He was the one righteous man his uncle Abraham prayed for, and the Lord saved from Sodom and Gomorrah. His wife, who was not named in the Bible, was turned into a pillar of salt.[546]

Genesis 19:16: *"And while he lingered, the men took hold of his hand, his wife's hand, and the hands of his two daughters, the Lord being merciful to him, and they brought him out and set him outside the city."*

Our human race is a family that shares one flesh and blood: descendants of Adam and the last Adam known as Jesus Christ. Remember, 'we are all of the body,' when prejudice enters your mind or hatred invades your feelings. Each person is a valuable and unique creation of God. Yet, by Adam and Eve's disobedience, after sin, God told Eve, "Your desire shall be for your husband, and he shall rule over you."[547] God changed the basic equality of man and woman, to benefit both in marriages to this day. Today, the original principle is distorted by modern myths of relationships and marriage.

---

[545] 2 Peter 2:7, 8
[546] See Life Application Study Bible, commentary. Lot's story is told in Genesis 11-14; 19 also mentioned in Deuteronomy 2:9; Luke 17:28-32; and 2 Peter 2: 7-8.
[547] Genesis 3:16

Begin Day 149:
Signs Before Marriage

You may have heard of people confusing the intense feelings of sex with true love, or believing great sex is love, and therefore it's a precursor to a great relationship. It's not true.

Good sex is described as physical stimulation performed with or without love. Usually, there are selfish motives, where some suffer from emotional or physically abusive relationships. Others believe if they have sex with their partner, they will never be lonely again. This one also is not true.

Likewise, "marriage makes one happier than they were before."

These are all myths that many young people believe will happen before marriage. Those who've been married can tell you otherwise.

After the sparks of romance, it fades to a day-to-day relationship of paying bills, feeding family members, health issues, caring for their property, and a host of other things that must be done. Marriage takes plenty of work, sacrifice and compromise. Statistics show that younger couples that marry are more likely to divorce. Teen marriages end in divorce by 78%. Part of the reason for this is that maturity in decision making doesn't come until one is in their twenties. Do not marry someone that you hardly know. Try to learn more about them for at least a year. After a one-year acquaintance, you will be able to understand how your marriage will be since you will have judged your compatibility. You can also decide if you are financially stable before raising a family and evaluate other important issues that will affect the future of your relationship, as well as that of any children who come along.

Here are some key factors why people get married for the wrong reasons:
- Pregnancy or already have had children as a couple;
- One is hoping marriage will cure loneliness, depression, and/or they are leaving their unhappy life;
- Their primary reason for marriage is to have sex;
  - Or, for women, their biological clock is ticking, and they'd better get married.

There are red flags to look out for in a relationship.
Observe how your potential mate treats their parents, their friends that are of the opposite sex, and family members. Furthermore, ask the family, co-workers, friends, and neighbors, to see if they have any problems or issues with your potential mate that you should be aware of. Respectful attitudes around other people, and not denigrating others in your presence is a great sign of a maturity of character.

Then you should evaluate the relationship for any 'danger signals' of possible violence or infidelity towards you. Verify if they abuse alcohol or any type of drugs, and beware of uncontrollable anger. Also be aware of any emotions they are unable to work through, even if you are offering reasonable ways out of their predicament.

It is imperative that you know each other's experiences with other people before committing to each other in marriage. How many relationships have they had, and what is going to make the relationship with you different?

Decide right now what character traits are game changers. What will you not handle well? Go into the relationship understanding that people do not change people. Only God does that. Pray to God for discernment to know if this is "the one" He wants for you.

Many people naively think that marriage will solve all their problems. Here are some problems that marriage will not solve: sexual proclivities, a need to satisfy one's deepest emotional demands, and a desire to eliminate life's difficulties.

Begin Day 150:
Commit

Marriage alone does not have the power to keep two people together, but commitment does. The commitment to Christ and to each other, despite conflicts and problems, must include a consideration of Christ's commission, and the purpose for the future. We are not to go about marriage as a temporary solution for our current loneliness. We must think of the good we can do, and the children who will be impacted by a solid family life. As wonderful as marriage sounds, it does not automatically solve every problem. Whether married or single, we must be content with our situation and focus on Christ, not on loved ones or friends to help address the problems that are in God's hands.[548]

Before considering someone as the person you will spend the rest of your life with, review their political, social, and cultural views, on guidance, rules, and individual affections. Regardless of our estrangement of affection, rebellious human mannerisms, or following our divine will (purpose), God desires obedience from His children to follow His will and purpose. Through obedience, we gain intuition, which guides us; a sense of any situation; help to resolve conflicting feelings; alternative images of the future; an assurance of the character in our relationships; and creativity.

God's Word gives us *convictional character*, which means we are given the motive and the courage to choose and act. If we are blessed with the experience of hearing God's will, it empowers within us the action to undertake the mission.

However, know that God's words can be distorted and perverted by our own desires or peculiar circumstances of our own hearing. Again, it is known that God speaks with clarity and wisdom, and we can find verification of what we set out to do by reading His words in the Bible.[549]

---

[548] Life Application Study Bible, NKJV, 1996.
[549] 1 Corinthians 14:33

Begin Day 151:
Pressure for Singles

Some single people feel tremendous pressure to be married. They think their lives can be complete only with a spouse. However, Paul, in 1 Corinthians 7 underlines the one advantage of being single is the potential of a greater focus on Christ and His work. In other words, if you are unmarried, you have the special opportunity to serve Christ wholeheartedly.[550]

When Paul says the unmarried person does even better, he is talking about the potential time available for service to God. The single person lacks the responsibility of caring for a spouse and raising a family. Singleness, however, does not ensure service to God. Involvement in service depends on the commitment of the individual. Paul's advice comes from the Holy Spirit, who guides and equips both single and married people to fulfill their roles.[551] He clearly distinguishes the words of Christ when he speaks to virgins and unmarried widows.[552] Although Paul is concerned with both celibate men and women, the attention here is on the women.

---

[550] Life Application Study Bible, NKJV, emphasis added by author.
[551] 1 Corinthians 7:40 –Life Application Study Bible, NKJV, 1996.
[552] Nelson Study Bible, NKJV, I Corinthians 7:25-40.

Begin Day 152:
Virgins

By the second century, the church had developed important offices for virgins, widows, and deaconesses. They were able to help the pastors and deacons in baptizing, ministering to the sick, and other works of mercy. In addition, a virgin would have lesser family responsibilities, and would not be deterred by the possibility of repercussions affecting her husband or children. Paul does not want to be understood as prohibiting marriage altogether. However, married couples are to dedicate themselves to God's work.

Another interpretation of Verses 36-38, any man has to speak to the father of an unmarried virgin. When she is past the *flower of youth,* shows that the virgin is approaching age at which marriage would be unlikely. It also refers to a fiancé, who is maintaining a celibate state. The Greek term, *she is past the flower of her youth,* is translated, he has strong passions. On the other hand, if he can control himself (has power over his own will), he should maintain his celibacy. If the man can control himself and keep himself from giving into immoral action, he should stay single. However, if the man's will is weak, he should go ahead and marry. Paul urges all believers to make the most of their time before Christ's return. Every person in every generation should have a sense of urgency about telling the Good News to others. Life is too short -- there is not much time.

Begin Day 153:
Perfect Mate

A perfect mate is compatible, lovable, and comprehensive to each other's needs. Moreover, the Holy Word describes our roles as husband and wife: to be a working relationship, where the husband is to love her, comfort her, honor and keep her in sickness and in health, and forsaking all others to keep only into her as long as they both will live. Duties and expectations of a good spouse are located in *Romans 3:10-18*, which further explains that no one is righteous, not one. Therefore, do not expect your spouse to be perfect.

We are to be thankful for His gift bestowed on you. *His gift bestowed on you* is the person He has chosen for you. Moreover, marriage is to glorify the Lord. God blessed us with the gift of matrimony.[553] Evidently, God has a divine lifetime plan: one woman and one man committed to each other for life.[554] God's solution for a man's desire is marriage, not dating. God did not see loneliness as the issue. Eve is described as a helper, translated as "succor," which is essential assistance. Marriage is a monogamous relationship when two become 'one flesh' as described in the Bible.

---

[553] Elisabeth Elliot
[554] Genesis 2:24

Begin Day 154:
Leave, Cleave, Covenant

The scriptures describe marriage as a decisive act of both detachment and attachment. One will leave his father and mother, and cleave to his wife, and they will be one flesh.[555] Furthermore, *leaving* means that the marriage relationship is to supersede that of the parent and the child. Leaving one's relationship with one's parents allows one to 'cleave' to another. Without this process, there is no firm foundation for marriage. *Cleaving*, the Hebrews term, means to stick to, to fasten, to join, and to hold onto. The closeness and strength of this bond illustrate the nature of the bond of marriage. Any attempt to break up this union can emotionally damage the couples in love. A man leaving his parents means that he establishes his home, and becomes the head of the marriage relationship. He is no longer a child.

Covenanting is a promise, in which married couples are bound together, and is spoken as a *covenant promise, being a* binding agreement known to God.[556] The relationship between husband and wife is connected with God's everlasting covenant with His people and the church.[557] Their commitment to each other is to take on the faithfulness and endurance that characterize God's covenant.[558] God and the couple's family and friends witness the covenant, which is also ratified in heaven.[559] The Christian couple understands that marriage is covenanted to be faithful to each other for as long as they both will live.

Biblically speaking, *becoming one flesh, figuratively* states that a married couple walks together, stands together, and shares a deep intimacy. *Oneness* refers to the physical union of marriage and to the intimate bond of mind and emotions that under grids the physical side of the relationship.

*"To become one **flesh** means that two persons become completely one with body, soul, and spirit, and yet there remain two different persons."*[560]

Intimacy in becoming *one flesh* involves sexual union: "Adam knew Eve, his wife, and she conceived."[561] Since the days of Adam and Eve, each couple reenacts the first love story. The act of sexual intimacy is the closest thing to a physical union, of which represents a closeness the couple can experience emotionally and spiritually too. Christian marriage is a mixture of love, warmth, joy, and delight.[562] Marriage is honorable among all and the bed undefiled.[563]

---

[555] Genesis 2:24, KJV
[556] Mal. 2:14; Proverbs 2:16, 17
[557] Ephesians 5:21-23
[558] Psalm 89:34; Lamentations 3:23
[559] Matthew 19:6
[560] *We Saw the Sun Rise Twice*, p. 213, Leona Amacher
[561] Genesis 4:1
[562] Proverbs 5:18, 19
[563] Hebrews 13:4

Begin Day 155:
Undefiled Bed

The Scripture clearly states that the joyous sexual expression of love between husband and wife is God's plan. *Undefiled* means not sinful and bed not soiled. It is a place of great honor in marriage, where husband and wife meet privately to celebrate their love for each other. It is meant to be both holy and intensely enjoyable. Moreover, sex is worship, it is a communion, and it is a marital duty ordained by God. Withholding sex to punish your mate is a sin.[564] Talk. Let your mate know your needs. Influence him or her to become a better lover. With unity of spirit, soul, and body—God is well-pleased and glorified. "Can two walk together, without agreeing?"[565] Clearly, this word of God, along with Paul's exhortation to not be yoked with unbelievers, warns you that marrying those who do not believe in Jesus Christ will cause issues with your faith life as you navigate the difficult waters of marriage.

True oneness demands an agreement such as one's beliefs and practices. To achieve the oneness God prescribes, people must marry others within their own communion. To become one flesh, two people must become completely loyal to each other. When one marries, one risks everything and accepts everything that comes with one's mate. Those who marry proclaim their willingness to share their mates' accountability and to stand with their mates against anything.

---

[564] Ephesians 4:26-27, NIV
[565] 2 Corinthians 6:14-16 KJV

Begin Day 156:
Religious Differences May Cause a Rift

Differences in religious experience can lead to differences in lifestyle and create deep tensions in a marriage. Marriage requires an active, pursuing love that will not give up. For instance, two people share everything they have, including not only their bodies, or material possessions, but also their thinking and feelings. Those may project in the relationship as a whole, which is not limited to their joy and their sufferings but also may include hopes and fears, successes, disappointments, and failures.

Instead of bringing up religious differences, we must focus on one's talents, abilities, good qualities, experiences, and other gifts, of which reflect and enhance the relationship that is becoming a partnership. Each person is responsible for developing these character imbalances. In other words, we are to make sure we are completely on track in the relationship. Consider the joy of your partner, and share the worship. You should have already discussed the future of your religious life if you share two different faiths. If your faiths do not mesh, you've given yourselves an extremely high bar.

For instance, if your mate is arguing over past incidents to start a conflict or confrontation, you are to remain calm and de-escalate the situation without causing more irritation. If you feel it is out of your hands, call the relationship to our Heavenly Father, to free us. Even if one sleeps on the couch until the heat of an argument has settled down, you cannot assume that settlement is impossible. You do not need to reply angrily to get your point across. It is not about you, it is about you and your spouse mending the relationship through compromise and understanding each other's feelings. Moreover, God designed human beings not to go through their life alone. God will meet our needs for a deserving relationship.

Don't fool yourself that marriage is 'peaches and cream,' since there are many times you will be on a 'rocky road.' Marriage has its difficult moments, conflicts, years spent and old experiences. In the time that you are getting to know one another intimately, there will be rejections, arguments, and feelings hurt. It can be a difficult task of accepting imperfections and immaturity. However, deception damages the relationship by lying to one another. Usually, the issue of deceit can be worked out unless one denies there is a problem. Sometimes, it is hard to be honest about feelings, disappointments, desires, likes or dislikes, pain, anger and hatred, sex, sins, failure, needs, and vulnerabilities. However, falsehood is not a way to protect or save the relationship since it can destroy any chance of recovery.

Begin Day 157:
Marital Love

Marital love is an unconditional, affectionate, and intimate devotion. It encourages mutual growth in the image of God in all aspects of each person: physical, emotional, intellectual, and spiritual. Because the future depends on a mutual goal, marital love seeks the growth of the relationship with God at the helm.

The *types of love* that operate in marriage are romantic, passionate times; highly sentimental times; comfortable times; companionable and sense-of-belonging times. *Agape love* comprises the foundation of true, lasting marital love.

Jesus manifested the highest form of this type of love when accepting the guilt and consequences for our sins when He died on the Cross. Paul describes this type of love in *1 Corinthians 13:4-8*. *Agape* means, one loves no matter what. No matter how unlovable the other person is, *agape* can keep on flowing. *Agape* is as unconditional as God's love is for us.

Begin Day 158:
Spiritual Responsibility

Responsibility is a mental attitude with a deliberate choice of will. When it comes to individual *spiritual responsibility,* marriage partners must bear the responsibility for the choices they make.[566] Taking such responsibility means that they will never blame the other person for what they themselves have done. They must also accept responsibility for their own spiritual growth since no one can rely on another's spiritual strength, nor should one partner expect more of his or her spouse when it comes that person's walk with God.

On the other hand, everyone's relationship with God can serve as a source of strength and encouragement to the other.[567] According to *Healing the Hurt in Your Marriage*, God's Word is full of instruction, admonition, and encouragement about our relationships on every level. The Bible provides clean instruction for resolving conflict and healing from hurt. A healthy fear of God is manifested in our trust in God. It will help deliver us from other fears that can damage our lives and marriage.[568]

There are two types of controllers known as active and passive. An *active controller* is someone that is in charge, controls the decision-making process, determines the course of action, and dominates what happens in his or her relationship. A *passive controller* has a low need for control and high need to please. During a conflict, they have opinions, needs, and suggestions, but tend to back off to keep the peace and make the spouse happy. Furthermore, they allow their partner to dominate the relationship, and they simmer under the surface. Learn to express yourself unequivocally, instead of struggling for dominance or power in the marriage.

---

[566] 2 Corinthians 5:10
[567] Seventh-Day Adventists Believe
[568] 2 Timothy 1:7

Begin Day 159:
Christian Marriage

In Ephesians, starting at chapter 5, verse 21, Paul gives husbands and wives rules by which they deal with three sets of household relationships; their relationship with each other; parents with their children; and masters with their slaves (bondservants). In each case, there is a mutual responsibility to submit and love; to obey and to encourage; to work hard while being fair. Examine your family and work relationships. Christian marriage involves mutual submission, subordinating our personal desires for the good of the loved one, and submitting ourselves to Christ as Lord. Consequently, children are to be handled with care. They need firm discipline administered with love. Do not alienate them by nagging, deriding, or destroying their self-respect so that they lose heart.[569]

---
[569] Life Application Study Bible, NKJV, 1996.

Begin Day 160:
Submit

Submitting to your husband is very important. When his wife is a godly woman, the man feels his heart, his results, and his emotions are safe with her. A woman contributes to his decisions by helping him cool down when he is upset. His flame should stir up his passion for God in his ambitions and in his home.

Consistency is a wife who is always there for him in heart, and someone he can always count on. This way, he knows what to expect from you because your character is sound and known. No man should have to worry about coming home to get on an emotional roller coaster, not knowing which "you" he will meet each day. He needs to have access to your heart, your softness and comforting words, reassurance as you counsel him, always his side, and vice versa.

Submit to God's authority by staying connected to God, knowing He has brought you from death to life.[570] Stay in God's love, keeping His presence close in your lives to limit sin and temptations. Overall, when we do not admit the truth about who we are, we give our spouse no chance to connect with us.[571] Testing your faith develops perseverance; it requires work to mature. If you can't see your own faults and shortcomings, you are not able to give them to God.[572]

---

[570] Romans 6:13
[571] 1 John 1:8
[572] James 1:25

Begin Day 161:
Concerns of those who are Married

Furthermore, Paul urges believers not to regard marriage, home, or financial security as the goal of life. We live unhindered by the cares of this world, not getting involved with burdensome mortgages, budgets, investments, or debts that might keep us from doing God's work. A married man or woman, as Paul points out, must take care of earthly responsibilities, but making every effort to keep them modest and manageable.[573]

1 Corinthians 7:33-34, NIV: *"But a married man is concerned about the affairs of this world—how he can please his wife[34] -- and his interests are divided. An unmarried woman or virgin is concerned about the Lord's affairs: Her aim is to be devoted to the Lord in both body and spirit. But a married woman is concerned about the affairs of this world—how she can please her husband."*

---

[573] Life Application Study Bible, NKJV, 1 Corinthians 7:33-34.

Begin Day 162:
Prudent Wife

Happy marriages display honest, open communication about conflicts by negotiation, compromise, and problem-solving. Communication makes relationships stronger, and deeper, by uncovering and resolving problem areas. One should be able to have humor and acceptance, forgiveness, treat one another as equals in decision-making and certain areas in life, and to be reliable and responsible adults in the marriage.

Proverbs 19:14, NKJV: *"Houses and riches are an inheritance from fathers, but a prudent wife is from the Lord."*

A *prudent wife* is a woman who demonstrates wisdom or skill. Finding the right spouse is a blessing from God, which further demonstrates that it is good to be married.[574] Today's marriage tends to emphasize an individual's freedom. Strong individuals are important, but strong marriages are important too. God created marriage for our enjoyment and views it as good.[575]

---

[574] Proverbs 18:22
[575] John 2:1-11 and Genesis 2:21-25

Begin Day 163:
Marriage:
Contractual Agreement And Covenant

Marriage is not only a contract— it is a covenant between couples and God, as *one flesh* or *union*. Marriage was God's idea.[576] Love is a decision consciously made, an act of will (emotion), and a sacrificial commitment.[577] The commitment level is that God is leading in this relationship on a spiritual or emotional oneness, which usually starts as intimate friendship before marriage after discernment. God brings spiritual power into a future marriage that will require a commitment to being 'set apart, holy and sanctified' in a personal relationship.

Marriage is an *unconditional commitment* to imperfect people:

> I will love you,
> I will honor you,
> I will cherish you,
> I will not be involved with anyone else,
> I will perform all the duties of a spouse,
> I will be loving and faithful through every circumstance,
>> for as long as the two of us live.

God's covenant is to abide by his plans for marriage. Are you committed to your mate? Are you willing to sign your name on the dotted line, and did God lead you into this matrimony? If so, God will fulfill and bless this marriage. This covenant is signed and honored by our Lord, Jesus Christ. Amen.

---

[576] Philippians 2:3
[577] John 15:3

Begin Day 164:
Set Boundaries In Marriage

Marriage requires discipleship. For couples to abide in discipleship, they first must understand the analogy of bridegroom and the bride. The husband is the maker, and the wife is the bride. Likewise, Christ showed the love for His Bride, His leadership, and her submission. No bride or groom can enter marriage without surrendering the right to "self."

According to *Boundaries in Marriage*, when two people are free to disagree, they are free to love. When they are not free, they live in fear, and love dies. Marriage is one of God's greatest gifts to humanity. However, we seem to overlook this gift as marriage being convenient, something to take away loneliness and depression, for financial support, or for all the wrong reasons. *Marriage* is also a lifetime of love and commitment to one person with whom we can share a life as one. *Marriage* is bonded together by caring, needing and companionship, and values shared between two people, who can overcome hurt, immaturity and selfishness, to form something much better than what a person can do alone.

There is a triangle of boundaries: freedom, responsibility, and love.[578] In essence, we live free, we take responsibility for our own freedom and love our Heavenly Father. Cloud and Townsend state that love only exists where freedom and responsibility are operating. Love creates more freedom, and that leads to more responsibility, which, in return, leads to a greater ability to love. In a marriage, some will view the church as evil since there are members that will gossip and spread rumors in the church and outside of the church to destroy the love you share for one another or will be jealous of that bond that you share as a couple. There may be people so new in the faith that they are jealous of the solid rock of a marriage that you have built. They may try to grab the person they think is stronger for themselves. Satan will set up other traps to lure you in. Share with each other when you notice such things, and discuss how to diffuse inappropriate actions by others.

The book, *Boundaries in Marriage,* is teaching married couples how to set boundaries to protect your relationship and learning more about yourself. It is not about setting boundaries for the other person. If we are setting boundaries for our mate, we are "controllers." Communication is the key factor in any type of relationship such as reading body language, gestures, facial expression, along with any verbal comments expressed. Truth is another important communication. God is the truth. Examples are: agree to not lie to one another; love one another faithfully and sacrificially; refusing to desire another person; covetousness; agreeing to give to others; to be more compassionate; and most of all, be able to forgive.

You cannot make your spouse "grow up," since it is between him/her and God. We do not have the power to change our spouse, nor any destructive behaviors and attitudes he or she has.[579] However, we do have some power and choices for ourselves. We can choose to tell the truth about our faults and bring those faults to the light of our relationship. We can choose

---

[578] Boundaries in Marriage
[579] Romans 7:15

to repent for these faults, work them out, and mature. Pray to God, instead of seeking approval from your mate.

Overall, boundaries are meant to protect our love, our freedom, allow ourselves to be imperfect people, and to stay connected as a married couple. Enter the process of boundary building as a team. Develop the self-control and patience needed to be humbler and self-connecting to your partner. Appreciate your mate for who they are instead of using them. Furthermore, respect the freedom from your spouse, and avoid withdrawing from your spouse. Other things to avoid are attacking them with complaints and making them feel guilty. Boundaries were not designed to end relationships, nor to preserve and deepen them, nor to escape from suffering or responsibility.[580] They are meant to open your freedom and capacity to love.

---

[580] Romans 5:3-4

Begin Day 165:
Emotional Makeup in Marriage

Marriage requires selflessness to succeed. It can be difficult not to snap at your spouse or children when you aren't feeling like being gracious. You might have been sick, or work didn't go well, or you simply forgot to do something in the morning to prepare for the evening. Yet, that emotional absence exposes our weaknesses and failure to relate to the other person. From time to time, couples struggle with judging, criticizing, and condemning each other. It becomes difficult in accepting these differences from others by misreading the person's actions out of a need to be loved and accepted. One might be disgusted with the sinful nature, but may also hate the sinner. This will eradicate the love in a marriage if one becomes so judgmental. God is the only One who can control and judge our decisions, except God does give us the freedom to choose how we react.

Emotional adultery is an affair with the heart when you desire someone other than your spouse in your mind and heart. God remains faithful. Do not let your spouse's failures be an excuse for your unfaithfulness. Consider discussing with your spouse the issue that is driving you to the point of acting out a fantasy. Why are you having difficulty? What could make it better? Having an affair will destroy you.[581] It will break the hearts of those who have faith in you and care about you. Remain faithful until the end. No failure is larger than God's grace.[582] You can expect failure even from the best people. God designed both spouses to invest continually in their love for each other. God says that you are equal in His eyes.[583]

---

[581] Proverbs 2:16-19; 5:3-20; 6:23-25
[582] Ecclesiastes 7:20; 1 John 3:4
[583] Ephesians 5:28-33

Begin Day 166:
Faithfulness in a Marriage

The requirement in marriage is oneness, which requires two complete people.[584]

Faithfulness is to trust one another in all areas, where one can be depended on what was promised, and to follow through on what your spouse has entrusted to you. As a couple or marriage, we are to be faithful with our bodies and our heart. Focus on the shared responsibility to God, to each other, and to the children around you.

---

[584] Boundaries in Marriage.

Begin Day 167:
Setting Limits Can Lead to Divorce

God does not want you to come into a relationship setting limits and expecting the other person to change. He wants you. When you confess your needs and faults to loving people, you will grow spiritually and emotionally. Forgive and let go of things in the past, do not masquerade with your broken dreams or promises, or continue to carry unnecessary baggage. People have a difficult time when their feelings are neglected and dismissed, and many people do not handle constant complaints or negativity well. While life changes people, other people often do not trigger that change.

God is the answer to proceed with your change. Validation and grace soften the burden of change. You may need to change even if your spouse does not.[585]

Ironically, over 50% of new marriages in America end in divorce. African-American marriages have a higher separation and divorce rate than Caucasians. Usually, 63% of women get custody of the children and two-thirds of the divorces are filed by women. Statistics show that children are better off with a happy single parent than in an unhappy household. If you're thinking about divorce or separation from your spouse, it is best to talk to a divorce lawyer on financial and other legal matters. You are urged to seek professional help from a counseling psychologist, a licensed counselor, a therapist, or even a psychiatrist before completing your divorce. There are Christian counselors for those who desire a therapeutic viewpoint grounded in Biblical principles.

Striking evidence shows that 50-70% of child mental health referrals show that emotional distress is caused by parents divorcing or separating. Of divorced fathers, 21-52 percent have no contact with their children. The best time to consider the children is before you commit to marriage. Their future and well-being, not your current desires, is the reason for marriage.

---

[585] Cloud, pp. 217, 221, 222, 223

Begin Day 168:
Restore your Marriage

Before resorting to divorce, there is a six-stage process for restoring your marriage:

1. Prepare your heart
2. Diffuse your anger
3. Communicate your concerns
4. Confront your conflicts
5. Forgive your spouse
6. Rebuild your trust

You must prepare your heart to receive love, give love, and welcome love. Let go of the unnecessary baggage carried for years, release and seek after Jesus' peace, and restore your marriage by releasing past hurts and pains you've carried for a period of time. Open your heart and mind to love your mate regardless of past incidents that troubled you. Reflect on why you married him or her in the first place. Seek every good quality that outdoes the bad.

Find ways to diffuse your anger. You may need to count to ten until the anger simmers. Hit a pillow until you can think clearly. Take deep breaths, inhale through your nose for four counts and exhale slowly through your mouth for five to seven counts, and follow your breathing. Focus on the wonderful things this person does to make you smile, or your heart flutter, and loved from the moment the two of you met. Seek counseling if you are unable to mend your differences, hopefully with your loved one. Consequently, if you refuse to acknowledge the hurt or pain, you will take it out on your spouse and your children without acknowledging all the pain built up inside. Instead, give it to God.[586] Remember that resentment only feeds anger. Resentment impairs the sense of understanding, undermines the healing of our hearts, and destroys the working of a gracious God in our lives. Forgiveness is requested, and then forgiveness is granted.

Communicating your concerns is a process of healing. Expressing your hearts to each other is another solution. Attempt, after thoughtful consideration, to connect with her or his heart; connect with the facts, not blame; and connect with a solution. Forgiveness is the key to resolving conflict in marriage. Confront all your conflicts and seek after beneficial results in each that leads to your restoration.

To rebuild the walls of marriage, we have to cry out to God through prayer by speaking honestly and wholeheartedly. First to Him, then to ourselves, and finally to our spouse. We must be willing to commit to healing. We can evaluate the damage *we*, (yes, "we"—remember that the Lord wants us to remove the beam from our own eye first) caused, and then formulate a plan to restore the relationship. Once we have formulated a plan, put this plan into action. Moreover, we have to trust God to bring forth the inevitable solution until it has been completed.[587]

---

[586] Matthew 11:28; 1 Peter 5:7; 2 Corinthians 5:19
[587] www.divorceproof.com or call 1-888-ROSBERG Divorce-proofing America's Marriage.

Begin Day 169:
Benefits for the Mother When she becomes a Parent

Pregnancy is a blessing for happily married couples who want children, especially those with financial resources to raise a family. Anyone who becomes pregnant, or decides to raise a child, needs to understand the enormous psychological and behavioral changes they will face.

One benefit for mothers that breastfeed: it will satisfy the baby's needs for intimacy, touch, interaction, and affection, as well as improve the mother's bond with her child. Also, breastfeeding will help a mother regain her physique, and the uterus will return to its normal size quicker. Breastfed infants are better able to fight infections and diseases, have less constipation and diarrhea, spit up less, and have smaller stools and fewer allergies than bottle-fed babies have. Breastfeeding also increases intelligence and avoids obesity. Breastfeeding is usually done six to twelve times a day.

Begin Day 170:
Choosing a Name for your Child

Parents can choose a name together, or the father or mother may choose a name for the child. Sometimes, a family member will select a name that has meaning, or the child will bear the name of a deceased relative.

In ancient times, names could not be separated from character. Today, we use nicknames to classify someone or a characteristic about a person. Names can bring a certain idea to mind such as Judas, Delilah, Jezebel, Hitler, Billy Graham, Martin Luther, Sadaam Hussein, Martin Luther King Jr., etc. What do people think about your name when they hear it?

Yet, Jesus still changes names. For example, God gave Pharaoh's sister the name for Moses, which means drawn out of the water. The name Jehovah is translated Lord, from YHWH or Yahweh. However, deeply religious Jews feared of violating God's name based on Scripture *Exodus 20:7*, and would not pronounce the sacred name or the primary name for God accurately. So, Jews submitted *Adonai* as God's sacred name. God is concerned about His name.

Conversely, we are to protect the name of our children.[588] Some names can give you power or a reputation. A person's death may be better than the day of birth if the name of that person has merited a lasting reputation and influence. For instance, names were given to both men and women in the Bible to provide a sense of connection to God. Children need definition. If people mispronounced their names or laughed at them, children were forced to defend their names and identities. A name is a 'spoken definition' of who you are and spiritual realm.[589]

Those naming children should be aware of the lasting effect of a name. Lay the foundation by entering a relationship with God, or reconnect with God. God will rename us to redefine our identity. Names also show how much God values us, specific significance, and to obtain a personal sense of value and purpose. Allow our Heavenly Father to name you. Picture your value and quiet those negative voices inside your head.

Several times in the Bible, God changed names to signify a change in calling, appointment, destiny, and even a change in nature.

---

[588] Ecclesiastes 7:1 and Proverbs 22:1
[589] Proverbs 18:21

Begin Day 171:
Determine God's Meaning of Names

My name is very difficult to find on babynames.com and other websites that dig into the meanings of a name. I was having a hard time understanding the meanings I found versus my character. A friend helped me to understand that God makes no mistakes on names, and sometimes the name is in parts. "Adri" in Hebrew means Flock of God.[590] The ending "Enna" means awe, fear, sword, or terror.[591] This is what she told me: "I believe you have your character here, caring for the flock of God with the Fear of the Lord." On another site, there is the spelling of "Adrina," which means 'happiness' derived from Italy.[592]

Most people shorten my name, calling me "Drina." Drina means 'watchful,'[593] however, on another site this name meant 'helper and defender of mankind.'[594] Or know my nickname (also stage name in the 1990s to the early 2000), "Deo." Deo meaning 'godlike, To God,' derived from the Latin phrase, *DEO Optimo Maximo*, meaning, 'To God, the greatest and best.'[595]

Now, you can see how the meaning of names can be determined, and how it translates or refers to a person's personality, characteristics, or behavior. I have come to realize that my name gives me purpose, true value, and an explanation of my characteristics as I have grown older and matured. I cannot wait until I enter the gates of Heaven, and God gives me a *new name* that I am worthy of, and I am clothed in my heavenly body for all eternity. [596]

Ecclesiastes 7:1, NKJV: *"A good name is better than precious ointment, and the day of death than the day of one's birth."*

Abraham's name was changed from Abram, meaning 'exalted father' to the meaning the *father of nations (or 'a multitude')* before he even had children.[597] Jacob, *deceiving one, supplanting one* was changed to *Israel*, which meant *he struggles with God* or *God prevails* because of his changed nature. God transformed Saul, who later was known as the *persecutor of the church* to Paul. There can be a shift in one's calling, functions, duties, and nature.[598]

The Bible renames you when you are born again and allows you to see yourself as God sees you. Your name is a sense of well-being and an accurate opinion of yourself. Allow God to show you just how much you mean to Him and to give you the proper image.

---

[590] http://www.biblical-baby-names.com/meaning-of-adri.html 11.15.2017
[591] http://texasactor.us/meaning-of-the-name/102525/what-does-the-name-enna-mean 11.15. 2017
[592] Babynames.com
[593] http://www.babynamesworld.com, author found name meaning on site 11.15.2007.
[594] http://www.babyhold.com, author found name meaning on site 11.15.2007.
[595] Webster Collegiate Dictionary, abbreviations and meanings.
[596] Revelation 2:7
[597] Genesis 17:4-5
[598] Acts 13:9

Proverbs 22:1, NKJV: *"A good name is to be chosen rather than great riches, loving favor rather than silver and gold."*

The proverb above points out that a reputation has more value than possessions or wealth. A name cannot be replaced easily. Please consider meanings when naming your children. Being aware of the meaning of the name will represent the child's character and allow that name to shape and bring forth life within. Do not let others call you by a different name other than the one that God gave you. Ask them to address you by your surname or the name your parents gave you.

God knew you before the foundation of this world, and He knows your name. When you walk in agreement with Him, your actions naturally correspond with your new identity. It identifies a perception of your behavior. Know your name. Introduce yourself. It is not by accident. God has a divine purpose for you. Remember, we are saved by faith, not by works. God love for us. A name is establishing a relationship with the Lord.[599]

---

[599] Nelson Study Bible, NKJV.

Begin Day 172:
Know your Worth

When a child knows who he or she is, and Whom he or she belongs to, their confidence shines through. They know what their parents will expect from them.

Confidence in God delivers you from needs since you have God, you will no longer think about needing others to make you whole. The object of God's love is each of His earthly creatures, and He loves us even more.[600]

---

[600] Psalm 139:16-17, Matthew 6:26-34

Begin Day 173:
Obedience: Honoring your Guardians (Parents)

Children are to obey their parents. However, if your parents ask you to do something that is opposite of God's commandments, it is best to obey God. Parents are representatives of the Lord.

Remember the *Fifth Commandment*: *Honor your father and your mother,* which is the *first commandment* with a promise. You need to leave things that are undone to honor your parents, which then follows with a reward. The reward or promise is to 'live long upon the earth.' Furthermore, this promise is for 'all children' who obey their parents. Honor increases esteem, value, reverence, respect for one another, and 'love.'

Obey your guardians since you are in the household of your parents, or until you pay your own bills in your own home. Even if you are a child who helps pay bills in your parents' household, does not mean that you have some control or power in the home. You still have to follow your parents' rules and regulations, but you are able to voice your opinion and try to compromise with your parents' wishes.

Begin Day 174:
Children Facing Conflicts & Rivalries

Despite parents' efforts and worries, conflicts between children in a family seem inevitable. Sibling relationships allow both competition and cooperation. Usually, a mixture of loving and fighting eventually creates a strong bond between brothers and sisters. It is not unusual, though parents might say, "They fight so much. I hope they don't kill each other before they grow up." Cain is an example of brotherly rivalries, where the troubling potential became a tragedy.

Primarily, a parent or guardian ought to praise their children daily and certain behaviors that are pleasing or appropriate to their parent(s). In addition, parents should have good communication with their children. Most of all, parents can focus on encouraging words, instead of bashing their children's negative behaviors. Show faith in your children's abilities, to develop their talents or gifts that God has blessed them with.

In contrast, anyone who made a *Corban* vow was required to dedicate money to God's temple.[601] It was a way to neglect parents, even though you are giving money to God and disregarding the care of needy parents. The *Corban* vow allowed children to disobey God's commandment, 'honor your parents.' In other words, they were respected for their earnings and not helping others, as Jesus requires of His followers. If children are excusing themselves from helping because their resources are already dedicated to God, this is also saying that children will not take care of their parents in their old age. Wouldn't you want to raise your children to be responsible adults, so when you get old, they will turn around and love to take care of you for all that you have done for them? This is one fine example of how a religious tradition governed people.

In Proverbs, parents are instructed to train children in the way they should go. The importance of parenthood is to love and nurture your children in the Word of the Lord. Later, out of love and respect, your child will take care of you.

---

[601] Mark 7:11, was the practice of Corban, an offering

Begin Day 175:
Parenting

Psalm 34:11-14, NLT: *"Come, my children, and listen to me, and I will teach you to fear the Lord. Does anyone want to live a life that is long and prosperous? Then keep your tongue from speaking evil and your lips from telling lies! Turn away from evil and do good. Search for peace, and work to maintain it."*[602]

Parents are very busy all day long and family life tends to become busier. As parents, we have to prepare meals, chores, help children with their homework from school, and other extracurricular activities. Parents carry the heaviest load, making sure everyone is clean and ready for the day, fed, and other time constraints.

However, children tend to take their parent(s) for granted by bickering and complaining.[603] Even though your work as a parent is difficult at times, maybe even exhausting and frustrating, God values our great efforts to parenthood.[604] Your parents are holding the family roles, and as a child, you will honor our Lord of the universe.[605]

God also gives the woman a dignified role as helper to her husband.[606] Today, there are many single-parent families, which tend to be more common than married couples are. Many single Christian parents are doing an admirable job of providing their household. But it is ideal for a family to have both parents.

Parents can learn about selfless love from Jesus' words on defiant people in *Matthew 23:27*. Jesus painted a vivid picture of a mother sheltering her young with her wings. Parents may learn from the protective instincts of a mother bird. Just like the mother bird, she will readily put herself at risk to protect her young from harm.[607] We would rather suffer harm than allow any harm to come to our children.

Further, we willingly make daily sacrifices to provide for our own. Many of us will rise early for work, at exhausting and frustrating jobs, to put food on the table, provide suitable shelter, and struggle to make sure our children have clean clothing and adequate education. In addition, we must keep this up day after day, and year after year, until they are able to tend for themselves. Even sometimes, when they are able to spread their own wings, we are still there when they need us most. Self-sacrifice and endurance please our Heavenly Father.[608]

---

[602] Also can refer to Psalm 34:11-22, on teaching your children from right and wrong
[603] Proverbs 22:15
[604] Ephesians 3:14, 15
[605] 1 Corinthians 10:31
[606] Genesis 2:18; Proverbs 31:13, 14, 16
[607] Proverbs 30:24
[608] Hebrews 13:16

Begin Day 176:
Faith needed in the Household

Paul further talks about how faith is required in the household.[609] He is referring to the family head, usually the father. In this Scripture, he was also speaking directly about the material needs of the family. In today's world, the head of the household will face many obstacles. Economic hardship can consist of layoffs, high unemployment rates, and the rising costs of living.

Moreover, a provider does well to remember that he or she is carrying out an assignment from God. Paul's inspired words give us hope in obeying God's commandments, if we refuse to abide by them, we have disowned the faith. However, many people today have 'no natural affection' by which they can work to build their family's faith.[610]

---

[609] 1 Timothy 5:8
[610] 2 Timothy 3:1, 3

Begin Day 177:
Fathers

Children should respect both parents. Some parents inform the children that they are co-parenting or co-parents. But throughout Scriptures, it points out that the father is taking the lead. *Father,* also known as husband, has the responsibility of being head and priest of the household.[611] The father represents Christ in his home, just like Christ is the head of the church. Husbands love your wives, just as Christ also loved the church.

Christ gave Himself for us (church) so that He might sanctify and cleanse us with the washing of the water of His Word. Also, Christ can present Himself a glorious church, not having spot or wrinkle, but that we are to be holy and without a blemish. Therefore, husbands ought to love their own bodies. He who loves his wife loves himself,[612] and will treat her individuality with the utmost respect. The husband is to lead his family sacrificially.

> *"Christ's rule is one of wisdom and love. When husbands fulfill their obligation to their wives, they will use their authority with the same tenderness as Christ uses toward the church. When the Spirit of Christ controls the husband, the wife's subjection will require from her to obey and honor her husband, and in the same way that Christ requires submission from the church...Husbands are to study the words of Christ on how he may have the mind of Christ. Then, he will become purified, refined, and fit to be the lord of his household."*[613]

The wise father spends time with his children. A child may learn many lessons from the father such as the love for God, the importance of prayer, love for other people, modesty, love for nature, and things God has made. If the father is never home, the child is deprived of this privilege and joy, and which is forced on the mother to try to take on the father's role as well as her own.

The Bible urges fathers to avoid exasperating their children that they do not become downhearted.[614] Fathers who are reluctant to express their feelings can look at God's example. Children draw much strength and courage from their parents' honest expressions of love and approval. Indeed, countless fathers shirk their responsibility, leaving their family in a lurch.

---

[611] Colossians 3:18-21; 1 Peter 3:1-8
[612] Ephesians 5:28
[613] Seventh-Day Adventist..., paraphrased by author
[614] Colossians 3:21

Begin Day 178:
Mothers

Motherhood is the closest thing on earth to being in partnership with God. Somebody in the family must bear the ultimate responsibility for the character of the children. Child training cannot be delegated to others, for no one feels quite the same about a child, as its parents do.

God created the mother with the ability to carry the child within her own body, to suckle the child, and to nurture and love it. However, extenuating circumstances of severe financial burdens or being a single parent, causes some mothers to be verbally and/or physically abusive to their children, instead of nurturing in love.

Today, both parents are working, even though the mother is supposed to be in the home to raise her children. However, most mothers are challenged to be a nurturer, express love to the children, and secure her finances in the household. Children are her priority besides her mate. Mothers have to balance work, playtime if any, children, husbands, and finances.

Paul, in 1 Corinthians 11: 2-16, writes of the roles of a woman in a marriage and worship. I suggest picking up *Excellent Wife: Biblical Perspective* by Martha Peace. This book is extremely helpful for single women thinking about marriage and even better for those who are married.

Begin Day 179:
Head of the Household

"The head of woman is man." The *head* is not used to show control or supremacy, but to lead her as Christ leads the Church. Because man was created first, the woman derives her existence from man, as man does from Christ and Christ from God.

Submission is a key element in the smooth functioning of any business, government, or family. God ordained submission in certain relationships to prevent chaos. Submission is not surrender, withdrawal, or apathy. It does not mean inferiority because God created all people in His image and because all have equal value. *Submission* is mutual commitment and cooperation.

God did not make man superior; He made a way for man and woman to work together. Jesus Christ, equal to God, the Father, submitted to God to carry out the plan for salvation. Just as Christ and God are equally divine, men and women are equal beings. Just as Jesus had to carry out different roles from the Heavenly Father, men and women have to share different roles.

Submission is by choice not force. Submission is not inferiority, but subordination. We serve God in these relationships by willingly submitting to others in our church, to our spouses, and to our government leaders.[615]

In the beginning, the first man did not come from a woman but created by the dust of the earth. He was molded by the hands of YHWH, our Creator. But woman came from man (Adam's rib): which is where the concept of 'helper' derives from and can be found in *Genesis 2:20*. This does not mean the woman is inferior to the man. It refers only to the purposes of God for man and woman in the creative order.[616] God created the lines of authority, for His created world to function smoothly. In the lines of authority, even in marriage, there should not be lines of superiority.

God created man and woman with unique and complementary characteristics. In other words, one sex is not better than the other is. We must not let the issue of authority and submission become a wedge to destroy oneness in marriage. We are to use our unique gifts to strengthen our marriages and to glorify the Lord.

---

[615] 1 Corinthians 11:3
[616] 1 Corinthians 11:7-9

Begin Day 180:
Cultural Differences

In many cultures, long hair on men is appropriate and masculine. In Corinth, it was a sign of male prostitution in the heathen temples. Women with short hair were labeled prostitutes. Paul was referring to the Corinthian culture, meaning that Christian women should keep their hair long, if short, would be hard to be a believable witness for Jesus Christ. Paul was not saying to accept all practices of the culture, but avoid appearances and behavior that detract from our goal of being believable witnesses for Jesus Christ, while demonstrating our faith.

Begin Day 181:
Conduct

There are proper attitudes and conduct in worship, including in marriage relationships, or the role of women in the church. Specific instructions are timeless, like respect for spouse, reverence, and appropriateness in worship and, focusing all of your life on God. If anything you do easily offends members and divide the church, then change your ways to promote church unity.

For example, Paul told the women who were not wearing a head covering to wear them, not because it was a scriptural command, but to keep the congregation from dividing over a petty issue that served only to take people's minds off Christ.[617]

Family heads may also find it helpful to contemplate Jesus' perfect example. Jesus is our *Eternal Father*.[618] Jesus is metaphorically signified as the last Adam, as the father that mankind who exercised faith.[619] Unlike Adam, who turned out to be a selfish, self-serving father, Jesus is the ideal father. The Bible speaks about Jesus in John 3:16. Jesus willingly offered up His own life for others. He also, on a day-to-day basis, put the needs of others ahead of His own.

---

[617] 1 Corinthians 11:2-16; 1 Peter 3:17
[618] Isaiah 9:6, 7
[619] 1 Corinthians 15:45

Begin Day 182:
Children's Spirituality

Jesus even speaks about providing for our children on a spiritual level.[620] What can parents do to teach their children about Jesus and the commandments?[621] Parents are first to cultivate their own spirituality, building their love for God, and taking His words to heart. We are students of God's Word, to develop a real understanding of and love for God's ways, principles, and laws. Our hearts will be full of fascinating Bible truths that will move you to feel joy and love for God. You can provide and will have an abundance of good things to impart to your children.[622] Spiritually strong parents are prepared to apply the counsel and to inculcate God's Words in their offspring at every opportunity.[623]

To *inculcate* means to teach and impress by the means of repetition. For example, when Jesus taught His disciples to be humble, instead of proud and competitive, He found various ways to repeat the same principle. He taught reasoning by illustrating, even demonstrating to those who were willing to listen.[624] Jesus never showed impatience. Therefore, parents need to find ways to teach basic truths to their children, patiently repeating Jesus' principles until the children absorb and apply to their lives.

Furthermore, Deuteronomy 6:7 shows, there are many occasions when parents can discuss spiritual things with their children. Whether traveling together, doing chores together, relaxing together, you may find opportunities to provide your children's spiritual needs. A regular, happy family Bible study is a mainstay of family spirituality. Try to keep your family conversations focused on a positive tone to build one's spiritual man or woman. Parents, engaging in conversations with your child(ren) will meet his or her spiritual need.

Parents also provide for their children's spiritual needs when praying. Jesus taught His disciples how to pray, and He prayed with them on many occasions.[625] They learned by joining in prayer with God's own Son. Children can learn a lot from your prayers. God wants us to speak to Him freely from the heart, approaching Him with any concern that we might have. Your prayers can help your children to learn a vital spiritual truth. They can have a relationship with their Heavenly Father.[626]

Children can also effectively share their faith with peers. These discussions develop greater interest in sharing what they are learning about Jesus. They may also see the ministry as happy and interesting work, producing great satisfaction and joy.[627] Through examples, your

---

[620] Matthew 4:4; 5:3
[621] Deuteronomy 6:5-7
[622] Luke 6:45
[623] Deuteronomy 6:7
[624] Matthew 18:1-4; 20:25-27; John 13:12-15
[625] Luke 11:1-13
[626] 1 Peter 5:7
[627] Acts 20:35

children are learning obedience: 'training a child in the way he or she should go, and when he or she is old, he or she will not depart from it.'[628]

---

[628] Proverbs 22:6

Begin Day 183:
Parent's Commitment

Other than a commitment to the Lord and their spouses, parents have no higher responsibility than to the children that they have brought into the world. Put their children's interests before their own advancement and comfort, for children did not choose to come into the world, and we are to give them the best start in life. Moreover, a parent's love is unconditional and sacrificial.

Children that demonstrate agape love will establish a positive self-image and emotional health throughout life. Children who have to win love, or who feel rejected and unimportant, will try to obtain their parents' love through undesirable behaviors that become ingrained and habitual. Children who are secure in their parents' love will reach out to others and teach how to glorify the Lord.

Christian parents are to dedicate their children to God's service at the earliest possible moment of life. In this service, the parents also dedicate themselves to educate the child in the way of the Lord, so that the image of God will be formed in the child. To reach this goal, parents will bring their children to church and religious school. Consistency with spiritual teaching from the parents is a continuing process that enters every phase of the child's life. Knowing God as a loving parent is vital to the children's Christian growth. Also, parents are to teach morals, guidance, education, and learn how to adapt to their environment.

Discipline implies far more than punishment. *Discipline* is a process in which the child is apprenticed to the parent for training, guidance, and teaching important principles such as loyalty, truth, equity, consistency, patience, order, mercy, generosity, and work.

Most language development is developed through socialization, which is when children learn the basic skills within their society. The language used in our homes and in schools needs careful monitoring since our children pick up the words we use, building up their vocabulary. Moreover, we need to control our tongues since it is like a sword and can verbally destroy the self-esteem of others. Our communication, or words spoken, can reveal our godly character. Children that hear frequent joyous and spontaneous expression of affection among family members will learn to praise to God.

Adults can teach them the beauty of their developing sexuality through correct and appropriate information. It is parents' responsibility to protect their children from sexual abuse.

Begin Day 184:
Children's Emotional Needs

Children also have emotional needs. God's Word tells parents how important it is to provide for them and to help them grow mentally sound.[629] It is sensible to show a child love, which teaches a child to love and brings lifelong benefits.

In contrast, a failure to show a child love is senseless. It causes great pain and represents a failure to imitate God, who shows us immense love, despite our imperfections.[630] *1 John 4:19* says, "He first loved us."

Take this initiative to build a loving bond with your children. A child learns the family's values and religious concepts from their parents or elders, so we need to be consistent. Since the family is the very soul of the church and society, Christian families responding to His call will build strong churches that reveal real Christianity. The churches made up of those families will grow, where their young people will not leave, and they will portray to the world a clear picture of God.

---

[629] Titus 2:4
[630] Psalm 103:8-14

Begin Day 185:
Modeling Behaviors

God created our children for His purpose, not for ours. In *Psalm 127:3-5*, children are a heritage in which defines children as God's gifts.[631] In ancient times, having many children was a symbol of strength (like arrows). Usually, the hands of children increased the productivity of the farmer. A full quiver was a mark of God's blessing. The blessing of a home in ancient times gave a person a measure of pride in the community.

However, children want to please their parents, but controlling parents make rebellious children. Parents should not be overly rigid with their children. Our children model their parents. We need to give them more time to grow and decide what they want to be when they are mature. If your child has not learned what you knew, then give them some more time and you will be surprised what God will teach them. We cannot make our children love God or do right; we can correct them. Avoid controlling them that can only be led by the Holy Spirit.

God has given us relationships with our children and/or husband for enjoyment, not for torment. Abundant life is to be content in the Lord. Do not look for the wrong in them, be encouraging and positive, look for the good in your children and magnify them. Do not focus on the negativity and harbor over it.

Overall, *parental love* is more than just mere words. Love is expressed primarily in action. Providing materially and spiritually is an expression of parental love, especially if love is the primary motivation. Additionally, discipline is a vital expression of parental love.[632]

In contrast, a failure to discipline is an expression of parental hatred.[633] Such balance is not always easy for imperfect parents to find. It is worth your every effort to strive for that balance. Firm, living discipline helps a child grow up to live a happy, productive life.[634]

When you do the important work God has assigned you as parents, which includes providing for your children's material, spiritual, and emotional needs, the rewards are great. Children are the best opportunity to 'choose life,' and thereafter, to 'keep alive.'[635] Those children who choose to serve God and stay on the path to life as they mature, bring their parents tremendous joy.[636] Unspeakable joy will last forever.

---

[631] Psalm 128:3
[632] Hebrews 12:6
[633] Proverbs 13:24, Jeremiah 46:28
[634] Proverbs 22:6
[635] Deuteronomy 30:19
[636] Psalm 127:3-5

Begin Day 186:
Obeying the Word

Joshua was a leader for thirty years. He led the nation by obeying God's Word. He meditated day and night on God's Word so that he would be successful in all things. This is what we need to do as parents, leaders, counselors, mentors, families, and communities if children are to live a life in obedience to God.

Joshua ruled a nation, raised his family, and ran an army. He led his home life to serve the Lord. Therefore, a father's responsibility is to teach his family the 'Word of God.' By setting examples, this will cause our children to emulate us unconsciously.

Joshua also spent time with the Lord, as we need to spend time with the Lord and raise and minister to our families. Families from generation to generation need to 'break the cycle,' not allowing demonic forces to take over our family happiness.

Has God shown you how to break the cycle from drug abuse, alcoholism, abusive relationships, etc.? Forgiveness is the key to getting over these hardships and demonic spiritual forces, which leaves no animosity or hostility.

Begin Day 187:
Satan's Plan

How did Satan wreck the first home? Adam and Eve sinned by disobedience to God. The first person God addressed after they heard God's voice and hid was 'Adam' (man). He was the leader of the household. Today, however, children are growing up in a single parent home where the mother is the leader of the household. In some households, the mother is the "boss" as you may have seen on the Yoplait commercial, where the father tells the daughter to go back to bed and wondering why she is up at this hour. She tells the father that she is getting a midnight snack and mom said it was okay. The father then tells her to put it back and go to bed. But she refuses because she says that mom is the "boss." Then he disagrees and tells his daughter that he is the "boss." The daughter flatly responds, "No you are not. Mom is the boss." He then comes to a compromising position and responds, "We are co-bosses." The daughter still argues, "No. Mom is the boss." He eventually gives in and eats the Yoplait yogurt with his daughter. Mom wins without being present. And some men are not present in their child's lives, where the mother is the boss. This is Satan's plan to divide the family roles, responsibilities, and headship.

There is a saying: 'You have not chosen me, I have chosen you.' In other words, God will choose us.[637] We may not choose our paths, or know our direction, or even choose God but He will definitely choose us for what He has divinely created us to become.

These are the tactics that Satan's uses: 5 D's are Doubt, Discouragement, Diversion, Defeat, and Delay. Review the chart for clarification.

Doubt	Makes you question God's Word
Discouragement	Makes you look at your problems rather than at God
Diversion	Makes the wrong things seem attractive so that you will want them more than the right things
Defeat	Makes you feel like a failure so that you don't even try
Delay	Makes you put off doing something so that it never gets done

Jesus paid for our sins on the Cross: suffered, been humiliated, and showed that nothing is too much.[638] Moreover, Pastor Malone mentions that people are blaming God when it is all about 'learning the lesson of our lives.' We are put through a test. Once we pass the test, we are to move on, and not faint over the suffering and pain we experienced through this trial. We are not to live or stay in the past.[639] Also, believers are to endure the chastening of the Lord.[640]

---

[637] Pastor Julius Malone sermon on *All Things That Created Are For God's Purpose*, June 6, 1998.
[638] Mark 10:17-32; Acts 4:12; John 14:6
[639] 1 Peter 4:12; 1 Peter 5:10
[640] Ephesians 3:11, 13, 16-21; 2 Corinthians 4:16; 2 Timothy 4:5; James 1:12; Jeremiah 29:11, 16; Isaiah 43:1, 2

Begin Day 188:
Chastening

Our elders, guardians and/or parents, can do the chastening. *Chastening* is teaching, educating, disciplining, and a learning process. Enough is enough. The purpose of chastening of the Lord is that believers are to be a part of God's holiness; to live in the Spirit; and to be children of the Lord, and not of Satan.[641]

---

[641] Pastor Julius Malone sermon: *All Are Created By God, But Not All Children Of God,* August 2, 1998.

Begin Day 189:
Keeping the Romance Alive

Most marriages fall apart when partners have not developed godly qualities such as the ability to love your mate, to serve, and the willingness to make sacrifices. God bestowed these qualities on you the moment you say 'I do.' You are able to develop these qualities by having a close relationship with God. His love flows through you once you are 'born-again.'

Men and women differ in many areas, like the usage of offensive words, and their views on sexuality. Men are more quickly aroused and satisfied sexually than their wives. In the book, *Love is a Decision* by Gary Smalley and John Trent, it says that men are fully enjoying the sexual experience, but a man should desire to meet a woman's emotional needs too. At times, men are stimulated and aroused by what they see (physical attraction), of which causes his manhood to stiffen. They may not be sensitive to a woman's feelings and emotions, just ready to meet their own sexual needs, instead of focusing on her needs. Usually, a woman longs to be kissed, sensual touching, and some form of foreplay to get her sexually aroused before his manhood enters inside of her.

Wives, do not minimize your husband's need for physical expression of sexual intimacy, even when he is slow to meet your emotional and relational needs. Try to open up to him, entice him, and show him what you want to be done in the bedroom. If he is not listening to your gentle words, or body language on how you desire to be aroused, most women will retaliate by using harsh words and bad-mouthing their mate. This can make him think that he is unable to please you, unable to meet your fantasies and wildest desires, and most of all, that he is unable to satisfy you. He wants to be all the man who you desire, and to please you sexually, financially, mentally, and emotionally. Women, please respect that some men are not as emotional and sensitive to meet your needs, but try to find other avenues to reach him.

According to **His Needs Her Needs** by William Harley, Jr., he says that the man's five most basic needs in marriage tend to be (1) Sexual fulfillment, (2) Recreational companionship, (3) Attractive spouse, (4) Domestic support, and (5) Admiration. The woman's five most basic needs in marriage tend to be (1) Affection, (2) Conversation, (3) Honesty and openness, (4) Financial support, and (5) Family commitment. In the book, *The Five Love Languages*, love is expressed by (1) Words of affirmation, (2) Quality time, (3) Receiving gifts, (4) Acts of service, and (5) Physical touch.

Marriage requires other ingredients to grow and thrive, like freedom and responsibility.[642] It is about promoting the relationship as a loving couple by learning your partner's good and bad behaviors and characteristics to avoid conflict. It is not about fixing, changing, or punishing your mate.

---

[642] 1 John 4:18

Begin Day 190:
Intimacy Lost

If intimacy is lost then so is love. Love and truth must exist together for the relationship to last. However, most couples are in denial and deny that the intimacy is gone. Instead, they turn to someone else or something else for comfort and intimacy. When they should be able to confront their partner and truthfully tell how they truly feel. You can open up with one another about anything. Usually, impure hearts will cause impure thoughts that eventually will cause this person to act these feelings out.

Overall, successful marriages follow God's principles and God's design for marriage. Ironically, if we focus on God's principles instead of pleasure, we end up having a very satisfying and pleasant marriage.[643]

---

[643] http://www.polynate.net/books/courtship/part1.html

Begin Day 192:
Responsibility

God gave Adam and Eve the responsibility to meet the needs of the earth, animals, and themselves. God empowered them to have the life all of us desire—one filled with love, beautiful surroundings, and many opportunities to use our abilities, talents, and spiritual gifts.

God also gave them the ability and opportunity to make the life they chose.[644] We need to take responsibility for our hearts, our love, our time, and our talents. We are to own our lives and live in God's light, growing up, and maturing of our character along the way.[645] We have to take the responsibility for growing our marriages. We are completely responsible to God for developing our souls—responsible for half of the marriage and all our soul, so, with God's help, set boundaries for yourself.[646]

Spouses must take full responsibility for their actions, and what is spoken that can make the relationship go sour.[647] Some things to look at in the relationship, when taking full responsibility:

Feelings	Choices
Thoughts	Love
Attitude	Behaviors
Desires	Limits
Talents/Gifts	Values

---

[644] Cloud, *Boundaries on Marriage, p.* 22.
[645] Ephesians 4:15
[646] Cloud, *Boundaries on Marriage,* pp. 64, 66.
[647] Cloud, *Boundaries in Marriage,* pp. 9, 11.

Begin Day 193:
See Your Mate in Heaven?

Some may ask, "Will I see my mate in Heaven? Will I still be married?" We do not need to be afraid of eternal life.[648] However, we can concentrate on our relationship with Christ right now because, in the New Kingdom, we will be with Him. If we learn to love and trust Christ now, we will not be afraid of what He has in store for us then. Jesus' statement does not mean that people will not recognize their partners in the coming kingdom. It simply means that God's new order will not be an extension of this life and that the same physical and natural rules will not apply. In other words, we will not be married once we go to heaven.

Jesus' response to the Sadducees' was His final word on marriage in heaven. Jesus did not want to fall into their trap. Therefore, sidestepping their question about the much-married woman, Jesus gave a definite answer to their question about resurrection. The Sadducees' real question was not about marriage, but about the doctrine of the resurrection. The Sadducees were an elite group of religious leaders, who denied the existence of angels, the immorality of the soul, and the resurrection. God's covenant with all people exists beyond death.

---

[648] Mark 12:18-25

Begin Day 194:
Bring God to the Workplace

First, those of us that have jobs, whether it is one, two or even three, we tend to forget who gave us the job in the first place. Second, we tend to complain about our boss, staff, employees or co-workers, and other issues relative to the job itself. Lastly, we need to ask ourselves, do we take God to the workplace? Do we pray and thank God for this job?

By the work of our hands, labor, and dedication, we are able to value our accomplishments, promotions, and salary increases. Also, your work glorifies the Lord, which depends on your choice of profession and whether you are sharing the gospel with others at your workplace.[649] It is a divine blessing to have a job.

In Proverbs 14:23 shows that all labor includes a profit. However, useless chatter only leads to poverty. *Useless chatter* is usually someone that talks about doing things, working on projects, and bragging about entrepreneurship. However, not seeking a position or employment opportunities leads to poverty. Furthermore, one can end up homeless because of only speaking about working, but not bringing any money in the household.

---

[649] Psalm 90:17, also can see Job 14:15, NKJV

Begin Day 195:
Laziness

In Proverbs 20:4, it speaks about laziness (*sluggard*). If you are a *sluggard*, you will not have anything to harvest. In other words, any money to replenish in the home is to pay bills and take care of the family, but if you are lazy, you may not seek work at all.[650] However, sometimes when we are fired from our jobs or laid off, we try so hard to find another job that pays more. After a month or two passes, even several months to years, we tend to get lazy. We pray. We hope. Moreover, we try, but we tend to give up and become lazy to the point that we no longer look for work. We give up on ourselves. We become sluggish, no enthusiasm when searching for a job, which causes us not to be able to pay the bills.[651]

Paul explains how others worked hard, buying what they needed, rather than becoming a burden to any of the believers. If we do not work, we will not eat. There is a difference between leisure and laziness.

Relaxation and recreation can be balanced throughout our weeks, but when it is time to work. Believers should work. We must make the most of our talent and time, doing all we can to provide for our dependents and ourselves.[652]

Furthermore, 2 Thessalonians 3:6-10 speaks against idleness or laziness and those who do not want to work.

2 Thessalonians 3:6-10, NLT: *"And now, dear brothers and sisters, we give you this command in the name of our Lord Jesus Christ: Stay away from all believers who live idle lives and don't follow the tradition they received from us. For you know that you ought to imitate us. We were not idle when we were with you. We never accepted food from anyone without paying for it. We worked hard day and night so we would not be a burden to any of you. We certainly had the right to ask you to feed us, but we wanted to give you an example to follow. Even while we were with you, we gave you this command: "Those unwilling to work will not get to eat."*

---

[650] also see Nehemiah 3:5
[651] Also refer to 2 Thessalonians 3:7-10
[652] Life Application Study Bible, NKJV.

Begin Day 196:
Diligence

The Bible speaks of laziness versus diligence. Minister Moore focuses on the Scriptures from Proverbs 30:24-31. *Nelson Study Bible* points out that these Scriptures refer to one's behavior. Each of these small creatures has a behavioral trait from which wise people can learn. *Life Application Bible* points out that these Scriptures demonstrates how the ant teaches us about preparation; badgers about wise building; locusts about cooperation and order; and spiders about fearlessness. Minister Morgan stated a vital part of wise living is by the work of our hands.[653] To serve God, it requires work on our part. There are two kinds of people: diligent and lazy. Which one are you?

---

[653] Minister Moore, *Changing Your World Ministries*, July 31, 2005.

Begin Day 197:
Behaviors of the Animals (Proverbs 30)

There are four behaviors or characteristics that each animal demonstrated in Proverbs 30:24-31, which shows us how we can be diligent workers to God:[654]

1. *Preparation:* We are busy doing our Father's business, just as the ants are prepared to gather food during the hot months since they will hibernate during cold. We are to be prepared to do God's will at any cost.
2. *Wise Builders*: Badgers are wise and able to protect themselves from their enemies. God can instill wisdom in us when we obey His Word and comprehend what He has set us to do. Whether it is ministry, evangelism or to serve others, let us have open ears and willing to carry the task God has placed on our hearts. We are not to have 'deaf ears.' Believers of Christ are set out to speak the Word to others who are lost and dead to God's existence.
3. *Cooperation and Order:* Locusts are leaders, even without a leader in charge. We have to be self-starters and go out to preach God's Word, even if others are not standing behind and helping us in our walk. Your calling may not be preaching, but our Heavenly Father will bless you with such gifts to get His message across. In addition, if your pastor is visiting other churches, it does not mean that you need to leave and wait for your pastor's return. Members can still go to church and receive God's message.
4. *Fearlessness:* Spiders are known to be in the king's palace and the owner of his own place. He does not show any fear of this occupancy. We need to believe and trust in the Lord to spread His word to each person and not fear such an outcome. Satan may fill your mind with doubt and fear, but you can overcome by trusting in God, just like Moses trusted in God when he was to deliver Israelites from slavery. He was afraid or feared for what was to come, a place he once knew and lived a life in luxury, but now has to go to Egypt to set his Hebrew people free. God assured Moses by saying, "I am the one that gave you the mouth to speak." When asked who God was, He replies, "I am who I am." Therefore, we can do it…no matter what it appears to look like, and imagine how God can move and change a person's life in an instant.

---

[654] Minister Moore, *Changing Your World Ministries*, July 31, 2005, emphasis added by author.

Begin Day 198:
Reap What You Sow

Remember what we sow, we will reap. This is the season for sowing and reaping. How do you think we make the wrong turn? To make the wrong turn is by allowing the fleshly desires take over us, even if God showed us the right way. God spoke to me through a dream about taking the wrong or right turns in our spiritual walk.

At the Woman-to-Woman conference in Milwaukee, WI, I gave my testimony. My dream can be titled, "Which Path Are You Taking?"

I was wandering down this unfamiliar road, where others were pacing back and forth. Then, I noticed traffic on a busy street, while I was walking on a sidewalk near a bridge and water below. Suddenly, there was a fork in the walkway, and decided that I might get to my destination quicker if I make a 'right turn.' After making a right turn, I see a couple of people ahead of me, laughing and appearing friendly, but we do not speak. Overhead, I see green pastures, plentiful homes next to each other, and a beautiful place. I wonder why I have never seen this roadway before. Before traveling further ahead, I stopped and was afraid maybe I am going the wrong way and would end up lost. However, I wavered back and forth, one foot forward and the other foot back to my previous destination. Finally, I decide to go back.

The meaning of this dream can take many forms. What path are you taking? Will you make the right turn or many wrong turns in your life? Will you turn back or stay forward on your journey? There is a narrow road, which few will take or follow. On the other hand, there is the wide road, which many will take. Today, we live in a society where we focus on what our peers or what the crowd is doing. We get lost in a mindset of worldly ways and thoughts, to think it is okay to do it. Just do it. Do what makes you feel good, will cause you to lose sight of God's path. In God's path, we are promised to live a life in abundance, peace, and obedience.

Earlier I mentioned that I started a path, wandering, and wondering what I will do, and where I will go. There are so many twists and turns, undecided in decision-making and no sense of direction. God says, if we follow His path in a life of obedience to do His will, we will see a life of green pastures, still waters, and abundance. Instead, I hesitated like most of us do and turned back in the dream. Don't turn back from the path God has you on to fulfill your dreams, visions, and the final road of your journey. Will you take the detour?

Sometimes, we can find ourselves in a heap of debt, seeking for debt counseling, or other means to pay our debts. No matter how long or how hard the situation is, God will open or close the doors for His children. He knows the job for you, if you believe and continue to pray to Him. I am a witness to how you can be at your lowest, and how God can bless you. I was out of work for ten to eleven months because of my supervisor jealous spirit after completing a master's degree, thinking I would take her position. At the time, I had a volunteer position and part-time job, of which barely paid the bills. I continued to look for work and started to become sluggish, not wanting to look for a job. I felt I had all these qualifications and degrees, but could not find a decent paying job with benefits. I did not give up on praying and trusting in God with other family members and friends praying too. If He had something else for me, I would be waiting with open ears to what He felt He had for me. The Lord told me that I would be blessed three-fold.

Although, I was down and out, bills steady on my mind. I used all my savings, took out a second loan, and suddenly my Chevy Metro car engine was blown. I prayed and cried, and then the heavens opened a blessing for me. My grandmother, Maxine Battle, was praying and then God spoke to her heart. He told her that I would see change within two weeks and God sticks to what He promises. I am blessed that people trusted and believed in God as much as I did. I know that God has a better plan for me. Later, God spoke to my heart, saying counseling. I continued to pray by asking God for insight. Finally, I was able to understand what God was trying to tell me. I thought that I would seek a doctoral degree in Psychology and understood why I was not getting accepted into the Ph.D. Counseling Psychology program. One night, God woke me up from my sleep to look in a Thesaurus on the term *counsel*. It was a breakthrough for me, where I realized that my true calling is to become an attorney. This was my original plan after completing my master's degree until I was unemployed for over ten months. Now, I am allowing God to move me into a challenging and competitive degree, and pray for financial stability before seeking this career path. God also promised me that I would be financially secure by staying in His will for my life.

Begin Day 199:
Work that Counts

Because our days are numbered, we want our work to count, or "to be effective and productive." [655] We desire to see God's eternal plan revealed now and for our work to reflect His permanence. If we feel dissatisfied with this life and all its imperfections, remember our desire to see our work established is placed there by God.[656] However, our desire can only be satisfied in eternity. Until then, we must apply ourselves to loving and serving God.[657]

Ecclesiastes 3:13, NLT: *"And people should eat and drink and enjoy the fruits of their labor, for these are gifts from God."*

Your ability to find satisfaction in your work depends on your attitude. You will become dissatisfied if you lose the sense of purpose God intended for your work. We can enjoy our work if we remember that God has given us *work* to do,[658] and the *fruit of our labor* is a gift from Him.

---

[655] see Psalm 104:23
[656] Ecclesiastes 3:11
[657] Life Application Study Bible, NKJV, 1996.
[658] See Ecclesiastes 3:10

Begin Day 200:
Labor Too Much

Review your labor like God does by finding a way to serve God.[659] Psalm 127 states, *Unless the Lord builds the house, the builder builds in vain.* The psalmist asserts here that life lived apart from God is not worth living. Even *building a house* is useless if the Lord is not in the process. The phrase *bread of sorrows* captures the essence of those of which removed a sense of the Lord in their lives. The food they earn should give them strength for life and a zest for living, instead of being in their miserable state.

In Nehemiah 6:15, the job was too big, and the problems were too great. Nevertheless, God's men and women joined for special tasks, solved huge problems, and accomplished great things. Do not let the size of a task, or the length of time needed to accomplish it, keep you from doing it.

God has *put eternity* in our hearts. This means that we can never be completely satisfied with earthly pleasures and pursuits. Because we are created in God's image, we have a spiritual thirst, and we have eternal value, and nothing but the eternal God can truly satisfy us. God has built in us a restless yearning for the perfect world that can only be found in His perfect rule. He has given us a glimpse of the perfection of His creation. However, it is only a glimpse since we cannot see into the future, or comprehend everything unless God reveals Himself through a vision or speaks to us in a dream. Therefore, we must proceed with His *work* on earth.

---

[659] Psalm 127:2

Begin Day 201:
Gossiping instead of Working

We do not want to be gossipers or busybodies.[660] The *Life Application Study Bible* states that a *busybody* is someone who gossips. An *idle person*, who does not work, ends up filling his or her time with less than helpful activities, like gossip. Rumors and hearsay are tantalizing and exciting to hear and make us feel like insiders. Conversely, they tear people down. If you often find your nose in other people's business, you may be unemployed.

---

[660] 2 Thessalonians 3:11-12

Begin Day 202:
Work on the Sabbath

Some religions forbid their followers from working on the Sabbath.[661] Exodus 16:23 shows that the Israelites were not to work on the Sabbath, not even to cook. You may be asking yourself why. God knows that the busy routine of daily living could distract people from worshipping Him. It is so easy to let work and family responsibilities, even recreation, to crowd our schedules that we do not take time to worship the Lord. Carefully guard your time with the Lord.

Check with your place of work for religious observance permission to request off from Friday sundown to Saturday sundown for Sabbath-observance. While Jesus said the Sabbath was made for man and not man for the Sabbath, we need our rest. God began the day at sundown, so, each day, we rest for the day ahead, not from the day behind. On the Sabbath, we rest for the week ahead. We need Him in our lives, and to rest is to reflect on His goodness for us, and worship Him. The purpose of Sabbath is to worship in the Lord and to give our Heavenly Father praise. We are not to cook, only heat up food, and not to buy or sell on the Sabbath day to glorify the Lord.

---

[661] Jeremiah 17:21-27

Begin Day 203:
Double Workload

In Exodus 5:6-18, we learn how the Israelites had a double workload. To punish Moses and Aaron for their perceived insolence, Pharaoh imposed severe measures on the Hebrew workers, who needed straw to strengthen the sun-dried bricks they were making. With no reduction in their daily quota, the people had to gather straw during their off-hours. Until that time, the Egyptians had provided it for them. Pharaoh felt that they had too much time on their hands—*free time*.[662] Hebrew leaders of the work gangs, as subordinate officials, complained about the new work rules. Pharaoh repeated his excuse that the people were idle and ordered them to continue. Hebrew crew chiefs were in a more precarious position than ever. Instead, they turned all their anger and complaints from Pharaoh and placed them on Moses and Aaron. *Let the Lord look on you and judge* is a harsh curse. They felt that Moses and Aaron's words to Pharaoh were futile and only hated them more. The word translated *abhorrent* means 'to cause to stink.'[663]

Just as Pharaoh increased the workload of the Hebrews, you may think that your workload has increased and you expect results. When God is at work in any situation, suffering, setbacks, and hardship still occur.

In James 1:2-4, we are encouraged to be happy when difficulties come our way. Problems develop our patience and character by teaching us to: trust God to do what is best for us; look for opportunities to honor God in our present situation; remember that God will not abandon us; and watch for God's plan in us.[664]

Perhaps you've felt caught in the middle at work, or in relationships with your family or church. Complaining or turning on the leadership does not solve the problem. For the Hebrews, God had a larger purpose in mind. So rather than turning on the leadership when you feel pressured by both sides, turn to God to see what else He might be doing in this situation.[665]

---

[662] Nelson Study Bible, NKJV.
[663] Nelson Study Bible, NKJV.
[664] Life Application Study Bible, NKJV, 1996.
[665] Life Application Study Bible, NKJV, 1996.

Begin Day 204:
Hard Work Pays

Another story of hard work is found in Ecclesiastes 2:18-23. Solomon emphasizes throughout that hard work bears no lasting fruit for those who work solely to earn money and gain possessions. Even though your possessions may be well cared for, all that was gained may be lost. Hard work done with proper motives such as caring for family and serving God is not wrong. We must work to survive. Moreover, we are responsible for the physical and spiritual well-being of those under our care. However, the fruit of hard work done to glorify only us will be passed on to those who may later lose or spoil it all. Such toil often leads to grief, while serving God leads to everlasting joy.

"Be strong and courageous, and do the work." [666] Judah's people had returned to worshipping God, in which God had promised to bless their efforts. However, it was time for them to work. We are people of prayer, Bible study, and worship, but eventually, we must get out and do what God has in mind for us. He wants to change the world through us. God has given you a job to do in the church, at your place of employment, and at home. The time has come to be strong and work because God is with you through discipleship.[667]

Sometimes God will give us a job to do as He did with Moses, Abraham, and Noah, just to name a few. Noah had a difficult and huge task that others found humorous since this was during a time that did not rain. He was building a large boat, ship, or ark. God took care of the details of the job Noah was called to do. For instance, Noah was required to build detail architecture craftwork with the proper equipment to build an ark, but God supplied everything that was needed for completion. Too many times, we worry about details over which we have no control while neglecting specific areas such as attitudes, relationships, and responsibilities that are under our control. Like Noah, concentrate on what God has given you to do and leave the rest to God.

In another situation, Joseph was a prisoner and a slave in Egypt. Joseph could have seen his situation as hopeless,[668] but Joseph did his best with each small task given to him. Once Joseph was thrown into prison, after being falsely accused of sexual conduct, he was the keeper of the prison and later promoted to prison administrator, showing diligence and demonstrating a positive attitude through his hardship. At work, at home, or at school, follow Joseph's example by taking each small task and doing your best. Remember how God turned Joseph's situation around. He will see your efforts and can reverse even overwhelming circumstance.[669]

Jehu did much of what the Lord told him to, but he did not obey Yahweh with all his heart. He had become God's instrument for carrying out justice, but he had not become God's servant. As a result, he gave only lip service to God, while permitting the worship of the golden calves. Gradually, God reduced the size of the nation of Israel. Check the condition of your heart

---

[666] 1 Chronicles 28:20; also can refer to 1 Chronicles 28:10; 2 Chronicles 15:7; Psalm 31:24
[667] Life Application Study Bible, NKJV, emphasis added by author.
[668] Genesis 39:21-23
[669] Life Application Study Bible, NKJV, emphasis added by author.

toward God. We can be very active in our work for God and still not give the heartfelt obedience He desires.[670]

---

[670] 2 Kings 10:30-31

Begin Day 205:
Will You Work Upon Jesus' Return?

Jesus is coming back. We know this to be true. Does this mean we must quit our jobs to serve God? No, it means we are to use our time, talents, and treasures diligently to serve God completely in whatever we do. For a few people, this may mean changing professions. For most of us, it means doing our daily work out of love for God.[671] Pray for your job, for your employer to blend with your personality, to be recognized and appreciated by others and your boss, and receive promotions and advancements in line with God's will.[672]

---

[671] Matthew 25:21
[672] Proverbs 14:23; Romans 12:11

Begin Day 206:
Work Dilemma

A particular job can be based on demographics, lifestyles we portray, and background we have acquired, whether it is through experience and/or education. *Occupation* is the single pursuit that dominates our lives since we normally will take our net income to buy groceries, personal items, clothing, household items, pay bills, pay for education or other extracurricular activities, tithing and offering, and to pay off other debts. Except according to the Word, God requests our tithes to come from our *gross income*, which is what we make before taxes, not our *net income*, what we bring home after taxes. However, there are those who work to live and those who live to work.

Most of us become burned out from our jobs or career choices that we have made over a span of time. We feel trapped in a job or career path, which we feel, we can neither escape nor derive psychological gratification. It can be from the long hours or stressful events while on the job. We are either workaholics or "hardly workers." *Workaholics* allow work to crowd out all other aspects of life.

'Hardly workers' know when to turn off the computers, to switch from the work environment to personal life affairs, and are able to leave work at work and home life at home. *Workaholics* find an emotional payoff in overwork and an adrenaline high from success, as *hardly workers* only meet the needs and requirements of the position. However, medical professionals classify job stress as an *occupational hazard*. This stress can cause ulcers and deep depression that can lead to suicide. The Japanese term is *karoshi*, meaning death from overwork.

Today, our work environment requires staff to be multitasked, detail-oriented, and provide resources to save the company tons of money. Therefore, it is cost-effective to hire someone that is able to carry the load of two or more people. In the unpredictable world we live in today, a combination of industrial and technological experience work is essential and fulfilling the obligations of your employer. Qualifications for most graduates and applicants can be discouraging.

When we consider our jobs, we need to also examine our attitudes about work. We cannot always change our circumstances. However, if you have been influenced by negative attitudes toward work, then you need to consider God's viewpoint and principles relative to your daily jobs.[673] God can measure the happiness and contentment we have with our work.

---

[673] Ecclesiastes 5:18

Begin Day 207:
Jesus at Work

God is a worker. In Genesis, God created the heavens and earth.[674] Think of all the roles God had when creating the earth itself: designer, organizer, engineer, artist, developer, information specialist, project manager and developer, chemist, biologist, zoologist, programmer, linguist, and the list continues.[675] Overall, the quality of God's work is very good.[676] His creation can glorify and praise God, for His marvelous works.[677]

God's work did not end with the creation of physical heavens and earth and the first human couple. Jesus said, "My Father has kept working until now."[678] More in-depth, *my father*. Jesus is "the only begotten Son" who is the unique Son of God. He is not only in a unique relationship with God, the Father but also equal with God in nature.

Since God continually does good works without allowing Himself to stop on the Sabbath, the Son does likewise since He is equal to God. If God stopped labor on the Sabbath, nature would fall into chaos, and sin would overrun the world. In *Genesis, 2:2*, states that God rested on the seventh day, but this cannot mean that He stopped doing things. Jesus continues to work by providing His people, sustaining His creation, and saving His faithful worshippers.[679]

---

[674] Genesis 1:1
[675] Proverbs 8:12, 22-31
[676] Genesis 1:4, 31
[677] Psalm 19:1; 148:1
[678] John 5:17
[679] Nehemiah 9:6; Psalm 36:6; 145:15, 16

Begin Day 208:
Jesus Assigns People to do His Work

God uses people. *His fellow workers* help with accomplishing certain tasks.[680] In other words, God's work involves many individuals with a variety of gifts and abilities. No superstars, only team members performing their own special roles. We can become useful members of God's team by setting aside our desires to receive glory for what we do. Do not seek the praise from people since it is worthless instead seek approval from God.

Since God is a hard worker, it's presumed that since humans are created in His image would also be diligent workers.[681] Our work assignment was given before God pronounced the words recorded in *Genesis 3:19*. If work were a curse and evil, God would have never encouraged people to engage in it. For example, Noah and his family had much work to do before and after the Flood. In the Christian era, Jesus' disciples are also urged to work.[682]

Quality and excellence in the workplace have always been praised. God does His work with excellence. For example, Bezalel and Oholiab's wisdom, understanding, and knowledge were enabling them to carry out specific artistic and practical tasks.[683] God took a special interest in the function, artisanship, design, and other details of Bezalel and Oholiab's labor.

---

[680] 1 Corinthians 3:9
[681] Genesis 1:26, 28; 2:15
[682] 1 Thessalonians 4:11
[683] Exodus 31:1-11

Begin Day 209:
Sweat from Our Brow (Burden Work)

In Genesis 3:17-19, some view that God punished Adam and Eve for their rebellion, by putting the burden of work on them. God said to Adam, "In the sweat of your face, you will eat bread until you return to the ground." Because of Adam and Eve's unfaithfulness, an extension of the Eden Paradise would not happen. The ground came under God's curse. Sweat and toil were required for a person to eke out a living from the soil.[684] *Futility* means 'vanity, emptiness,' which refers to the curse on creation,[685] and creation waits for the coming glory because it also will be delivered. The bondage of corruption describes the *futility* in *Genesis 3:20*. Nature is a slave to decay and death, because of sin.

However, work can be a burden caused by stress, hazards, boredom, disappointment, competition, and deception. Injustices are those 'thorns and thistles' relative to the curse bestowed on Adam and Eve, for their disobedience in the Garden of Eden.

Believers are well-equipped to deal with work-generated stress. The Bible provides numerous fundamental principles to carry us through difficult times, with a positive effect on our spiritual and emotional well-being. For example, Jesus told us not to be anxious for nothing. The encouragement is to focus on today's problems, not tomorrow's. We are to avoid blowing things out of proportion; even our problems, troubles, and situations will only increase the sense of pressure and stress.[686]

Christians ultimately can rely on God's strength in our dreadful and tiresome situations. When we think that we are at that breaking point, God can give us peace and joy in our hearts, and provide us with wisdom to deal with any hardship.[687] Even stressful circumstances can produce positive results. Trials can make us turn to God. It can also prompt us to continue cultivating a Christian personality and the ability to preserve under pressure.[688]

---

[684] Romans 8:20, 21
[685] Genesis 3:17-19
[686] Matthew 6:25-34
[687] Ephesians 6:10; Philippians 4:7
[688] Romans 5:3, 4

Begin Day 210:
Work Performance

Perception of our personal abilities and work habits will help us see them as gifts from God. God will review our performance.[689] Since creation, God has given us work. We can perform our jobs without complaining or resentment.

Furthermore, the *reward of inheritance* is a strong motivation to serve someone. Our future reward is to spend eternity with Jesus Christ, which He treasures those who are faithful in His service. We normally think that we receive eternal rewards for spiritual practices such as reading the Bible, prayer, or even evangelism. Paul asserts that all work done to the honor of Christ will bring an eternal reward.[690]

We are to have a godly attitude, good behavior and a Christ-like perspective on the job so that our message of the Bible will be attractive to coworkers and others we are in touch with from day to day. Remember, there is always room for improvement.[691] For instance, King Solomon, who worked hard, enjoyed all the riches and comforts that life had to offer said, "Fear God and keep His commandments, for this is the whole duty of man." This clearly states that we must consider God's will in whatever we do, even if it is work. If we do not consider God's will, we will suffer from the pain of despair, loneliness, and emptiness. Doing work that pleases our Creator will not leave us dissatisfied. To Jesus, the work Jehovah assigned Him was as nourishing, satisfying, and refreshing as food.[692]

God will alert us to the areas where we need to grow in faith.[693] Those who are working hard to serve God can look forward to the time when He will restore a new earth and new heavens. Our deep-rooted faith and spirituality can supply much-needed strength. Once we learn what God's will is for our lives, and work in harmony with it, we may be blessed and always see well in our work.

---

[689] Colossians 3:23
[690] see Colossians 1:22-23
[691] Proverbs 10:4; 22:29
[692] John 4:34; 5:36
[693] 1 Corinthians 16:13-14

Begin Day 211:
Please God with your Work

The Corinthians continued steadfastly in the work of Christ because of the resurrection. Your *labor is not in vain* is stating that all the work that we do for Christ will be rewarded.[694] Sometimes, we hesitate to do good because we do not see or expect any results. Nevertheless, if we can maintain a heavenly perspective, we will understand that we often will not see the results of our efforts.

If we truly believe that Christ has won the ultimate victory, this should affect the way we live right now. Do not allow discouragement over an apparent lack of results keep you from working. Do good things that you have an opportunity to do and know that your work will have eternal results.[695] Moreover, Paul said that no good work is ever in vain. In 1 Corinthian 16, Paul elaborates on some practical work that has value for all believers.

1 Thessalonians 1:3, NKJV: *"Remembering without ceasing your work of faith, labor of love, and patience of hope in our Lord Jesus Christ in the sight of our God and Father."*

Paul commended these young believers for their work produced by faith, labor prompted by love, and endurance inspired by hope. These characteristics are the marks of effective believers in any age.

---

[694] see 2 Corinthians 5:10
[695] 1 Corinthians 15:58

Begin Day 212:
Faith through Family Isn't Enough

Jesus' hearers were shocked when he said that being Abraham's descendants was not enough for God. The religious leaders relied more on their family lines (tradition) than standing for God, which is not handed down from our parents to their children. Jesus' harshest words were to the respectable religious leaders, who lacked the desire for real change. Religious leaders wanted to be known as authoritative leadership, but they did not want to change their minds. Therefore, their lives were unproductive. Repentance is tied to action, or it is not real. Following Jesus means more than saying the right words, it means acting on what He says.[696] Everyone commits to God on his or her own. Do not rely on someone else's faith for your salvation. Put your own faith in Jesus and then exercise it every day.

For instance, the book of James emphasizes faith in action. God-fearing servants living are the evidence and result of faith. The church should serve with compassion, speak lovingly and truthfully, live in obedience to God's commands, and have love for one another. The body of believers ought to be an example of heaven on earth and draw people to Christ through love for God and for each other. If we truly believe God's Word, we will live by it daily. God's Word is not merely something we read or think about, but something we do. Belief, faith, and trust must have hands and feet – ours.[697] Faith without works is dead.[698]

Do not think good works will get you in the gateway of Heaven.[699] Jesus spoke against this way of thinking. Faith is to believe that Jesus Christ will come through for you, and His grace will give us salvation if we only believe. Do not think you will get into heaven because you are a *good person*. We are to work as believers of Jesus Christ to help others find salvation, for we are so blessed to have, by believing and receiving Jesus Christ in our lives.

---

[696] Life Application Study Bible, Luke 3:8-9, NKJV.
[697] Life Application Study Bible NKJV, emphasis added by author.
[698] James 2:14-26
[699] Ephesians 2:8-9

Begin Day 213:
Job Confirmation

Ask God what type of job He has for you, trust in Him always, and He will bring you through as He has done in the past to let you succeed in this task. God has blessed you with talents and gifts. If you are not sure, pray and ask Him. He will let it be known to you through either visions or dreams. His voice will speak to your heart and mind, or through others. Ask for confirmation to make sure it is a word from God.

Begin Day 214:
Prayer Life

God (Jesus) has no 'correct' name. He has only the name you give Him since His name changes from time to time, from place to place, and from person to person. However, God remains the same and never changes, long as you give Him the praise that He deserves. Even the angels in heaven praise and worship the Lord to the highest, Lucifer even worshipped God. God created all things, even the angels to worship Him.

But Lucifer's name had changed to Satan because of his pride, desiring others to worship and praise him instead of God. Some of us want praise and to be worshipped. There is no middle ground. We either are for YHWH or against YHWH. We are either children of YHWH God, or we are children of Satan.

Are you a child of God, or a follower of Satan? The Bible speaks of the differences. We are all God's creation, which would make us one He died for, but our lifestyle and actions can determine which father we truly emulate.

Begin Day 215:
Prayer

Matthew 6:25-34, Verse 33, NKJV: *"But seek first the Kingdom of God and His righteousness and all these things shall be added to you."*

What is prayer? Is it communication with God? Prayer is a two-way thing. We come to God in prayer, and He speaks to us through different means, especially through His Word. It is imperative to be in the Word on a consistent basis, and meditate on it day and night.

Who can pray? The church is to pray. As believers, we are those made righteous by His blood, and we were once sinners, saved by God's grace.

When can we pray? Always and all day long, we can pray. Thanking God for our meals we eat. In the morning, noonday, and when the sun goes down. When we are sick or ill, we can pray to God for healing. Most of us, pray when we are facing death.

Where should I pray? Pray in groups, while engaged or involved in church ministries, Bible study, work, home studies, and other meetings or seminars. You can pray in your closet, or in secrecy. You can pray in one's home. You can pray in church either publicly or corporately.

How should I pray? A.C.T.S.:
    A-Adoration: Magnify God for who He is.
    C-Confession: Forgiveness for our sins.
    T-Thanksgiving: Personal blessings.
    S-Supplication: Petitioning God's throne for others and ourselves.

What are things that can hinder my prayers? Some things that can hinder our prayers are sinful, an unforgiving spirit, and an empty repetition prayer. Other hindrances are family problems,[700] such as a husband taking advantage of his wife's submission, and spouses failing to honor and respect one another. *Hypocritical prayer* is praying with the wrong motive, self-righteousness, or pride just as Lucifer did, can also hinder your prayers.

Some would argue, "I do not have a prayer life with God." Do you talk to Him? Do you praise Him? Do you thank Him for what He has blessed you with? Do you thank Him for the food on the table? Do you thank Him for the car you drive? Thank Him for making a way out of no way to pay your bills and blessing you with a job? Do you pray to God and praise Him at the same time. However, if you do not have a relationship with God, then why would you pray? Once you receive and believe in Jesus Christ, you have a relationship with Christ. You will find your prayers coming easily.

---

[700] 1 Peter 3:7

Begin Day 216:
Prayer Changes Things

Praying to God will change the person, change their situation, and make a difference in our lives. Ask the Lord for wisdom. After you are willing to change by allowing God in and to do His will, your situation will change.

When we pray in the Holy Spirit, it will edify (build) our souls. Prayer spoken in tongues will likely be in utterance and may surprise you.[701] Each prayer language is different, which Satan may have a problem translating. Paul states that the spirit prays when we don't know how to pray.

Only God will never give us a bad gift.[702] It is diligent to seek God when we pray. *Prayer* is a deeper, more intimate way to reach the Lord. God will reveal Himself – manifest Himself. We must learn to wait on Him and pray. Others are willing to fast and pray to get an answer from God. God will manifest His presence in many ways.

When we are full of ourselves, biblically speaking, we are full of death and darkness. When were full of God, we are full of light and life. Pray like Paul did, he prayed until he knew God's power and who God is. If we pray this way, it will help us from trying to manipulate people into doing what we want them to do, and from throwing fits when things do not go our way. We will be more patient and more open to hearing God's voice. Furthermore, He is the perfect one to show us how to handle these issues that we are going through. Jesus continually intercedes for us, as He sits at the right hand of God.[703]

Keep in mind that not all of us pray alike and God created us that way. Not one of us are alike in appearance, and unless you are identical twins, you do not share the same DNA, personalities, characteristics, or behavior, so we are going to pray to our Heavenly Father differently. Whether you fast, use blessed oil or holy water, pray on your knees, standing, bow, or lie on the floor to pray to our Creator, He wants to hear from you.

---

[701] Romans 8:26
[702] 1 Corinthians 12:30
[703] Hebrews 7:25; Romans 8:34

Begin Day 217:
Promises through Prayer

When we are praying and trusting in God's promises for our lives,[704] we first must seek the Word of God for the promises. We will receive all the good things that God has promised us in His Word when we believe and obey the Lord wholeheartedly. Here are some of the promises listed in His Holy Word:

Deliverance	Healing	Peace
Prosperity	Eternal Life	Health
Guidance	Life	Protection
Abundance	Revival	Wisdom
Truth	Love	Victory
Freedom	Happiness	Blessings

To obtain these promises, we need to know God, trust the love of God, believe in God, live for the Lord, and pray to God. However, sometimes it requires patience.[705] Next, we need to be obedient to the Lord's Commandments and things that He requires from us.[706] We need faith.[707] We are to be strong and courageous.[708] We are to be active in God's Word and to do His will.[709] We are to put God first in everything we do.[710]

Prayer is an avenue that takes us:
from our problems to God's promise,
from doubt to discovery,
from the valley to the mountaintop,
from giving up to hope,
from discouragement to encouragement,
from fear to faith,
from despair to happiness,
from lies to truth,
from confusion to wisdom, and
from losses to gains.

Prayer brings life, peace, joy, and victory to every area of our lives.[711]

---

[704] Acts 6:4
[705] Hebrews 10:36-37
[706] Deuteronomy 11:22-23
[707] Hebrews 11:6
[708] Joshua 1:7
[709] Hebrews 6:12
[710] Matthew 6:33
[711] Praying God's Promises

Begin Day 218:
6 Simple Steps to Prayer

Step 1: Know God's Word. God's Word is implanted in our hearts to keep us from sins, also our sword where the Holy Spirit will always slay the enemy.[712]

Step 2: Believe in God's Word. It builds faith in our hearts.[713] God keeps His Word, and He does not lie. No matter how dismal circumstances might seem, keep your thoughts and focus on Him, because His compassion will renew itself each day.[714]

Step 3: Receive God's Word. Receive His promises, which makes it essential to know what they are. As we read, study, memorize and meditate on God's Word, it brings the promises to life for us.[715]

Step 4: Personalize the Word. The Bible is more personal than any other book. It is a message from our Heavenly Father's heart to us. It enables us to claim God's promises to meet our every need. The bible personalizes God's promise, being able to touch everyone from a different perspective – and meet them from the perspective of the Holy Spirit.[716] Keep reading the Word, as your experiences will frame and reveal to you the things you do not understand.

Step 5: Pray the Promise. Once you have immersed yourself in the Word of God and allowed its truths to saturate deeply within your spirit, be ready to walk by faith and not by sight. For example, studying the Word of God opens your eyes to deeper truths of God.[717] *Spiritual freedom* enables you to believe God's Word and trust His promises implicitly.[718] God will lead you every step of the way. Personalized faith and promised prayer life (all forms of prayer to pray the promises of God -- 1 John 5:14-15). Praying accordingly to God's will -- whole counsel of God is praying what He wants us to pray and believe, pray His Word. He hears us and answers us.

Step 6: Answered prayers are when God meets every human need. We can apply to every aspect: physically, financially, family, relationally, emotionally, mentally, sexually, vocationally, and spiritually. Furthermore, the Bible contains every need, praying His Word, actualizes those answers through faith. Through prayers, we are building faith in our hearts. *Prayer* is also a stepping-stone to new spiritual discoveries. Prayer will change your life in radical ways. All God's blessings will come to you as you enter this exciting way to pray. The promises that God wants us to claim as our own through faith and prayer.[719]
 "I pray for the anointing of God. Stir your people to action. Strengthen your people! Encourage! Give us the power to overcome the appetites which try to take control over our spiritual life.

---

[712] Ephesians 6:17
[713] Romans 10:17
[714] Lamentations 3:22-25
[715] 1 Corinthians 2:9-10
[716] 1 Corinthians 2:14
[717] John 8:32
[718] Proverbs 3:5-6
[719] 2 Corinthians 1:20

Give us purpose and direction to follow you obediently and faithfully. In Jesus Name, Amen!"—
Author, Adrienna Dionna Turner

Adrienna Dionna Turner

Begin Day 219:
<u>Meditation</u>

Meditation is a prayerful consideration and a continuous thought, according to Joshua.[720] *Meditation* helps you get in touch with who you really are, after asking God all the questions.

Steps to Meditation:
First, clear your mind. Breathe deeply and slowly. It will be okay if you fall asleep while meditating. This will give you the frame of mind to remember His Word. Then, you should forget all the questions that you wanted to address to God. Require no answers just breathe, and let Him bring those answers to you. *Meditation* is being able to go the one place where the answers and questions are. If you expect an answer, you will not get one, because instead of letting Him fill your mind, your focus is on the question you have before Him. If the answer comes to you, accept the answer from God. *Meditation* is not a mental process; it is simply the absence of the mental process. Continue to breathe deeply and trust in Him. Praise Him, remember who He is, and thank Him for being a part of you, and allowing you in. In other words, it is not thinking or expecting anything, just pure relaxation and focusing on the Lord.

If you meditate daily, according to the scripture, and you ask God to make moves in your life, in your walk, in your talk, change your ways to become more like Christ, watch God move into action. Some think that God speaks through your imagination. We need to have the channels of communication open to God by talking or praying to Him every day. This is the remedy to ward off selfish thoughts such as doubt, worry, fear or discouragement. In living without expectations, you will avoid disappointment.

Memorize
    Emphasize
        Visualize
            Personalize

Find a prayer time and remain faithful to that 'prayer watch.'

Five components of Meditation:
Worship (thanksgiving)
Confession (repentance)
Intercession (focus on the needs of others)
Petition (prayer for your edification)
Communion (listening to hear God)

---

[720] Joshua 1:8

Begin Day 220:
Prayer Helps with Attacks

According to Stormie Omartian's book, *Lord I Want to Be Whole*, she lists several steps to follow when the enemy attacks:

1. Are you proclaiming the Lord in every area of your life? Sometimes, we exclude Jesus without realizing it. Name specifically the area Satan is attacking and give God the credit.
2. Saturate yourself with God's Word.
3. Prayer. Ask God to reveal the truth of your situation to you. Ask God for guidance, protection, and strength for whatever you are facing.
4. Continue to praise the Lord in the midst of whatever is happening.
5. Ask God to show you if there are any points of obedience that you have not taken, in which the lack of obedience always opens us up to the enemy's attack.
6. Fast and pray, which is a powerful weapon for breaking down enemy strongholds.
7. Resist Satan since Jesus lives in you. You have full authority and power over Satan.
8. Rest in the Lord. Jesus is the victor and fights all our battles.

Begin Day 221:
Unanswered Prayers

There are times when our prayers will not be answered, or not exactly the way we prayed for it to happen based on our timetable. If that happens, trust that God knows what is best. There can be painful consequences of unanswered prayers, and there can be consequences to an answered prayer. This is just a matter of waiting on God.

On the other hand, our prayers can be answered without realizing it. We can pray without realizing it. If a prayer takes so long to be answered, we tend to give up on hope. Then, we become discouraged and fear God has forgotten us. Next, you will stop praying, stop reading the Holy Word, and stop going to church. We tend to feel, what is the point of praying if they are not answered? Most of us do not like to wait a day, a month, or even years, for the answer to come. But it will. When you pray, consider the outcome you are asking for. Do you really want that prayer answered?

Begin Day 222:
Lord's Prayer

Jesus taught the disciples how to pray and teaches us how to pray to the Lord. Here is our daily prayer:

"Our Father in heaven,
Hallowed be Your name.
Your kingdom come,
Your will be done,
On earth as it is in heaven.
Give us, day by day, our daily bread.
And forgive us our sins.
For we also forgive everyone who is indebted to us.
And do not lead us into temptation.
But deliver us from the evil one (Luke 11:1-4)."

Matthew 6:9 adds to this, "For Yours is the Kingdom, the Power, and the Glory forever. Amen."

Begin Day 223:
Enjoy Life

God wants us to enjoy life. When we have the proper view of God, we discover that real pleasure is enjoying whatever we have as gifts from God, not in what we accumulate.[721] God also wants to lead us deeper into the waters of surrender and consecration.

We become whatever we choose to be. We are not what we feel, or what we might do or say in a single impulsive moment of our life. We are what we will be, growing into the fullness of our Savior. We cannot always control our emotions, but we can control our own will. God has granted us 'free will.' Usually, our feelings have nothing to do with the truth of God. It is not your feelings or emotions that make you a child of God, but the doing of God's will.

Moreover, your battle is with self, and when you become willing, God will give you victory over your situation and your carnal enemy.[722] Before you can have, you must give away. Before you can be full, you must be empty. Before you can live, you must die. In other words, the *old man or woman* must lay down the fleshly desires. Before you have the victory, you must surrender to God. In the weakness of the flesh, we find ourselves bound in mind and body by the superior strength of our spiritual enemy. We struggle to extricate ourselves from the bondage, but the harder we try, the deeper we sink into the mire. Without the transforming grace of the new birth, we will live our lives with a carnal mind.[723]

---

[721] Ecclesiastes 3:12—Life Application Study Bible, NKJV.
[722] 1 Corinthians 15:57
[723] Romans 8:7

Begin Day 224:
Struggles as a Believer

About Romans 6—there is no other chapter in the Bible that gives assurance to a struggling Christian. God will never do anything in our spiritual lives that we are not willing for Him to do. He never coerces the will or pressures us into any actions to which we have not given consent. God gives us a choice to follow Him, and we are free and sovereign. Nothing will force us into any life choice that we have not willingly accepted.

Fatal delusion depends on trying harder and struggling longer to get the victory over sin. The secret is trusting instead of trying. Trying, over time will only make a young sinner into an old sinner. We must admit that, without God, we are not as strong as our adversary, Satan. We are to surrender our dependence on human strength and effort to God since He provides the glorious gift of victory. Jesus stated we could do nothing without Him.[724] Philippians 4:13 states, *"I can do all things through Christ, which strengthens me."*

---

[724] John 5:15

Begin Day 225:
Sinners

Sinners do things willfully, breaking the commandments of God, hurting other people, creating discord, and usually end up hurting themselves in the bargain. *Sin* is also an attitude of pride, or arrogance of your thoughts, which starts within our minds. We ought to let the Holy Spirit captivate our minds. Sin is not just a private matter.[725] Everything we do affects others, and we must think of them constantly.

God created us to be interdependent, instead of independent. We, who are strong in our faith, without pride or condescension, must treat others with love, patience, and self-restraint.

Overcoming sin is the possibility that rests with God and the responsibility that rests with us. When we begin to act against the sin, God provides the power to break the habits of sin. By yielding our will to the higher powers from above, we can be delivered from the bondage of the flesh. Then, our wholeness is captive to the Spirit of God, and we can discern His thoughts. Paul declares that we partake of the divine nature and have the mind of Christ. The process of this is to surrender our will and give up our own way.

---

[725] Romans 14:20-21

Begin Day 226:
Believers

As believers, we are to *edify* or *build up* each other. Paul has already exhorted mature believers to have consideration for the weak believers. In Romans 14, Paul exhorts the mature believer to identify ways to build up those weaker in their faith. Alternatively, there is a little distinction between the words "stumble," "offended," and "someone who is weak." Paul uses all three to reiterate that a mature believer should not cause the downfall of another believer.[726]

On the other hand, Paul does not require the strong to abandon their convictions about things not condemned by the law. Instead, he encourages them to have faith about such issues. Although believers may refrain from eating meat in front of weaker believers, they can still believe that Christ gives them the freedom to eat all types of food privately before Him.[727] Nevertheless, this does not infer that drinking wine is okay in the privacy of your home and with God.

Christ is the ultimate model for the strong believer and someone to Whom the weak can turn. Let Jesus make you strong. We try to avoid actions forbidden by the Scripture, of course, but sometimes the Scripture is silent. Then, we are to follow our conscience. When God shows us that something is wrong for us, we must avoid it. However, we are not to judge other believers who exercise their freedom.[728]

---

[726] Nelson Study Bible, NKJV, Romans 14: 20-21.
[727] Romans 14: 2, 5
[728] Romans 14:23

Begin Day 227:
People Pleasers

If we merely set out to please our neighbors and other people, we are labeled people-pleasers. Peer pressure can be difficult and a touchy situation, so we want to do our best to be a part of the crowd and be loved by them. However, Jesus was not a people-pleaser, but pleasing the will of God. As believers of Jesus Christ, we can please God instead of people. God will bless us.

Paul was opposed to seeing people trying so hard to please other people.[729] We are to set aside willfulness and self-pleasing aggrandizement for the sake of building others up. Our Christian convictions must be a substitute for coldhearted and dismissive treatment of our brothers and sisters, and to support their growth in Christ.[730]

---

[729] Galatians 1:10
[730] Romans 15:2

Begin Day 228:
Exalt Self

Satan's strongest efforts are aimed at the exaltation of self. Satan can only control the individuals who continue to feed the carnal nature. Self-related indulgences are those Satan constantly holds to the fallen human race. The most appealing subtleties are self-righteousness, self-dependence, self-seeking, self-pleasing, self-will, self-defense, and self-glory.

However, counselors urge us to improve our self-worth and our self-esteem. Even ministers preach sermons to that effect around their interpretation of loving our neighbors as we love ourselves.

We need to recognize our value in the sight of God. The Lord has counted every one of us as more precious than *His own life*. He gave us our esteem. God can love us despite our genetic weakness and indulged carnal appetites, but the closer we come to Jesus, we become less charmed with our own selfish ways. We enter the converted life through the Holy Spirit; the confidence we placed in the flesh will be wholly shifted to the Savior, our Lord. The truth is that egocentric nature of a baby, child, or as an adult, is to have its own way. This nature needs to be crucified, and under the new spiritual nature, our affections are set on Jesus. Self is no longer important where the flesh has no control over life to fulfill its own will.

The subject of the will is not achieved by any decision since the self will never make the choice to put itself to death. Only the Holy Spirit can create the desire to escape from the domination of a sin-loving nature. It can bring us to the point of being willing to give up every indulgence of that corrupt, fallen nature. Self makes the Christian path seem dark and fearsome, but when the self is surrendered and crucified, the narrow road is filled with joy unspeakable. Ironically, you would think believers of Jesus Christ should be the happiest people in the world. If they are not, it is because the self has not been surrendered and crucified.

Begin Day 229:
Insight to do what is Right

God gives us insight and warning signs, and we need to pay attention to them to keep out of trouble. We tend to blame our unhappiness on many things that really are not at fault. Adam blamed Eve. Eve blamed the serpent. This is just the syndrome of the 'blame game.' We need to repent for each sin we have committed, to have maturity and balance.

Sometimes, we are tempted to do things other than what our heart and/or mind want to do. God has been speaking to you about some changes in your life, but you are afraid. Whether it is minor or major, and whether you think that you are able to proceed or not, you can accomplish this task at hand. Making many mistakes in the past does not justify ending your relationship with God. Ask for forgiveness through repentance by confessing your sins. Do not look back at your sin, wishing you could have done things differently. If you lost your direction, where you are unable to see the full path or picture, let God lead your steps. We are appointed in due time.[731]

---

[731] 1 Peter 5:6 and Genesis 18:14 also talks about the proper time (Galatians 4:4).

Begin Day 230:
Test everything, even Movies

Paul tells us to test everything, to hold on to the good, and to avoid all appearance of evil in the world.[732] In our modern lives, 1 Thessalonians 5:21-22 refers to the evil scary movies that we watch, video games that we play, and sexual images or content in movies or magazines. It can be joining others on social media to create a clique that puts down people and banishes them from your ideas of who God will accept into heaven, or even draw you into a worship of someone to substitute for God. These images can play in your mind; and you may act it out and your actions, including thoughts that are against God. Alternatively, Jesus warned the undiscerning people to stop judging according to mere appearance and to make right judgments.[733] For example, Harry Potter books are a facet of occult, alchemy, astrology, spells, mediums, and other pagan practices. Potter books desensitize children and others to the forbidden and dangerous world of pagan magic.[734] Besides Potter series or movies, there are other witchcraft related shows such as *Sabrina the Teenage Witch*, *Charmed*, and *Buffy the Vampire Slayer*.

Other horror movies showcase deadly creatures of the night like ghouls and demons. A *ghoul*, according to the occult legend, is an evil spirit to rob graves and feed on human corpses. *The Hindu vetala* are demons that haunt cemeteries and animate dead bodies as for *rakshasas* and are a whole order of evil demons that disturb sacrifices.

This generation is becoming desensitized to the occult. The Bible gives a biblical perspective on the occult and explains how followers of Jesus Christ resist the encroachment of darkness into our increasingly pagan culture. However, if we are lovers of Jesus Christ, we can walk in the Spirit's wisdom and strength, to tackle many spiritual counterfeits.[735]

Unbelievably, being entertained by evil and pornography movies can release an evil spirit in your home, in your mind, in your spirit, and in your life. We can repent to God, asking for forgiveness for watching such movies or television shows and rebuke some evil spirits that linger. We must repent and rebuke because we allowed them a window to come in.

---

[732] 1 Thessalonians 5:21-22
[733] John 7:24
[734] Deuteronomy 18:9-14; Galatians 5:20; Revelation 22:15
[735] 1 John 4:4

Begin Day 231:
Spiritual Footwear

God gives us spiritual footwear, known as the *gospel of peace*.[736] It symbolizes both a readiness of spirit and a commandment to share God's good news of salvation. Believers of Jesus Christ will be protected from many fiery arrows of persecution by the armor of God. Our most potent weapon against evil is God's Word, described as the *sword of the spirit,*[737] which divides the truth from error in the most confusing situations.[738]

---

[736] Ephesians 6:15
[737] Ephesians 6:17
[738] Hebrews 4:12

Begin Day 232:
Spiritual Dangers

Some believers are inaccurate about certain things because they misinterpret the Bible to fit their needs and wants. Misinterpretation can be spiritually dangerous. Christians who believe and receive Jesus Christ as their personal savior will enjoy eternal bliss.[739] Others will suffer eternal separation from God by not accepting Jesus Christ as their personal savior.[740] This is why the Bible instructs Christians to overcome evil with good.[741]

We also must avoid seeking revenge.[742] Instead, Jesus tells us to pray for your enemies,[743] consider others more important than ourselves,[744] view all people as inherently equals,[745] and to reject lies.[746] Other habits we can turn away from are drunkenness,[747] flee from hypocrisy,[748] refrain from using corrupt and vulgar communication,[749] and avoid activities like occultism that leads away from God.[750] Now we can live a life in honesty,[751] walk with integrity,[752] and forgive those who hurt us.[753]

Overall, we say we are followers of Jesus Christ, but want to openly watch anything and listen to everything, and feel we are strong enough to withstand all evil. It's part of our childish eagerness to explore the world around us. Paul explains in 1Corinthians that we need to put off our childish ways. *Evil* is the substance of a higher power, supernatural power, emanating from the fallen angel Satan and his demons (a third of the angels who fell from heaven). These *fallen angels* are also known as demons or devils that are deceiving and trying to steal your joy and happiness. As mentioned in the previous chapter concerning 'prayer,' if we pray to God, God's Holy Spirit points to the activity or sin He wants you to get right.

---

[739] Romans 10:9; 1 John 5:11-13
[740] Luke 16:19-30; John 3:16; Revelation 20:11-15
[741] Romans 12:21
[742] Leviticus 19:18; Romans 12:17, 19; 1 Peter 3:9
[743] Luke 6:27
[744] Philippians 2:3
[745] Acts 17:26; Galatians 3:28
[746] Proverbs 12:22; Ephesians 4:25; Colossians 3:9
[747] Ephesians 5:18
[748] Luke 6:42; Romans 12:9; James 3:17
[749] Colossians 3:8; 4:6; Titus 2:8
[750] Isaiah 44:25; Galatians 5:20; Revelation 21:8
[751] Hebrews 13:18
[752] Psalm 15:2; 26:1; Proverbs 11:3
[753] Matthew 6:14-15; Ephesians 4:32

Begin Day 233:
Unconfessed Sin

Unconfessed sin is a prime reason we do not know God's will or purpose on the pathway of life.[754] According to 2 Timothy 3:9, sin has consequences, and no one will get away with it forever. Live each day as if it is your last, and your actions will be brought into the light. Now is the time to change, and confess to anything you would not want to be revealed later.

Pray during the time of temptation and difficulty, God will bring a verse or Scripture that will give you a clear indication of your sin, and how to overcome this sin by making godly choices according to His will. Shout 'Amen' that our Heavenly Father loves us so much, that he not only overlooks our sin once we confess and repent, but is also willing to help us overcome our battles.

---

[754] Isaiah 59:2

Begin Day 234:
Should We Drink Liquor?

Some would argue that Jesus drank wine, so how is it forbidden for us to drink if Jesus did it?

I always thought it was fine to drink if we did not overly indulge or get overly intoxicated because a couple drinks would not hurt anybody. A majority would believe that one is able to drink moderately, just not excessively. The third argument is that alcohol is addictive and destructive.

The Scripture references to Jesus' drinking wine were similar to drinking grape juice today without the fermentation. It was fresh grapes crushed into a liquid. *New wine*, in a biblical sense, refers to the *new* or fresh juice of grapes. Other times, the Bible describes *wine* as the aged or fermented product known as alcohol. However, most translators never used 'grape juice.' The word *tiyrosh* is used for new unfermented wine, and *yayin* is used for fermented wine, but there are exceptions.[755] However, in the New Testament, only one Greek word, *oinis*, is used to describe both fermented and fresh grape juice. In *Luke 5:37-39*, it speaks about 'old and new wine.' This context is also referring to grape juice, not alcohol.

Mark 2:22, NKJV: *"And no one puts new wine into old wineskins; or else the new wine bursts the wineskins, the wine is spilled, and the wineskins are ruined. But new wine must be put into new wineskins."*

Apparently, the *new wine* is referring to fresh unfermented wine. Isaiah 65:8 speaks of *new wine* that is simply grape juice. In these Scriptures, some tend to think wine is what we get from the liquor store, or if served at parties and clubs is acceptable to drink since Jesus' speaks of drinking 'new wine' in some of the Scriptures mentioned above. However, He is referring to wine that has not sat out for a period to turn into alcohol. Instead, it is fresh grapes crushed into a liquid form and drank before fermented. Yet, others would argue that Jesus drank wine with His disciples at the Last Supper.[756] Jesus uses new wine as a new covenant with His people. He also calls wine *fruit of the vine*.

Fermentation is the identical process of leavening.[757] In the Bible reference to bread without leaven, the leaven is a type of sin so we can be assured that *wine* is a symbol of Jesus blood. A symbolic illustration of Jesus' blood was part of the conversation with His disciples at the Last Supper. The perfect, sinless blood of Jesus would never be symbolized by corrupt and putrefying old wine.

The first time *wine* was mentioned in the Book of Genesis, was in the story of Noah, after the flood, where Noah grew a vineyard and created the original fermented grape juice.[758] During this time, Noah drank and stumbled around naked and shamefully exposed himself to his sons. Lot also drank and was easily seduced into having incestuous relationships with his

---

[755] Isaiah 16:10
[756] Matthew 26:28-29
[757] Exodus 12:19
[758] Genesis 9:20-23

daughters.[759] His offspring of these relationships became the nations of Moab and Amnon, the mortal enemies of God's people.

This is another time when we should care about a weaker brother or someone who cannot control their intake of wine or alcohol.

For some people, the mere presence of that which entices them will send them into the trap of addiction. So, even if you handle life with an appropriate amount of alcohol, do not take the opportunity in the presence of others who may not be as strong as you.

---

[759] Genesis 19:33

Begin Day 235:
Strong Drink(s)

Strong drink is translated from the word, *shekar,* and is condemned by Solomon as *a brawler.*[760] This strong drink was prohibited from the priests[761] and Nazarenes.[762] *Shekar* is called a sweet wine or syrup. *Shechar* is a luscious, saccharin drink or sweet syrup in its fresh and unfermented state. Sugar and cider are from *shekar*. *Shekar* can be either a sweet unfermented drink or intoxicating drink. We must never interpret the Word that it is okay to drink shekar or any strong alcoholic beverage.[763] For example, the children of Israel drank alcohol, stripped naked and worshipped a golden calf.[764] Some of these stories seem exotic or nauseating, but it lets you imagine some of the things we could be capable of doing if we indulge in alcoholic beverages. What will be our excuse? It was only a drink.

Amnon, the son of David, was another strong drinker who raped his half-sister, Tamar. Because of his incestuous act, he lost his life at the hands of his enraged half-brother while intoxicated.[765] Think about how many drive-bys are under the influence of alcohol and bad decision-making. Think about all the rape victims: the person who was violated was either drunk by her personal choice or influenced by the substances, date-rape drugs or psychotics. One who uses common sense will neither be in the position to consume these substances, or in the position to attempt to use them to hurt someone else. Even if a believer encourages you to attend where alcohol is used or served, do not go.

Think about how many fights usually occur at house parties, college parties, clubs, and other events that have alcoholic beverages. There are other terrible repercussions involving alcohol found in the Bible.[766] How would believers of Christ argue in defense if they are actively drinking and in ungodly environments? Many people are convicted of manslaughter because they were present (culpable) when someone died under the influence of alcohol.

Alcohols can be classified as poisons, of which are toxins to the human body. Beer, wine, and brandy are ethanol, or C_2H_5OH, which is a clear, highly flammable liquid that has a burning taste and a characteristic odor. If one consumes this type of alcohol, death can occur if the concentration of ethanol exceeds about five percent. Those who drink it sparingly, there are immediate behavioral changes, impairment of vision, and unconsciousness can occur. It has the same effect on your body as if you used heroin or even marijuana.

On the other hand, Native Americans consider alcohol or liquor as *evil spirits* since it caused them to sin, changing their whole way of thinking—pure evil.

Think about what people do today when they drink liquor. Whether it is *moonshine*, a potent distilled drink of high alcohol content usually made illegally. Many people associate it with the

---

[760] Proverbs 20:1, also can refer to Isaiah 5:11
[761] Leviticus 10:9-11
[762] Numbers 6:2-4 and Judges 13:3-5
[763] Deuteronomy 14: 26
[764] Exodus 32:6, 25
[765] 2 Samuel 13:28
[766] 2 Samuel 13:28 and Job 1:13-19

past because of movies and old television shows. *Moonshine* can also be considered a hard drink served at a bar or club setting. What are people's thoughts or actions after consuming alcohol? Some may run out on the streets naked while blurting out bizarre things. Some may go back to someone's home and have one-night stands. Afterwards, they blame their actions on what they drank. Imagine what other excuses and things we might do when we drink fermented wine or other alcoholic beverages. Ironically, people will look everywhere but to God for excitement and true meaning. Instead, we prefer to go to the club and bars, concerts, and other special events that usually have alcohol available at our leisure.

Today, we can get caught up being in touch with people in a place where alcohol is served, thinking that we are "doing God's will," taking an example from Jesus being in the bars of His day. Do we really think that drinking in a bar is going to help someone if we are not strong enough to avoid the temptations such an environment presents? We are not God. We must depend on Him. There is a difference in what God expects from us.

Begin Day 236:
Drunkenness/Alcoholic(s)

In Isaiah 5:8-25, God condemns six sins: (1) exploiting others;[767] (2) drunkenness;[768] (3) taking sarcastic pride to commit a sin;[769] (4) confusing moral standards;[770] (5) being conceited;[771] and (6) perverting justice.[772] Because of these sins, God punished Israel with destruction by Assyria.[773] A similar fate was awaiting Judah if they did not turn away from these sins. These people spent many hours drinking and partying, but Isaiah predicted that eventually many would die of hunger and thirst. Ironically, our pleasures, if we do not have God's blessings, may destroy us. Leaving God out, allows sin to come in. God wants us to enjoy life,[774] but to avoid those activities that could lead us away from Him.

If we pray to God after having a few beers to drink, would this be convincing and uplifting to the Heavenly Father? This is confusing, especially to our children, since we are sending mixed signals. God tells us to come out from among them, which are people who are following the morals and rationale of the world, and to be separate.[775] If a Christian begins to drink alcohol, they show that they are not separated from worldly things.

In 1 Timothy 3:2, *temperate* means without wine, sober or clearheaded. *Sober-minded* means that an overseer must have control of his or her body and mind. It is a balanced state of mind, arising out of self-restraint. 1 Timothy 3:3, where Timothy points out, *not given to wine* means not addicted to wine. Paul speaks of not being drunk with wine, wherein is excess, but to be filled with the Holy Spirit. Most think the passage refers to not drinking too much. The word *excess* in Greek is *asotia*, which is translated as riot or riotous living.[776] We are called to be sacred vessels filled with God's Spirit.

God approves a moderate use that is good for our bodies and spirit. However, gluttony, whether it is drinking or eating, is condemned in the Bible.[777] Additionally, Jesus describes gluttony as one of the primary sins of the people destroyed by the flood.[778] In contrast, moderate drinking is not God's answer–abstinence is. Jesus did not drink a portion of wine mingled with myrrh to quench his thirst while he was on the Cross, which was intended to numb the pain. Jesus refused it, choosing to suffer the complete pain.[779]

---

[767] Isaiah 5:8-10
[768] Isaiah 5:11-12
[769] Isaiah 5:18, 19
[770] Isaiah 5:20
[771] Isaiah 5:21
[772] Isaiah 5:22-24
[773] Isaiah 5:25-30
[774] 1 Timothy 6:17
[775] 2 Corinthians 6:17
[776] Ephesians 5:18; 1 Peter 4:4; Luke 15:13
[777] Deuteronomy 21:20 and Proverbs 25:27
[778] Matthew 24:38
[779] Matthew 27:34; Mark 15:23

Every alcoholic sip starts their downward path with one or two drinks, which is considered as a *moderate drinker*. Drunkenness might be excusable for dying people in great pain, but it is inexcusable for national leaders.[780] Alcohol clouds minds, and can lead to injustice and poor decisions. Leaders have better things to do than anesthetizing themselves with alcohol.

---

[780] Proverbs 31:6, 7

Begin Day 237:
Jewish Wedding: Finest Wine

At a Jewish wedding, one of the guests served as a *governor of the feast*, similar to the master of ceremonies at a banquet. The *headwaiter* was responsible for seating the guests and the correct running of the feast. Then, good wine or better wine was served first. Then, after the guests were dulled, the everyday wine was served. However, this wine was so good that the master of the feast was surprised at how late it was served during a celebration.

In the Gospel of John, the miracles of Jesus were called signs, showing that they pointed to His messiahship. John records seven signs in the book of Revelation. Jesus first sign (miracle) signified Christ's glory, His deity. Jesus first miracle was when he transformed water into wine. He clearly demonstrated His power.[781] In *John 2:6*, it explains how much water it took to make the finest wine for such a feast. Each water pot held 20-30 gallons, for a total of 120-180 gallons of the finest wine.[782]

For some reason, people expected God to be dull and lifeless, just as many do today. Jesus saved the best wine for last at the Jewish wedding, which demonstrates *that a life with Jesus is better than life on our own.*[783]

When the disciples saw Jesus' miracle, they believed. This miracle showed His power over nature and revealed the way to go about His ministry—helping others, speaking with authority, and being in personal touch with people.

---

[781] John 2:9-11, Nelson Study Bible, NKJV.
[782] John 2:10
[783] Life Application Study Bible, NKJV, 1996.

Begin Day 238:
Woe (Alcohol)

Woe means deep distress, or misery, which is usually caused by grief or wretchedness. Here are a few Scriptures that use the term *woe*, referring to alcohol.

Isaiah 5:11, **NKJV**: *"Woe to those who rise early in the morning, that they may follow intoxicating drink; who continue until night, till wine inflames them!"*

Proverbs 23:29-30, **NLT**: *"Who has anguish (woe)? Who has sorrow? Who is always fighting? Who is always complaining? Who has unnecessary bruises? Who has bloodshot eyes? It is the one who spends long hours in the taverns, trying out new drinks."*

Habakkuk 2:15, **NKJV**: *"Woe to him who gives drink to his neighbor, pressing him to your bottle, even to make him drunk, that you may look on his nakedness!"*

Begin Day 239:
Drinks Defile the Body

Daniel would not defile his body with wine.[784] He was offered wine while in the king's palace and other delicacies that Jews would not eat such as swine. Therefore, he carefully requested to eat only fruits and vegetables for a week, proving that he would not be weak but strong while the other men under the king's care continued to eat the foods and wines offered to them. He succeeded with his diet, leaving King Nebuchadnezzar and his advisors in awe.

Sour wine mixed with gall would have dulled Jesus' pain and consciousness.[785] Jesus refused it. He wanted to drink His cup of suffering.[786] *Gall* is generally understood to be a narcotic that was used to deaden pain. Jesus chose to fully suffer while conscious and needed to do so with a clear mind. What if he'd taken that drug? What would the message have been if He had died without conveying the loss of fellowship from the Father? Would it have been as powerful to those who looked on?

Would He have been able to let people understand that the Sin of the World, which He took upon Himself, separates people from the Love of God?

At the ninth hour, Jesus cried with a loud voice, "My God, My God, why have You forsaken me?"[787]

Therefore, as a Christian, God is making a clear statement about alcohol consumption. In other words, when in doubt, is it representing what God is all about? Consumption does not glorify the Lord. Instead, it destroys the mind and body, which is a clear violation of the *Sixth Commandment.*

Remember when Jesus was on the cross, dying for our sins, He had wanted something to quench his thirst. The Roman soldiers offered him wine to drink, but Jesus refused. He would not risk any wrongful judgment by drinking a mouthful of wine to quench His thirst. Would Jesus expect less of us?

Nevertheless, why do we continue to offer Him less of us?

---

[784] Daniel 1:8
[785] Matthew 27:34
[786] Psalm 22:18-24
[787] Matthew 27:46

Begin Day 240:
Drinking is like a Cancer

A quote attributed to Abraham Lincoln states: "Drink is a cancer in human society, eating out its vitals threatening its destruction." What good has alcohol done in one's life? It usually breaks up homes, breaks up marriages, causes loss of confidence and self-esteem, and people end up losing jobs, categorized as *alcoholics*. Usually, once you are labeled an *alcoholic* in your work environment, you may be requested to attend Alcoholics Anonymous to keep your current position.

As an addictive substance that takes your ability to think clearly, alcohol can lead to drunk driving, ultimately destroying other people's lives and families because you've caused the loss of a loved one. Drinking to excess can also lead to various transmitted diseases by having unprotected sex with multiple partners and other deadly measures.

Alcohol was described as destroying nations in Jeremiah 13:12-15. Think about all the crimes in the nation today because of the consumption of alcohol beverages or influenced by other drug substances. Imagine how many people see psychologists, counselors, and other community services for alcohol abuse and other drug substances.

Micah also warned of lying and false prophets, who condone wine and strong drinks.[788] Alternatively, some congregations or preachers teach 'moderation,' but the Scriptures show, throughout, that it can be addictive and lead to much destruction. Refer to Romans 14:21, describing how excessive alcohol makes your brother weak and stumble. If you truly love your family member, a close friend, or sister or brother that is struggling with alcohol and/or other intoxicating substances, how can we tell them it is okay to drink by doing it in their presence? Paul said he would neither eat flesh, or drink wine, or do anything to offend a brother.[789]

Let us make this simple and plain: it lowers a Christian's mortality and weakens the resolve in resisting temptation. We already have a hard time removing ourselves from the pleasures of the world, and sin or alcohol just makes an excuse for others and ourselves in doing it or trying it. Do you really want to make it easier for the Devil to lure his way in your life?

Romans 13:13-14, NLT: *"Because we belong to the day, we must live decent lives for all to see. Don't participate in the darkness of wild parties and drunkenness, or in sexual promiscuity and immoral living, or in quarreling and jealousy. Instead, clothe yourself with the presence of the Lord Jesus Christ. And don't let yourself think about ways to indulge your evil desires [of sinful nature]."*

---

[788] Micah 2:11
[789] Romans 14:21

Begin Day 241:
Should we Smoke?

In another sense, cigarette smoking and alcohol is a slow death (or suicide) in small increments such as a payment plan in installments. One puff, one more drink, is taking the life out of you and you will die sooner. Some would argue, "Who cares since we are all born to die because of Adam and Eve's fallen sin that messed up the entire generations to come? At least, I can enjoy my life to the fullest until that day comes."

How does this sound? Isn't it sassing the home you welcome His Spirit to? Giving in to the flesh, in spite of the Bible's warnings to the contrary?

On another note, tobacco-use injures the health and defiles the body of a smoker.[790] In addition, tobacco is unclean.[791] *Nicotine* is an addictive substance that enslaves people. We become servants to whomever or whatever we yield ourselves to.[792] For instance, tobacco users are servants of nicotine. It is not only a chemical addiction but also a psychological addiction that supports a cigarette habit. On the other hand, tobacco is a waste of money.[793] We are God's stewards of the money given us. It is required in stewards that a man is found faithful.[794] The use of tobacco never draws anyone close to Christ.

In 1 Peter 2:11, *"Abstain from fleshly lusts, which war against the soul."* Tobacco-use is a fleshly lust or desire. Furthermore, the use of tobacco shortens the lifespan by one-third.

Even though is a slow suicide, it is still murder. One of the best ways to postpone your funeral is to quit using tobacco or smoking cigarettes.

God is the truth, He wants you to open your eyes and see the truth. Let it be revealed in your body to convince you to stop smoking cigarettes and harsh chemicals in vaping as well as marijuana. Follow the ways of Christ. Consider other good things to drink and replace cigarettes with items that will nourish your body.

---

[790] 1 Corinthians 3:16-17
[791] 2 Corinthians 6:17
[792] Romans 6:16
[793] Isaiah 55:2
[794] 1 Corinthians 4:2

Begin Day 242:
Night Activities

Night in Romans 13:12, is referring to the present day while we live in Satan's dark dominion or during evil times. We are to put on the "Armor of Light (Jesus)."

Day is the beginning of a new life with Christ in His glorious reign or the time of Christ's return.

At hand, means Christ can return at any time.[795] Note that Paul puts strife and envy on the same level as drunkenness and lusts. Put on the Lord Jesus, believers clothe themselves with Christ-like characteristics such as righteousness,[796] truth,[797] and peace.[798]

Just as Jesus said in His Sermon on the Mount, Paul considers attitudes as important as actions.[799] Just as hatred leads to murder, envy leads to strife and lusts to adultery. When Christ returns, He wants to find His people clean on the inside, and on the outside.

A person whose life changes radically at conversion may experience contempt from his or her old friends. He may be scorned, not only because he refuses to participate in certain activities, but also because his priorities have changed and he is now heading in the opposite direction. His life incriminates their sinful activities. Mature believers can help new believers resist pressures of opposition by encouraging them to be faithful to Christ. *Dissipation* refers to wasteful expenditure and an intemperate pursuit of pleasure, especially of drinking to excess and partying.[800]

Some of us would go to the club on Friday and Saturday, and whether you had a hangover that Saturday, would attend church on Sunday, praising the Lord as if nothing went down the night before. Some believers get drunk as a skunk. Go club-hopping and dancing, and unmarried couples are having sex on Friday and Saturday nights. On Sunday mornings, these same Christians attend church, singing hymns, and clapping their hands, which is so hypocritical to the Word. Instead of engaging in sinful acts against what the Word says, we are to be modeling Jesus Christ. This is why Peter charges us to remain sober.[801] The devil is already on our case attempting to make things so that we will not face Jesus Christ when He returns. Satan wants to see us suffer, struggle, and keep us from ever turning to Christ. Jesus Christ can bail His followers out to receive salvation for our past sins.

---

[795] Philippians 4:5; James 5:8; 1 Peter 4:7
[796] 1 Corinthians 1:30
[797] John 14:16
[798] Galatians 5:22, 23; Ephesians 2:14; 6:10-17
[799] Matthew 5-7
[800] 1 Peter 4:3, 4 –Life Application Study Bible, NJKV.
[801] 1 Peter 5:8

Begin Day 243:
Dress Code

Do you intentionally leave your home wearing the shortest skirt or dress, the tightest jeans or outfit, and revealing more than meets the eye in the club scene? Sometimes men walk out of their house, trying to look thuggish or gangster by wearing sagging or baggy pants down to their knees, showing their behinds. We must put on our armor, including how we dress.

Both non-believers and believers are guilty of dressing provocatively or unholy.[802] Whom are you trying to attract? Who will be impressed? The clothing you wear should draw attention to your face, not your body. This does not mean you shouldn't dress well, but to pray and ask God to show you the right thing to wear. This is a challenge for all of us. The change in how you dress can be a starting point to show that you really want to live for God. It is possible that someone will open an opportunity to hear about Him if you are dressed well.

---

[802] Romans 12:1-2

Begin Day 244:
Substances can Cause Abusive Habits

Drug-using parents often transmit their weaknesses to their children. Parents' drug abuse habits can be passed down to the third and fourth generation because of their unruliness.[803] The children and grandchildren inherit the bad habits and weakened, sickly bodies when their mother or father defy God. Ask yourself: is this what you want for your children, grandchildren, and great-grandchildren? If you are using drugs, smoking, or drinking alcohol, it usually follows a pattern until someone breaks the cycle or habit.

The church will not condone drinking or using any harmful substance or drugs. Some congregations teach that it is permissible to drink a little wine. Instead, the church must uphold the clear position of the Word of God, knowing that Jesus is the Word that made flesh and comes to dwell among us. God's issue on alcohol is clear—it is unholy and unclean. Partaking of the worldly drink to drunkenness[804] can only compromise God's high standards for our lives. If you have a problem with alcohol, seek counseling or appropriate help, but trust in God and pray that He will deliver you from this addiction.

The Bible speaks against drugs.[805] Most people are running from their problems and think getting high or drunk will eliminate their pain and misery. Overall, you will only have a hangover and became more depressed in the end, then find yourself shortchanging your budget due to buying liquor or drugs. This can lead to losing your family, home, and losing your life since it can lead to addiction, or to hurt someone or someone's property while under the influence. This addiction generally takes control of you, where you no longer have self-control over this situation since your body is craving alcohol, drugs, or any other harmful substance.

---

[803] Deuteronomy 12:24, 25 and Exodus 20:5, Proverbs 20:1
[804] Ephesians 5:8
[805] in Matthew 27:34 (CEV) and Mark 15:23 (LB)

Begin Day 245:
Put on Christ

How do we *put on* the Lord Jesus Christ?

- First, we identify with Christ by being baptized.[806] This shows our solidarity with other believers, and with the death, burial, and resurrection of Jesus Christ.

- Second, we exemplify the qualities Jesus showed while He was here on earth, of which are love, humility, truth, and service. We role-play what Jesus would do in our situation.[807]

- Last, we must not give our desires any opportunity to lead us into sin. Avoid those situations that open the door to gratifying sinful desires. Christ should satisfy our needs and wants.[808]

---

[806] Galatians 3:27
[807] Ephesians 4:24-32 and Colossians 3:10-17
[808] John 6:35

Begin Day 246:
Addictions: Where Can It Take You?

With addictions, there could be an argument that psychological or medications are needed to stop addictions. However, on a spiritual level, we can gain His help to fight addictions and get out of bondage.[809]

Christ made us free! We do not have to be caught up in bondage with sin. In other words, Christ died to set us free from our sins, including the old laws and regulations. Even though Christ set us free from sin, does not mean that we can continue to sin because we are saved by grace. In other words, there is no excuse to go back into our own selfish desires. Those who only want to be free, yet, continue to live and fulfill our fleshly needs, will fall back into sin.

If you are caught in addiction, recognize that you are weak and that the strength in you comes from Christ. Once that becomes a reality in your life, you are enviably closer to Christ, because your walk is a moment-by-moment victory. Those who've been free of addiction were following what the Bible affirms.

"I am powerless to beat my addiction alone."
"I need God's help."
"I need people who are like-minded to lift me up when I am weak. I will seek them out."
"I recognize that my power to be loving and giving and caring is in my Savior, who walks with me."

---

[809] Philippians 4:13 and Galatians 5:1

Begin Day 247:
Saved by Faith

It is wrong to judge or place the burden on Christians, haranguing them about following God's laws. These laws are laid on our hearts as Christians; to obey God's commands and decrees. We must stand against those who would enslave us with rules, methods, or special conditions for being saved while growing in Christ.[810] Keeping the law without God's grace and being saved by grace are two different approaches. You will not profit anything if you are trying to save yourself. We need Christ's provision and protection. Obeying the law does not make it any easier for God to save us. All we can do is accept His gracious gift through faith. Our deeds must never be used to try to earn God's love or favor.[811]

Who is weak in their faith? Who is strong in their faith? We are all weak in some areas and stronger in other areas. Our faith is strong; we can survive contact with unbelievers without falling into the same old patterns. In our areas of strength, we will not fear being defiled by the world. Rather, we continue to serve God. If we have strong faith but shelter it, we are not doing Christ's work in the world. If we are weak, we must avoid those activities that would cause us to fall to protect our spiritual life. It is important to take a self-inventory to find out our strengths and weaknesses. In the areas of weakness, we need to be cautious. If we have a weak faith but expose it by assuming we know all, we are extremely foolish. One must be deeply knowledgeable of the character of Him who died on the Cross. Without reading the Bible, without listening for His guidance, we cannot stand strong. Whenever we are in doubt, we should ask, "Can I go without sinning? Can I influence others for good, rather than being influenced by them?"[812]

---

[810] Life Application Study Bible, NKJV, emphasis added by author.
[811] Life Application Study Bible, NKJV, 1996.
[812] Romans 14:1

Begin Day 248:
Conscience Leads to Repentance

A sinner's conscience will lead to either guilt resulting in repentance or headlong into sinful acts because of a refusal to repent. The more guilt he or she feels, the more likely he or she is to turn to God and repent. Sometimes, when we as believers continue to repeat a particular sin, we fall further away from repentance instead of turning to God for help to break the dependency.

If we meet someone who is deep in sin and interfere with the natural consequences of his or her actions, we make it easier for them to continue to indulge in their sin. The same goes for you. Here are the words to speak to the sinner (including ourselves). "Please turn to God, trust and believe that He has forgiven you. Get out of the habit of believing that 'once I sin, God will forgive me without repenting to Christ anymore.'" It's easy to think, 'He sees and knows all, so He will automatically forgive me because I am saved.' Remember, God wants us to confess our sins to Him, repent, and move forward, not looking back at that sin. When you think or feel that you cannot fight addictions such as lust, sexual immorality, anger, and so forth, remember that we have a higher power looking over us and can bring us through.[813]

Matthew 19:26, NKJV: *"But Jesus looked at them and said to them, 'With men this is impossible, but with God all things are possible.'"*

---

[813] See also Philippians 4:13 and Matthew 19:26

Begin Day 249:
Non-believers

Non-believers cannot understand God, and they cannot grasp that God's Spirit lives in believers.[814] Do not expect many people to approve of, or understand your decision to follow Christ. It all seems so silly to them. Don't worry about it. They cannot receive God's message if they continue to reject Him.

Sometimes Jesus believers can get sidetracked by mingling people caught up in the way of the world, or by enjoying time with things that do not glorify God (remember the commandment to not place anything or anyone in God's place). Then, because we do that, we tend to fall further away from Christ and are no longer focused on the prize of our Heavenly Father. Satan would love us to be lost forever from our Savior Jesus Christ, who died on the cross for our sins.

On the other hand, it is funny how so many philosophers, religious leaders, and books like *The DaVinci Code* question Christ's coming and going. They'll ask questions, like "Where is Jesus' body? Did Jesus really die on the cross? How did He suffer? Was Jesus married?" All these remarkable stories were broadcast on ABC around March 2004. A year later, a movie on *The DaVinci Code* was featured. The real answers lie in the Bible and having an intimate relationship with Christ will help those answers reside in your heart.

---

[814] 1 Corinthians 2:14-16

Begin Day 250:
Don't Be Fooled

You will have people who will try to influence you to sin. There will be temptations presented to you. Even your friends may have an influence over you to do things that you know are wrong. Others will try to convince you that another's opinion justifies your well-being. Overall, we are to turn to God for guidance and reassurance in our decision-making, seeking His wisdom in areas we are not confident in and remain righteous.

In your social life, pray about it, then search the Scriptures for answers because everything you do is viewed in the eyes of God. God will bring it to light. Do not say, "I cannot do it." If you gave your life to Christ, "Yes, you can."

If you enjoy going to clubs to dance, then learn to dance for Christ and join a praise dance at your local church or recreation center within your community. If you love hip-hop music, listen to gospel and gospel rap artists such as Cross Movement, Canton Jones, Righteous Riders, Ton3x (was Tonex, pronounced Toe-nay), Kirk Franklin, and many others by tapping into this genre of music until you find one to suit you. There is a variety of praise music available in all genres from Jazz, R&B, Hip-Hop, Reggae, Christian Rock, Contemporary Christian, and Gospel, to name a few.

If you like to drink, smoke, or get high, instead, get high on the Word. The spiritual high through meditation and prayer can take you higher than any drink, drug, or marijuana.

If you crave porno tapes, or certain movies, or games to entertain yourself, turn to God for the remedy.

Conclude that Satan and his demons are always lurking for an opportunity, whether it is through music, videos, movies, and even pornography. This can be an open door for Satan and his fallen angels, giving them permission to manipulate and to possess your soul. Give it over to Christ by allowing the Holy Spirit to convict you.

Begin Day 251:
Contentment

Paul was content because he could see life from God's point of view. Paul focused on what he was supposed to do, not what he felt he should have. He had his priorities straight. He was grateful for everything God had given him. He was also able to detach himself from the non-essentials so that he could concentrate on the eternal. Often the desire for more or better possessions is a longing to fill an empty place in a person's life.

How can you find true contentment? The answer lies in your perspective, your priorities, and your source of power.[815] Can we really do all things? The power we receive, union with Christ, is sufficient to do His will.

Furthermore, we can face the challenge that arises from our commitment to press forward. He does not grant us superhuman ability to accomplish anything we can imagine without regard to His interests. As we contend for the faith, we will face troubles, pressures, and trials. When these difficulties come, ask Christ to strengthen you.[816]

---

[815] Life Application Study Bible, NKJV, 1996.
[816] Life Application Study Bible, NKJV, emphasis added by author.

Begin Day 252:
How Do We Live A Christian Life?

Some roadblocks keep us from living a Christian life. Some people portray themselves as followers of Jesus Christ. However, Christ does not live there. God speaks about obedience by following His commandments and rules that He demonstrates throughout the Holy Bible. We are not saved by keeping God's rules alone.[817] Trying to live a Christian life by just going to church weekly is not enough. Fellowship is essential in the Christian life. However, we need a daily relationship with God. Some of us try to live a Christian life by doing what is good. We are not saved by our ability to do good works.[818]

2 Peter 1:5-6, NKJV: *"But also for this very reason giving all diligence, add to your faith virtue, to virtue knowledge, to knowledge self-control, to self-control perseverance, to perseverance godliness."*

We need to understand God's part for living a Christian life. God does not expect us to live a Christian life through our own understanding and knowledge.[819] In 2 Peter 1:1-14, God has shown us what we need to do to live a Christian life. These attributes consist of faith, help, grace, peace, knowledge of God, a source of divine power from God, and promises from God. God does not expect us to live this life by being a spectator. Our responsibility for living a Christian life or prerequisites is to trust in God, which is depending on God. Another prerequisite is diligence, which is an effort to do our part. Both of these must be present to live a successful Christian life.

---

[817] Galatians 3:1-5
[818] Ephesians 2:8-9
[819] Proverbs 3:5-6

Begin Day 253:
7 Steps to Living a Christian Life

Seven Steps to Living a Christian life:[820]
1. *Virtue -- excellence*: We cannot produce a virtuous character ourselves. Do we desire to live right and please the Lord?
2. *Knowledge -- practical wisdom*: Once we desire to do what is right, we now need to know what is right. We learn what God expects from the Scripture. What questions should we ask as we study the Scripture? What is God like? What does God disapprove and approve? What did Christ do for us?
3. *Self-control -- practice*: Knowing all the answers means nothing if our life is not in shape with Jesus. Self-control results from the Holy Spirit. Thinking and meditating on the Scripture is a start, but not enough since we have to put it into practice (action speaks louder than words).
4. *Perseverance -- endurance*: In life, we will face troubles and problems. This gives us the ability to complete what we have started. It develops character and faith through spiritual maturity.
5. *Godliness -- focus*: We live for God and not for ourselves. Our focus, therefore, is becoming more like Christ.
6. *Brotherly -- kindness*: Godliness requires us to do what God does. As God shows kindness to us, we must show kindness to others.
7. *Love – agape*: God's love is agape, unconditional love no matter what we do or say. We are to love people despite how they treat us. We are sacrificing ourselves for the good of others.

The results of living a Christian life is to be productive, not to be shortsighted and blinded to the point that we have foresight what Christ has done for us.[821] We will not stumble. We can look forward to greater rewards in heaven.

---

[820] 2 Peter 1:5-7
[821] See 2 Peter 1:8-11

Begin Day 254:
Stay Focused

God must be your focus on everything you do. We are able to make choices since God has blessed us with free will. However, this does not mean once we are saved that we are able to do what we want to do. Every time you are not sure what to do in a situation, just think, *What Would Jesus Do (WWJD)*. If fear continues to run your life, God says if we believe, we will receive. We can be delivered from 'fear' if we only ask God.

Begin Day 255:
Command

When we are asked to do something for God such as evangelism, singing in choir, musicians, and ministering to others, just to name a few, imagine what God can do to you and for you. If you do what God commands, imagine all the blessings you can receive in the Kingdom of Heaven and receive here on Earth. If we do not follow His commands, imagine a soul that is lost to the Lord and burning in Hell for eternity.

Remember, you cannot force God on the timing of His command. Just plant the seed, pray that God will be the focus in other's lives, and watch them grow spiritually. If you feel fear, ask God to make you fearless like the 'spider,' so you can conquer to do His will.

For instance, I feared writing this book, but I realize that it is more important to reach and save souls by spreading God's Word then sitting back to pray that someone will be reached, and subsequently saved. I will still pray for those souls, but my point here is, we need to act when God shows us our calling. I feel, when you have fear or doubt and ask Him, you will see God's purpose in your lives. If you open the door and let God in, you will get past your fear. You may think that it is hard work to do God's business, but it really is not. You simply haven't arrived at the next step in your mission.

Begin Day 256:
Glorify the Lord

Glory is the manifestation, or Hebrews word *doxa*, of God's excellence and goodness. We all want to experience His glory because the Spirit of Grace lives inside of us as believers in Jesus Christ.[822]

1 Corinthians 6:20, NLT: *"for God bought you with a high price. So you must honor God with your body."*

Romans 8:16, 17: *Indication of believers' son-ship* is that the Holy Spirit bears witness. When believers cry out to the Father in prayer, *Romans 8:15*, and the Holy Spirit intercedes for them.

According to *Vine Dictionary*, *glory* means *God's essential nature*. Those who still live under the Old covenant, rituals, and formulas or following the dead letter of the law,[823] will not enjoy life. To live a life under the grace of God, we are expecting glory and to be filled with the Holy Spirit in which we should be excited about life. If we are excited about our lives, where we are living a life for Jesus Christ, it will make things better, easier, and more enjoyable, including being able to overlook the evil in the world since we have complete joy knowing we have surrendered to Christ and bear His yoke. We can experience remarkable joy, *Dancing in the Son*, a song by Ton3x.[824]

---

[822] Colossians 1:27
[823] 2 Corinthians 3:6
[824] emphasis added by the author

Begin Day 257:
Joint Heirs (Inheritance)

Romans 8:16-17, NLT: *"For his Spirit joins with our spirit to affirm that we are God's children. ¹⁷ And since we are his children, we are his heirs. In fact, together with Christ we are heirs of God's glory. But if we are to share his glory, we must also share his suffering."*

Romans 15:26. Heirs: All of God's children have an inheritance based on their relationship to God, which is incorruptible, undefiled, and reserved in heaven.[825] Their inheritance includes an expectation of eternal life.[826] As joint heirs with Christ they share His suffering now[827] and will share His glory later.[828] First, Christ must live in us. Otherwise, we are unable to experience the glory of God. We all want to experience God's glory on a continuous basis. If we ask, then we shall receive it.[829]

Psalm 119:175, NLT: *"Let me live so I can praise you, and may your regulations help me."*

---

[825] 1 Peter 1:4
[826] Titus 3:4-7
[827] Philippians 3:10
[828] Philippians 3:11-14
[829] Matthew 7:7

Begin Day 258:
Surrendering to Worship

We are to surrender everything to God. Some refer to surrendering to God in worship as bowing, which is done by standing, lying straight down, or on your knees. Bowing may be in private, which is worshipping the Lord in your secret place. Worshipping God involves acknowledgment of His divine perfections.

Direct address is adoration, thanksgiving, or service to God, and can be in private or in a corporate function. In worship, praise, and/or glorifying the Lord, we must fear the Lord with all our heart, mind, body, and soul.

Begin Day 259:
Fearing the Lord

Fearing the Lord is another keyword to 'loving the Lord.' If we love the Lord, we will follow His commandments. Proverbs 9:10 says, "The fear of the Lord is the beginning of wisdom, and knowledge of the Holy One is the beginning of understanding." Contrast this with Jesus' promise of the Holy Spirit in John 16:13, guiding us "into all truth."

If we love the Lord, we will follow His will. If we love the Lord, we will read, study, and meditate on His Holy Word. God is greatly to be feared in the assembly of the saints and to be held in reverence by all those around Him. Moreover, to serve the Lord, God focuses on our hearts, not our physical appearance. Jesus is the way, the truth, and the light.[830]

---

[830] John 14:6; 17:7

Begin Day 260:
Forms of Worship

There are several ways to worship, and they are all demonstrated in the Bible. God will lie on your heart and can be expressed through praise dance. Other ways are the admiration of God's creation, thanksgiving for the blessings He has administered, and through songs and hymns including poetry/lyrics. We can give God praise through our service, with our announcements or testimonies and glorifying the Lord. We can start as early as the morning, when we first open our eyes, and before getting out of bed. We can rest on our beds for the day ahead and welcome Him as we go to sleep, meditating on Him.

It is a true blessing to see another day. We are blessed to have our health, family, and roof over our heads. We ought to worship and thank the Lord throughout the day and until the end of our day before dosing off to sleep. Give God the praise for your life having coped another day in our toxic world of sinful acts and thoughts and in the air we breathe (toxic chemicals).

We can also exhibit worship in a corporate setting through prophetic sermons, concerts, prayer meetings, Bible study, and church services.

Begin Day 261:
Worship also Calls the Angels

There is another reason for glorifying and worshiping the Lord. It gets God's attention to enlist the help of His angels. You will hear some people say, 'I know that I have a guardian angel.' Angels are prompted when God commands them to do so.

God will be there for His children when they call, and His sheep will be able to hear His voice. He will take care of their enemies. "Vengeance is mine," says the Lord. Praise God for taking care of your enemies and the ultimate enemy of them all—Satan. Furthermore, Satan is the fallen angel responsible for first two humans to fall and lead us all into sin. Since the fall, we are all born into sin but can be saved through our Lord and Savior. We have a second chance, but Satan and his followers do not.

For example, God released His angel when Daniel continued to praise and pray to God at the same time every day, instead of worshipping the idol King Darius wanted everyone in his kingdom to worship. Due to refusing the King's command, Daniel was thrown into the Lion's Den with hungry, ferocious lions. Nevertheless, he knelt in the den to pray to God, what do you think happened? Some imagine the worse. Some just simply do not know. If you read the story, there was a victory from beyond that cage he was trapped in, facing hungry animals that would eat flesh. The angel was inside tame and calm down the lions, and they did not touch a hair on Daniel. Through prayer, Daniel worshipped the Lord, no matter what the situation was.[831]

Another example is the Good News about the birth of a child named Jesus. Joseph prayed that his fiancé would make it to his birth land unharmed.

The Corinthians prayed for Peter while he was held captive in prison. After God heard their sincere prayers, He sent angels to come to Peter's rescue to release him from prison without disturbing the guards at the post. The chains fell off Peter's hands and feet as the prison gates flew open and he walked quietly pass the sleeping guards.[832] Look at what prayer can do!

Remember that vague prayers will get vague answers. Tell God the desires of your heart, and wait and watch how God will shower you with blessings beyond your wildest dreams.[833]

---

[831] Daniel 6
[832] Acts 12
[833] John 5:14; Psalm 37:4-5

Begin Day 262:
14 Reasons to Worship & Praise God

1. He forgives my iniquities
2. He heals all my diseases
3. He redeems my life from destruction
4. His loving kindness
5. He satisfies my mouth with good things
6. He executes righteousness and justice for the oppressed
7. He makes his ways known to us
8. He is merciful and everlasting
9. He is gracious
10. He is slow to anger
11. He removes our transgressions from us
12. He takes pity on us
13. We have obedient fellowship
14. He rules us all, and His throne is established

Begin Day 263:
Surrendering Attitude

We can have an *attitude of surrender*, which means putting God first. Submitting to His rulership will make all the difference. A simple prayer to God: "I surrender my relationship, my finances, my work, recreation, my decisions, my time, my body, my mind, my soul, my desires, and my dreams. I put them all in Your hands so they can be used for Your glory."[834]

Philippians 2:9-11: *"Therefore God also has highly exalted Him and given Him the name which is above every name, that at the name of Jesus every knee should bow, of those in heaven, and of those on earth, and of those under the earth, and that every tongue should confess that Jesus Christ is the Lord, to the glory of the Father."*

Every knee: Only those who put their faith in Him will have an everlasting relationship with Him after death.

Those under the earth: Paul refers to those who will already have died before the time of Christ's second return on earth. Those who were saved and lived a righteous life will be raised first when Christ returns. Second, He will rapture those who will still be living on earth.

Confess: Paul uses a strong, intensive verb, agree with or say the same thing. Paul is saying that everyone will unanimously affirm what God, the Father, has already stated; that Jesus is Christ the Lord.[835]

---

[834] Refer to the following Scriptures: Galatians 2:20; Luke 9:23-24; Romans 14:8; 1 Peter 5:6-7
[835] Isaiah 45:23

Begin Day 264:
Judgment Comes

At the last judgment, even those who are condemned will recognize Jesus' authority and right to rule.[836] People can choose to consider Jesus as Lord and Savior this very day. This shows a step of willing and loving commitment to follow Christ. Or you will acknowledge Him as Lord when He returns, and it will be too late for your salvation. In that case, it will break your heart. Christ may return at any moment. Are you prepared to meet Him?

---

[836] Philippians 2:9-11

Begin Day 265:
God's versus Moses' Law

Remember: Believers are not *lucky*; we are *blessed*.

God's Law:
1. Love the Lord with all your heart, mind, soul and body
2. Love your neighbor

Law of Moses:
1. Has penalties for not following the law
2. We have to make a choice of which law we will follow
3. Led by the Spirit: Will you love your family? Will you follow and live for the Lord, regardless of the law?
4. Some people only concerned about themselves -- not the Lord
5. Satan will have you focusing on one extreme or the other
6. Learning how to fight the Adversary
7. God will not leave you alone
8. Fear and intimidation = Devil concentrates on
9. *James 4:7:* Resistance and Satan will flee from us, Devil fear
10. Head knowledge: learning and studying more, but we need personal experience

Begin Day 266:
Guidance

The book, *Choosing God's Best* says that God's guidance will never go against the Scripture. The Bible is a record of God's revelation of Himself to man. If you seek the Spirit alone for guidance without confirming it with the Word, you can open yourself up for possible deception.

If you look at circumstances alone without the Word, you can be deceived. In seeking God's direction, in prayer, in Scriptures, through circumstances, and the counsel of other believers agree in the direction that God is leading you. You are unable to see the agreement of God's will and advice from non-believers.[837] Allow God to purify your spirit and mind to make you strong and secure in all that you do, build you up, restoring your soul and mind, to refresh your spirit, and most importantly, to grow in Christ.[838]

---

[837] Micah 4:2
[838] 2 Timothy 2:5

Begin Day 267:
Conquerors

No athlete or competitor is crowned unless he competed within the confines of the rules. We are conquerors. However, we need to follow God's laws to preserve and conquer any spiritual warfare or battles that come in our path. Faithful believers will receive a victor's crown, which is the royal crown that belongs to Jesus. In other words, spiritual activity must be conducted within the directives of biblical faith and doctrine.[839]

Review Psalm 119:165-166, 174-176.

---

[839] Nelson's Study Bible, NKJ, emphasis added by author.

Begin Day 268:
God's Love

Do we love the Lord? God says in His Word: God is love. Once we know that God loves us and we love Him, we will obey His commandments, laws, decrees, or anything He asks of us to do—we will do. Lastly, we know that His love will never fail.[840] We ought to be delighted to serve the Lord because He cares about the welfare of His children.

We were like lost sheep, unable to find our way to the Father, but if we seek the Lord and truly love Him, we will not forget His commandments that He set forth. We cannot ignore or run away from the commandments as believers of the Word. Blessed are those who keep the Word of God, who are able to hear the Word and keep it.

---

[840] 1 Corinthians 13:8

Begin Day 269:
Walk in Holiness

The Word of God will set a person free from bondage. We are able to see the areas that need to be improved – *walk in holiness*. Be an anchor in the Lord. Hear the gospel so we can be doers of the Word. Doers of the Word manifest themselves through service or ministry.

Begin Day 270:
God Blesses

God promises to bless our health through salvation and obedience. God will continue to bless you and show you His will through obedience and willingness to listen to Him. Obedient servants will not fall short of God's glory. We stand boldly in confidence and peace by abiding by His laws and commandments. *Please Lord; show me Your steps so I can trust Your guidance in everything.*[841]

God will pour on the blessings that we are meant to receive. Furthermore, God wants us to pray, praise, glorify, and turn to Him in everything we do daily. We need to meditate on His law (precepts) and take in (contemplate) God's ways. *Contemplate,*[842] means consider purpose, reflect on, study, think of, think about seriously, and plan. God will show us His purpose. We are to reflect on studying the Bible and having a personal relationship with God. We need to think about God's plan and take it seriously. Through obedience, we will be blessed and satisfied.

---

[841] Philippians 4:13
[842] Roget's Thesaurus.

Begin Day 271:
The Song of the Commandments

David wrote eloquently on walking with God and following the commandments. One can find these and more in the Book of Psalms.

Psalm 119:10, NLT: *"I have tried hard to find you—don't let me wander from your commands."*

Psalm 119:11, NLT: *"I have hidden your word in my heart, that I might not sin against you."*

Psalm 119:15-16, NLT: *"I will study your commandments and reflect on your ways. I will delight in your decrees and not forget your word."*

Psalm 119:17-21, NKJV: *"…That I may live and keep Your word. Open my eyes, that I may see wondrous things from Your law. I am a stranger in the earth; do not hide Your commandments from me. My soul breaks with longing for Your judgments at all times, you rebuke the proud—the cursed, who stray from Your commandments."*

Begin Day 272:
Open with God through Confession

We must admit that we have sin that God is not pleased with. Otherwise, we only deceive ourselves, and the truth is not in us. If we confess our sins, God is faithful and just to forgive us of our sins and cleanse us from all unrighteousness. Allow God to reveal to you, all your faults, shortcomings, mistakes, and sins.

Sin is one's desires that fulfill the wants of the flesh and willingness to proceed with an act, thought, or desire to satisfy self. Unfortunately, some of us are bonded in chains of the world, of our flesh, and not seeking the Holy Spirit for correction and direction. Before making decisions, seek God first to direct our path, our choices, and in everything we do in the name of Jesus Christ.

Begin Day 273:
Shepherd

Jesus is the Shepherd of His sheep, as His sheep, we hear our Master's voice and clear instructions from the Lord. Additionally, we will be able to decipher right from wrong, especially things that are not like Jesus Christ, our Lord.[843]

---

[843] also can refer to these Scriptures—1 John 3:22-24; Luke 11:28; John 14:21

Adrienna Dionna Turner

Reviews Are In

AAMBC (Africans on the Move Book Club)
Gretchen Tolbert, 5 out of 5 stars.

The Day Begins with Christ puts me in the mind of a theologian properly dissecting the bible so that others can better understand Christ and develop a relationship with him. This book analysis God's relationship with his people and helps the reader to further develop and cultivate their relationship with Christ. We all are here for a purpose and for a season. That season and purpose involves God's love and guidance to properly understand and pursue. One must first be able to hear God's voice and know what his voice sounds like to you. Afterwards, one must be able to take heed and follow after Christ with passion and convection that will lead to salvation and further trust in God. As a non-fictional reader of Christian-related information for a passion, I found the book to be very informative and easy to read and non-threatening.

Christians are looking for a following guide or something to aid in their walk as they grow in God. This journal/booklet provides this ultimately to the readers. Each day provided enriching elements of what God expects from his people consistently. I agree with Adrienna Turner that without the knowledge of the expectations of Christ, his people perish or do not live life to the fullest and to their best capability.

Author Wright, Historical Romance (Lavina: The Saga of an African Princess) and Biblical Fiction (Ruth of Moab: Triumph of a Daughter's Love) gave 5 out of 5 stars.

Posted **(August 2009-August 2010)**

Often, the full impact of God's sovereign grace for fallen man is hidden in the writing style and expressions of many biblical scholars and teachers. However, the exhortation from our Lord and Savior to lead a righteous and holy life is still as relevant in our lives today as it has ever been. As Christians, we should always have God's amazing love as we walk in Faith from day to day. It is his transforming love which brings us to the true expression of his will. The Day Begins with Christ is a marvelous work of God guiding the hands and heart of his servant Adrienna. In her powerful book, she makes the power and purpose of our Lord's death abundantly clear and accessible in her lucid discussions of life and salvation. She stresses that through Jesus' death alone, the power over sin and death has been conquered. In her gracious writings, she tells her readers that mastery and dominion of sin have been broken once and forever. Then, she patiently leads them into the perfect will of God. The Day Begins with Christ, along with the Holy Bible, should be in every home so that one could learn how to live the successful walk of Faith.

Other Spiritual Books and Novels

Nonfiction Reads & Poetry:
From The Depths of My Soul: Collection of Poetry and Songs
Gospel/Religious Version

Unleashing the Spirits, Volumes 1-3

Desire at Will

God is in the Equation

Novels:

Miss the Mark Series: Book 1: *Tormented Dreams*
Miss the Mark Series: Book 2: *Outcry, Shalom!*

Mirror Beware! (Revised version entitled: *Mirrors Lie*) as Dream Summore

Nonfiction Future Books:
Vessel 4 Christ Series: Disciple Me
Vessel 4 Christ Series: Counsel Me
Vessel 4 Christ Series: Friend & Follow Me
Vessel 4 Christ Series: Lead Me

Who Will I Serve?

More About the Author

Adrienna Turner is an award-winning author for female author of the year: *Day Begins with Christ* (former title), nonfiction. She has a graduate certificate in Legal Studies, Master's Degree in Library Information Science with honors as magna cum laude and a Bachelor's Degree in Information Resources. She enjoys working as a state law librarian.

She's a prolific writer and working diligently on an apocalyptic thriller series; a fantasy thriller series; and other nonfictional works. She has also penned as Dream Summore, with debut inspirational drama novel, entitled *Mirrors Lie* (Book 1 of the Mirror Saga Series).

As she writes, she (and others) notice these works seem to be a gift from God, meant for those who have lost their way and are seeking for a place for their soul to rest, restoring their faith, their hope, and their love.

She has a virtual ministry and radio program called Dream Your Reality Prophecies (DYRP). She was honored to serve under her former Pastors Wilke as a Bible Study teacher at Spirit Life Church (Milwaukee, WI). She has taught teleclasses: Dream Experience Series (DES). She was a featured speaker at Revolutionary Christian Literary Conference—RCLC 2012.

She has been nominated for Outstanding Community by BBCRA (Black Books Club Rocks Award, 2009) and best book reviewer (Dream 4 More Reviews); and literary talk show (Adrienna Turner Show) for 2010 AAMBC Literary Award also Host of the Year with Facebook Urban Literary Award.

APPENDICES FOR FURTHER STUDIES

BEGIN DAY 32
Contrast Of Moral And Ceremonial Laws

Moral Law	*Ritual or Ceremonial Law*
Royal Law of Liberty—James 2:8-12	Law…contained in ordinances—Ephesians 2:15
Spoken by God—Deuteronomy 4:12	Spoken by Moses—Leviticus 1:1-3
Written by God on stone—Exodus 24:12; 31:18	Written by Moses in book—2 Chronicles 35:12
Placed in the Ark—Hebrews 9:4; Exodus 40:20	Placed in the side of the Ark—Deuteronomy 31:24-26
To stand forever—Psalm 111:7,8	Ended at the cross—Colossians 2:14-17
Gives the knowledge of sin—Romans 3:20; 7:7	Was given because of sin—Galatians 3:19
Not grievous—I John 5:3	Contrary to us—Colossians 2:14-17
Judges all men—James 2:10-12	Judges no man—Colossians 2:14-17
Spiritual—Romans 7:14	Carnal—Hebrews 9:10

BEGIN DAY 40
Dietary Fiber In Food

Breads & Crackers	Amount	Fiber (grams)
Graham Crackers	2 squares	1.5
Pumpernickel	¾ slice	1.5
Rye Bread	1 slice	1.0
Whole-Wheat Bread	1 slice	0
Whole-Wheat cracker	6 crackers	2.0
Whole-Wheat roll	¾ roll	1.0

For other bread/crackers products, check the Dietary Fiber intake.

Cereal	Amount	Fiber (grams)
All Bran 100%	1/3 cup	8.5
Bran Chex	½ cup	4.0
Corn Bran	½ cup	4.5
Corn Flakes	¾ cup	2.5
Grape Nuts Flakes	2/3 cup	2.5
Grape Nuts	3 tbsp	2.5
Oatmeal	¾ pkg	2.5
Shredded Wheat	1 biscuit	3.0
Wheaties	¾ cup	2.5

For other Cereals, check the Dietary Fiber intake.

Fruit	Amount	Fiber (grams)
Apple	½ large	2.0
Apricot	2	1.5
Banana	½ medium	1.5
Blackberries	¾ cup	6.5
Cantaloupe	1 cup	1.5
Cherries	10 large	1.0
Dates (dried)	2	1.5
Figs (dried)	1 medium	3.5
Grapes (white)	10	.5

Grapefruit	½	1.0
Honeydew Melon	1 cup	1.5
Orange	Small	1.5
Peach	1 medium	2.5
Pear	½ medium	2.0
Pineapple	½	1.0
Plum	3 small	2.0
Prunes (dried)	2	2.5
Raisins	1 ½ Tbsp	1.0
Strawberries	1 cup	3.0
Tangerine	1 large	2.0
Watermelon	1 cup	1.5

Meat, Milk, Eggs	Amount	Fiber
Beef, Pork	1 ounce	0
Chicken, Turkey	1 ounce	0
Cheese	¾ ounce	0
Cold cuts, Franks	1 ounce	0
Egg	1 large	0
Fish	2 ounces	0
Ice cream	1 cup	0
Milk	1 cup	0
Yogurt	5 ounces	0

Rice	Amount	Fiber (grams)
Brown Rice (cooked)	1/3 cup	1.5
White Rice (cooked)	1/3 cup	0.5
Leaf Vegetables	Amount	Fiber (grams)
Broccoli	½ cup	3.5
Brussel Sprouts	½ cup	2.5
Cabbage	½ cup	2.0
Cauliflower	½ cup	1.5
Celery	½ cup	1.0
Lettuce	1 cup	1.0
Spinach (raw)	1 cup	.5
Turnip Greens	½ cup	3.5

Root Vegetables	Amount	Fiber (grams)
Beets	½ cup	2.0
Carrots	½ cup	2.5
Potatoes (baked)	½ medium	2.0
Radishes	½ cup	1.5
Sweet Potatoes (baked)	½ medium	2.0

Other Vegetables	Amount	Fiber (grams)
Green Beans	½ cup	2.0
String Beans	½ cup	2.0
Cucumber	½ cup	1.0

Eggplant	½ cup	2.5
Lentils (cooked)	½ cup	4.0
Mushrooms	½ cup	1.0
Onions	½ cup	1.0
Tomato	1 small	1.5
Winter Squash	½ cup	3.5
Zucchini Squash	½ cup	2.0

This is a general guide provided by the Nutrition Therapy Department at Milwaukee Medical Clinic. If you have more questions or concerns, please contact your dietitian or doctor.

30 Fat Burning Foods

Apples	Jam (sugar-free, low cal only)
Bananas	Leeks
Beans	Lettuce
Bread (plain, preferably wheat)	Melons
Broccoflower	Pasta (low-fat, whole grain)
Broccoli	Pears
Cabbage	Peas (all types)
Cauliflower	Peppers
Celery	Pineapple
Citrus Fruits (lemons, oranges, grapefruit)	Root Vegetables
Corn (also air-popped popcorn)	Cranberries
Grains and Grain products	Tomatoes (salt-free, sugar-free sauce and salsa)
Grapes	Waffles and Pancakes (low-fat and frozen)
Zucchini	Spinach

BEGIN DAY 40

Unclean (forbidden foods)	*Clean foods*
Eagle	Chicken
Vulture	Duck
Buzzard	Goose
Red Kite (all kinds)	Grouse
Falcon	Partridge
Raven (all kinds)	Pheasant
Ostrich	Quail
Owls	Turkey
Sea Gull	Song Birds
Hawk	Fish: Anchovy, Barracuda, Bass, Bowfin, Buffalo
Jackdaw	Deer: Roe deer (male deer)
Stork	Antelope
Hoopoe	Gazelle
Bat	Hart (male red deer), Fallow
Flying Insects: creep on all fours and leap on the earth	Carp, Tarpon, Trout, Tuna, Whitefish, Sole, Snapper
Camel or Donkey	Cod (fish)
Rock Hyrax	Darter (fish)
Swine or Pig	Sardine (fish)

Humans (flesh)	Salmon (fish)
Carcass: food with outer shell such as oysters, clams, crabs, lobsters	Haddock (fish)
Creep on the earth: mole, mouse, lizard, gecko, sand reptile, chameleon, snake, hamsters	Other fish: Grayling, Flounder, Halibut, Herring, Jack, Mackerel, Minnow, Mullet, Perch, Pike, Shad, Sunfish
Hare (Rabbit)	Lamb or Sheep
Fish: Catfish, Eels, Swordfish, Sturgeons, Shellfish, Shrimp	Beef (Cow or Oxen)
Eel	Goat

Four	Body	Types	Exercise	Other
Endomorph	High percentage of body fat and gains weight easily	Gains mainly in the lower body	Aerobics, power walking, jump rope, biking at low intensity (60 % of maximum heart rate) for 40-60 minutes, 4 days a week. Strength training for 15 minutes, 2 to 3 days a week. Lower abdominal exercises. Stretch for 5 min before and after every workout.	Aerobics to reduce body fat and maintain optimum weight. To lose weight, increase your aerobic activity to 5 days a week. Avoid step aerobics, ankle weights, and stair climbing. Focus on upper body to draw away from heavier body
Mesomorph	Large chest and thick waist with narrow hips and slender legs. Usually have tight joints, prone to exercise-related injuries.	Tends to be muscular with a lower body-fat % and a lean physique.	Aerobics include running, step classes, and stair climbing at high intensity (70% to 85% for maximum heart rate for 30 minutes, 3 to 4 days a week. Strength training for 15 minutes, 3 days a week, focusing on your lower body to balance your physique.	To lose weight, add an extra day of aerobics since your upper body is naturally muscular, avoid rowing machines and swimming. Develop flexibility by doing yoga or Tai Chi or stretch-oriented classes, at least 15 minutes, 5 days a week.

Ectomorph	Hips and chest are in proportion, but inflexible and lack strength.	Quick metabolism and an athletic, wiry physique.	All types of aerobics including running, swimming, rowing machine, and step aerobics at medium intensity (60 % maximum heart rate) for 20 minutes, 3 to 4 days a week.	For weight loss, add an extra day of aerobics. Emphasize strength training using heavier weights for upper and lower body for 30-40 minutes, 3-4 days a week. Focus on abdominal strengthening exercises at least 15 minutes before and after every workout. More prone for back injuries.
Meso-endomorph	Hips and chest are in proportion.	Lean muscles with body fat and good flexibility.	All types of aerobics including swimming, power walking, and biking at low intensity (60% of your maximum heart rate) for 40-60 minutes, 4 days a week. Use light weights with multiple repetitions for 15 minutes, 3 days a week. Focus on lower abdominal exercise. Stretch for at least 5 *minutes before and after every workout.	Increase to 5 days for weight loss.

Step 1

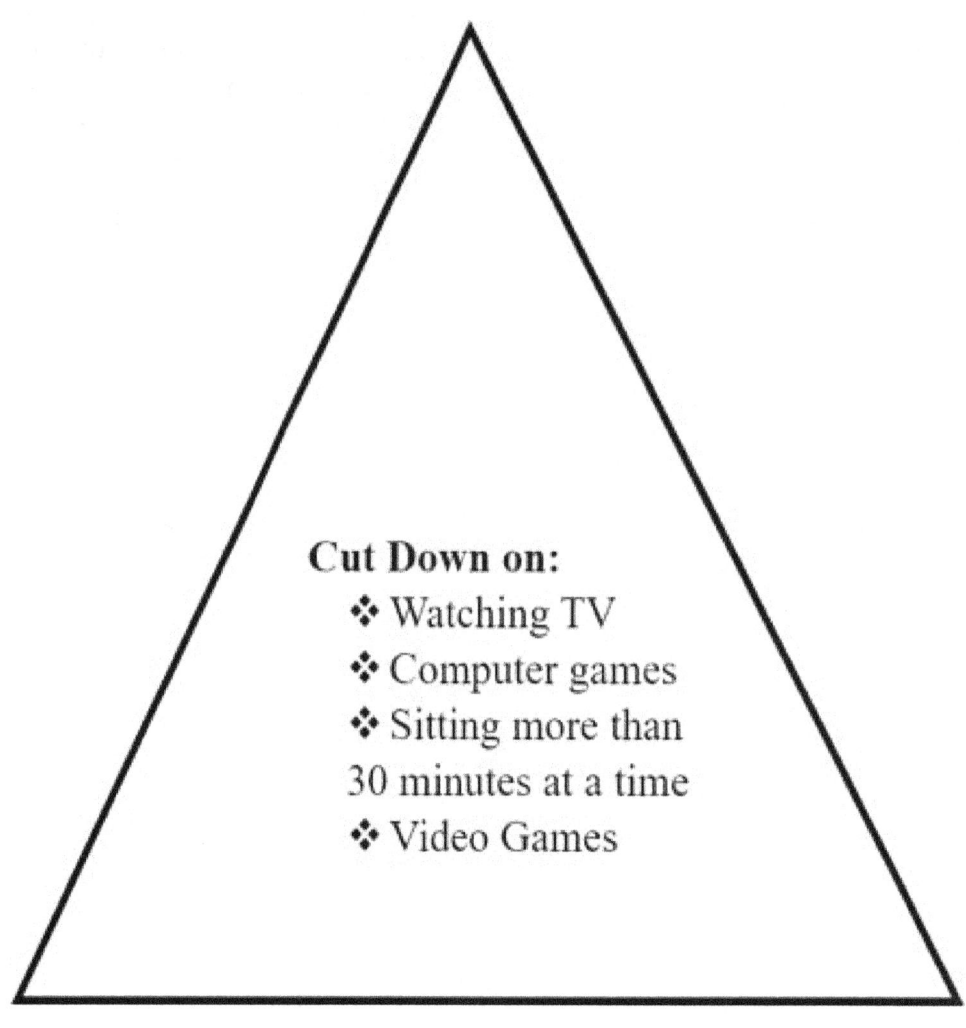

The Activity Chart
Step 2

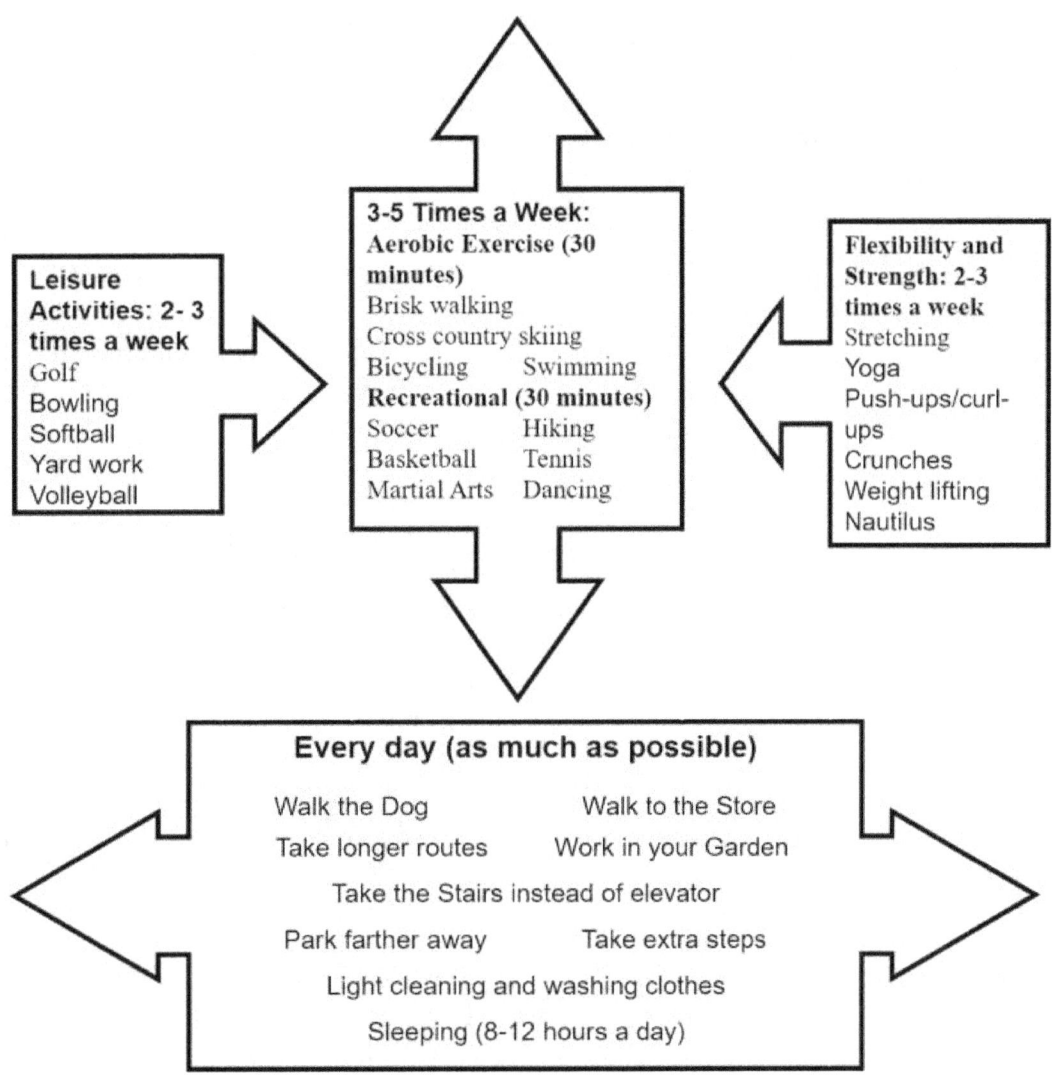

Dubious Diets: Beware Of The Pitfalls Of Some Of The Most Popular Diets

The Diet	The Concerns
Low-Calorie Diets: (Under 1200 calories per day) Limited amounts of food: protein, complex carbohydrates, and fat.	- RDA guidelines for daily nutrients often are not met - Although weight loss is often two to three pounds a week, it is usually water weight, and gaining it back more likely than with slower loss diets
High Carbohydrate and High Fiber Diets: Whole grains, cereals, raw fruits, and vegetables, some protein, and dairy products. Highly processed foods are discouraged.	- High amounts of fiber may reduce the absorption of minerals
Liquid Diets: Powers and liquids are consumed as a meal replacement.	- Most people quit due to lack of variety - Healthful eating habits are not established - Can cause constipation - May cause menstrual problems if calorie level is too low - Due to large amounts of water lost with very low-calorie liquid diets, when normal eating is resumed, the body compensates by retaining massive amounts of fluid, which can dilute the body's potassium, causing abnormal heart rhythms - Use of these products is safer if used daily for one meal only, with two meals of regular foods
High Protein Diets: High protein foods, such as chicken and cottage cheese are emphasized.	- Can increase levels of blood fat and cholesterol - May cause menstrual problems - Dehydration - Osteoporosis - Aggravation of gout - Kidney stones or kidney failure
Single Food Diets: Only one type of food such as grapefruit or rice is allowed.	- RDA guidelines for daily nutrients often are not met or are excessive in some areas - Most people quit due to lack of variety

	✦ Healthful eating habits are not established
Fasting: Water and any beverages without calories are allowed.	✦ RDA guidelines for daily nutrients often are not met ✦ Low blood pressure ✦ Emotional disturbances ✦ Death if prolonged ✦ Healthful eating habits are not established
Do not fall for the diet gimmicks: it does not melt away extra weight, and they can be costly. The safety of many gimmicks could be an issue. If losing weight were that easy, we would be a nation of very slender people.	✦ A daily program of healthy, well-balanced diet and regular exercise is what works -- there are no overnight, instant or magic cures for weight loss

--Betty Crocker's New Eat and Lose Weight, 1996

Parenting (www.christiannet.com):

Parenting Resources	Scriptures
Children heritage and blessings from God	Psalm 127:3,4
Children can teach adults	Matthew 18:1-4
Children's personality	Proverbs 22:15
Reasoning with children removes foolishness	Proverbs 22:15
Parents responsibility for their children to live for God	1 Thessalonians 2:11-12
Discipline our children	Proverbs 13:24
Wise child accepts reproof from father	Proverbs 15:5
Children are joy	Proverbs 23:24-25
Children's obedience brings blessings	Ephesians 6:1-3
Children enter covenant with God	Deuteronomy 29:10-12
Discipline: child on the right path	Proverbs 22:6
Authority and pacify conflict through strict words	Proverbs 15:1
Do not provoke anger or aggravate	Ephesians 6:4
Obey parents	Ephesians 6:1-3
Parent bear children's burdens	Galatians 6:5-9
David's sin hurt his family	2 Samuel 12:9-10
God's warning: not to follow in your parent's footsteps	Ezekiel 20:18
1Jesus taught	Matthew 18:5-6
Passing Christian heritage to our children	Psalm 78:4-7
Parents provide	2 Corinthians 12:14
God has given us children: bless them	Genesis 48:8-10
Fatherly love	Genesis 37:3-4
Inheritance	Proverbs 13:22

Encourage children to learn God's commandments	Deuteronomy 6:6-9
Fear the Lord	Proverbs 14:26
Corrects his children	Proverbs 22:15; 3:11-12; 29:17
Wild friends bring shame on the parents	Proverbs 28:7
Foolishness of a child affects the father	Proverbs 17:21
Building home	Psalm 127:1
Troubled Home	Proverbs 15:27
Joy	Proverbs 23:24
Bore child in old age	Genesis 17:17-19; 22:15-17
Birthright	Genesis 25:29-33
Love one child more than the rest	Genesis 37:3-4
Twelve Tribes of Israel	Genesis 49:28
Sons death and still worshipped God	2 Samuel 12:19-20
Footsteps of God	Ezekiel 20:18-19
Stepfather	Matthew 1:18
Evil in the sight of God	2 Chronicles 33:22-24
Courageous Father	Mark 5:22, 24, 41
Honor Parents	Deuteronomy 5:16

Respect mothers	Leviticus 19:3
Love God more than parents and children	Matthew 10:37
Virtuous woman	Proverbs 31:10
Beauty in vain	Proverbs 31:30
Blessing and Praises	Proverbs 31:28
Household	Proverbs 31:13-15
Training (raise a child)	Proverbs 22:6
Pain in childbirth	Genesis 3:16
Birth of child	John 16:21
Elders	Titus 2:3-5
Death or cursed parents	Exodus 21:15
Discipline	Proverbs 1:8
First twins	Genesis 25:21-23
Adoption	Exodus 2:10
Nurse child (breastfeed)	Exodus 2:5-9
Prayed for a child	1 Samuel 1:11
Child not his	Matthew 1:19
Movement in womb	Luke 1:41-42
First miracle	John 2:1-5
Death of son	John 19:25
Mother taken care of	John 19:27

Below is a list of **all** the names our Creator has been given for various reasons and/or purposes.

Abba	Romans 8:15	Advocate	1 John 2:1 (KJV); John 14:26
Almighty	Psalm 68:14; Matthew 28:18; Revelation 1:8	Alpha	Revelation 22:13; 1: 8-13
Amen	Revelation 3:14	Ancient of Days	Daniel 7
Anointed One	Psalm 2:2	Apostle	Hebrews 3:1
Arm of the Lord	Isaiah 53:1	Atoning Sacrifice of our Sins	1 John 2:2
Author of Life	Acts 3:15	Author of our Faith	Hebrews 12:2
Author and Perfecter of our Faith	Hebrews 2:10	Author of our Salvation	Hebrews 2:10
Beginning (and End)	Revelation 3:14; 21:6; 22:13	Blessed and Holy (only) Ruler	1 Timothy 6:15
Branch	Jeremiah 33:15	Bread of God	John 6:33
Bread of Life	John 6:35, 48	Bridegroom	Isaiah 62:5
Bright Morning Star	Revelation 22:16	Chief Shepherd	1 Peter 5:4
Chief Cornerstone	Ephesians 2:20; Acts 4:11; Isaiah 28:16; 1 Peter 2:7	Christ	Matthew 22:42; 1 John 2:22; Revelation 20:4
Chosen One	Isaiah 42:1	Christ the Lord	Luke 2:11
Christ of God	Luke 9:20	Consolation of Israel	Luke 2:25
Christ, Son of Living God	Matthew 16:16	Deliverer	Romans 11:26
Commander	Isaiah 55:4	Door	John 10:7 (KJV)
Consuming Fire	Deuteronomy 4:24; Hebrews 12:29	Eternal God	Deuteronomy 33:27; 1 John 1:2; 5:20
Creator	1 Peter 4:19; John 1:3	Faithful and True Witness	Revelation 3:14
Desired of all Nations	Haggai 2:7	Father	Matthew 6:9
Faithful and True	Revelation 19:11	First Risen from the Dead	Revelation 1:5
Everlasting Father and Counselor	Isaiah 9:6	First Fruits	1 Corinthians 15:20-23
Faithful Witness	Revelation 1:5	Foundations	

First and Last	Revelation 1:8,11,13; 1:17; 2:8; 22:13		1 Corinthians 3:11
Firstborn	Revelation 1:5; Romans 8:29; Colossians 1:15	*Gentle Whisper*	1 Kings 19:12
Friend of Tax Collectors and Sinners	Matthew 11:19	*Gift of God*	John 4:10
Gate	John 10:9	*God*	Genesis 1:1; John 1:1; 20:28; Hebrews 1:8; Romans 9:5; 2 Peter 1:1; 1 John 5:20
Gift of God	John 4:10	*God over All*	Romans 9:5
Glory of the Lord	Isaiah 40:5	*Good Shepherd*	John 10:11, 14
God Almighty	Genesis 17:1	*Great Shepherd*	Hebrews 13:20
God who sees me	Genesis 16:13	*He searches the thoughts of everyone*	Revelation 2:23
Great High Priest	Hebrews 4:14	*He opens and closes doors, no man can shut*	Revelation 3:7
He resurrects	Revelation 1:13, 18	*Heir of all Things*	Hebrews 1:2
He holds the seven stars and golden lampstands	Revelation 2:1	*High Priest Forever*	Hebrews 6:20
He is the Seven Spirits (of God)	Revelation 3:1	*Holy One*	Acts 3:14; 2:27
He carries the sharp sword with two edges	Revelation 2:12	*Hope*	Titus 2:13; 1 Timothy 1:1
Guide	Psalm 48:14	*Horn of Salvation*	Luke 1:69
Head of the Church	Ephesians 1:22; 4:15; 5:23; Colossians 1:18	*Image of God*	2 Corinthians 4:4
High Priest	Hebrews 2:17; 3:1	*Immanuel*	Isaiah 7:14
Holy and True	Revelation 3:7	*Jesus*	Matthew 1:21
Holy One of Israel	Isaiah 49:7	*Jesus Christ our Lord*	Romans 6:23
Hope of Glory	Colossians 1:27	*King*	Zechariah 9:9
I Am	John 8:58; Exodus 3:14	*King of Israel*	John 1:49

Image of His Person	Hebrews 1:3 (KJV)	*King of Kings*	1 Timothy 6:15; Revelation 19:16
Jehovah	Psalm 83:18 (KJV)	*Lamb*	Revelation 13:8; 5:8,9
Jesus Christ	Revelation 1:1	*Lamb of God*	John 1:29
Judge	Isaiah 33:22; Acts 10:42	*Last Adam*	1 Corinthians 15:45
King Eternal	1 Timothy 1:17	*Leader*	Isaiah 55:4
King of the Jews	Matthew 27:11	*Light of the World*	John 8:12
King of the Ages	Revelation 15:3	*Lilly of the Valleys*	Song 2:1
Lamb slain	Revelation 5:8-9	*Living One*	Revelation 1:18
Lamb Without Blemish	1 Peter 1:19	*Living Water*	John 4:10
Law Giver	Isaiah 33:22	*Lord God Almighty*	Revelation 15:3
Life	John 14:6; Colossians 3:4	*Lord Jesus Christ*	1 Corinthians 15:57
Like an Eagle	Deuteronomy 32:11	*Lord of Glory*	1 Corinthians 2:8
Lion of the Tribe of Judah	Revelation 5:5	*Lord (YHWH) our Righteousness*	Jeremiah 23:6
Living Stone	1 Peter 2:4, 6	*Man from Heaven*	1 Corinthians 15:48
Lord	John 13:13; 2 Peter 2:20; Revelation 4:11	*Master*	Luke 5:5
Lord God of the Holy Prophets	Revelation 22:6	*Mediator of the New Covenant*	Hebrews 9:15
Lord of All	Acts 10:36	*Messenger of the Covenant*	Malachi 3:1
Lord of Lords	1 Timothy 6:15; Revelation 19:16	*Mighty God*	Isaiah 9:6
Love	1 John 4:8	*Nazarene*	Matthew 2:23
Man of Sorrows	Isaiah 53:3	*Omega*	Revelation 22:13
Mediator	1 Timothy 2:5	*Our Passover Lamb*	1 Corinthians 5:7
Merciful God	Jeremiah 3:12	*Our Holiness*	1 Corinthians 1:30
Messiah	John 4:25	*Our Peace*	Ephesians 2:14
Offspring of David	Revelation 22:16	*Our Redemption*	1 Corinthians 1:30
Only Son of God	John 1:18 (KJV); 1 John 4:9	*Power of God*	1 Corinthians 1:24
Our Great God and Savior	Titus 2:13	*Prince of Peace*	Isaiah 9:6
Our Husband	2 Corinthians 11:2	*Purifier*	Malachi 3:3
Our Protection	2 Thessalonians 3:3; Genesis 15:1	*Radiance of God's Glory*	Hebrews 1:3

Our Righteousness	1 Corinthians 1:30	*Refiner's Fire*	Malachi 3:2
Potter	Isaiah 64:8	*Rider of White Horse*	Revelation 19:11
Prophet	Acts 3:22	*Righteous Branch*	Jeremiah 23:5
Rabboni (Teacher)	John 20:16	*Rock*	1 Corinthians 10:4
Redeemer	Job 19:25	*Rose of Sharon*	Song 2:1
Resurrection (and the Life)	John 11:25	*Ruler over all Kings of Earth*	Revelation 1:5
Righteous One	1 John 2:1; Acts 7:52	*Savior*	Luke 2:11; Ephesians 5:23; Titus 1:4; 3:6; 2 Peter 2:20
Root of David	Revelation 5:5, 9; 22:16	*Seed*	Genesis 3:15
Ruler over Israel	Micah 5:2	*Shepherd of Our Souls*	1 Peter 2:25
Scepter out of Israel	Numbers 24:17	*Son of David*	Luke 18:39; Matthew 1:1
Servant	Isaiah 42:1	*Son of Man*	Matthew 8:20; Revelation 1:13
Son of God	John 1:49; Hebrews 4:14; Matthew 27:54; Revelation 2:18	*Source (of Eternal Salvation)*	Hebrews 5:9
Son of the Most High God	Luke 1:32	*Star out of Jacob*	Numbers 24:17
Spirit of God	Genesis 1:2	*Sun of Righteousness*	Malachi 4:2
Stone	1 Peter 2:8	*The One Mediator*	1 Timothy 2:5
Teacher	John 13:13	*True Bread*	John 6:32
The Stone the Builders rejected	Acts 4:11	*Truth and the Way*	John 14:6
True Light	John 1:9	*Witness among the people*	Isaiah 55:4
True Vine	John 15:1, 5	*Wisdom of God*	1 Corinthians 1:24
Word	John 1:1	*Word of God*	Revelation 19:13-16

Resources Used

Betty Crocker's New Eat And Lose Weight: Three Steps to Lose Weight And Feel Great! Minneapolis: General Mills, Inc., 1996.

Life Application Study Bible, New King James Version. Wheaton: Tyndale House Publishers Inc., 1996.

Webster's New World College Dictionary. 3rd ed. MacMillan, 1996.

Women's Devotional Bible: A New Collection Of Daily Devotions From Godly Women. New International Version. Grand Rapids: Zondervan Publishing House, 1995.

Anonymous. Bible Quizzes, "Sex." http://www.christianet.com.

Anonymous. *Operation Timothy*. Chattanooga: CBMC, 1985.

Anonymous. *Praying God's Promises.* Tulsa: Victory House, Inc., 1998.

Anonymous. "Work A Blessing Or A Curse?" *The Watchtower,* 15 June 2005, 3-7, 18-31.

Abanes, Richard. *Harry Potter And The Bible: The Menace Behind The Magick.* CampHill: Horizon Books, 2001.

Anderson, Ken. *Where To Find It In The Bible: The Ultimate A to Z Resource.* Nashville: Thomas Nelson, Inc., 1996.

Bacchiocchi, Samuele. *The Sabbath in John.* Website: http://www.biblicalperspectives.com/endtimesissues/eti_110.html

Batchelor, Doug. *The Christian And Alcohol.* Roseville: Amazing Facts, Inc., 2002.

Braybrooke, Marcus. *The Wisdom Of Jesus.* New York: Readers Digest Association, Inc., 1997.

Cloud, Dr. Henry and Dr. John Townsend. *Boundaries In Marriage.* Grand Rapids: Zondervan Publishing House, 1999.

Crews, Joe. *The Surrender Of Self.* Roseville: Amazing Facts, Inc., 1992.

Elliot, Elisabeth. *Loneliness.* Nashville: Thomas Nelson Publishing, 1988.

Evans, Anthony T. *The Philosophy Of Church Ministry.* Dallas: The Urban Alternative, 2000.

Evans, Tony. *The Battle Is The Lord's: Waging Victorious Spiritual Warfare.* Chicago: Moody Press, 1998.

Falcon, Chuck T. *Family Desk Reference to Psychology: Practical, Expert, And Counseling Advice At Your Fingertips!* Lafeyette: Sensible Psychology Press, 2002.

Gray, John. *Mars & Venus On A Date: A Guide For Navigating The 5 Stages Of Dating To*

Create A Loving & Lasting Relationship. New York: Harper Collins Publishers, 1997.

Hammond McKinney, Michelle. *The Power Of Feminity: Rediscovering The Art Of Being A Woman.* EuGenesise: Harvest House Publishers, 1999.

Jameson, Judy. *Fat Burning Foods And Other Weight-Loss Secrets.* Owings Mills: Ottenheimer Publishers, Inc., 1994.

King, J.L. *On The Down Low: A Journey Into The Lives Of 'Straight' Black Men Who Sleep With Men.* New York: Broadway Books, 2004.

Kipfer, Barbara Ann. *Roget's 21st Century Thesaurus In Dictionary Form.* New York: Dell Publishing, 1993.

Malone, Julius. *Introduction To The Ten Commandments.* Sermon at New Testament Church Milwaukee, WI, 2004.

Ministerial Association. *Seventh-Day Adventist Believe: A Biblical Exposition of 27 Fundamental Doctrines.* Hagerstown: Review and Herald Publishing Association, 1988.

Omartian, Stormie. *Lord, I Want To Be Whole: The Power Of Prayer And Scripture In Emotional Healing.* Nashville: Thomas Nelson Publishers, 2000.

Omartian, Stormie. *The Power of a Praying Woman.* Waterville: Thorndike Press, 2002.

Radmacher, Earl D., Ronald B. Allen, and H. Wayne House. *Nelson Study Bible: New King James Version.* Nashville: Thomas Nelson Publishers, 1997.

Rannibar, Don. *Choosing God's Best: Wisdom for Lifelong Romance.* New York: Multnomah Publishing Inc., 1998.

Rosberg, Gary, and Barbara Rosberg. *Healing The Hurt In Your Marriage.* Wheaton: Tyndale House Publishers, Inc., 2004.

Shelton, Danny. *The Forgotten Commandment: A Battle For Our Loyalty To Christ Or Man.* Nampa: Pacific Press Publishing Association, 2001.

Sper, David. *How Do You Live The Christian Life?* Grand Rapids: RBC Ministries, 1986.

Vander Lugt, Herb. *How Can I Break the Silence?* Grand Rapids: RBC Ministries, 1988.

Viden, Holly and Michelle McKinney Hammond. *If Singleness Is A Gift What's The Return Policy?* Nashville: Thomas Nelson Publishers, 2003.

Water, Mark. *Sharing Your Faith Made Easy.* Peabody: Hendrickson Publishers, Inc., 1999.

Walsch, Donald Neale. *Questions And Answers On Conversations With God.* Charlesville: Hampton Roads, 1999.

Whitelaw, Daniel. *Biblical Reasons To Wait For Sexual Fulfillment.* Wisconsin Dells: 2001.

Whitelaw, Daniel. *Health And Emotional Reasons For Waiting For Sexual Fulfillment.* Wisconsin Dells: 2001.

www.ingramcontent.com/pod-product-compliance
Lightning Source LLC
Chambersburg PA
CBHW080725230426
43665CB00020B/2618